$29.95   OCT -- 2011

OCPL SOULE BRANCH
101 SPRINGFIELD RD

WITHDRAWN

If Our Lives Be Spared

*A Saga of the Collin Family Settlers
in Early New York State*

Terrance Keenan

Syracuse University Press

Copyright © 2007 by Syracuse University Press

Syracuse, New York 13244-5160

All Rights Reserved

First Edition 2007

07 08 09 10 11 12   6 5 4 3 2 1

Excerpts from the text of *A History of New York State,* revised edition, edited by David M. Ellis, James A. Frost, Harold C. Syrett, and Harry J. Carman, copyright © 1957 Cornell University, are used by permission of the publisher, Cornell University Press. Permission is gratefully acknowledged. Unless otherwise stated, all illustrations courtesy of the Onondaga Historical Association Museum and Research Center, Syracuse, N.Y.

The paper used in this publication meets the minimum requirements of American National Standard for Information Sciences—Permanence of Paper for Printed Library Materials, ANSI Z39.48–1984. ∞™

For a listing of books published and distributed by Syracuse University Press, visit our Web site at SyracuseUniversityPress.syr.edu.

ISBN-13: 978-0-8156-0860-8   ISBN-10: 0-8156-0860-8

Library of Congress Cataloging-in-Publication Data

Keenan, Terrance, 1947–

If our lives be spared : a saga of the Collin family settlers in early New York State / Terrance Keenan. — 1st ed.

p. cm.

Includes bibliographical references.

ISBN 978-0-8156-0860-8 (hardcover : alk. paper)

1. Collin, David, 1794–1884. 2. Collin, David, 1794–1884—Family. 3. Pioneers—New York (State)—Fayetteville—Biography. 4. Frontier and pioneer life—New York (State)—Fayetteville. 5. Farm life—New York (State)—Fayetteville—History. 6. Wills—New York (State)—Fayetteville—History. 7. Fayetteville (N.Y.)—Biography. 8. Fayetteville (N.Y.)—Social life and customs. 9. New York (State)—History—Civil War, 1861–1865—Biography. 10. United States—History—Civil War, 1861–1865—Biography. I. Title.

F129.F23K44 2007   974.7'041092—dc22   [B]   2007005607

Manufactured in the United States of America

*For the late Betsy Knapp
and for my mentor, Antje B. Lemke*

Terrance Keenan is a former teacher, bookseller, and librarian. For seven years he owned an independent bookstore in a small upstate New York college town. For fourteen years he worked as special collections librarian in the Department of Special Collections at the Syracuse University Library.

In May 1994 he was ordained as a Rinzai Zen Buddhist priest. He later served as adjunct Buddhist chaplain at Syracuse University and meditation chaplain at Tully Hill Treatment Center, teaching meditation to alcoholics and addicts just entering recovery.

He has authored four books of poems, the most recent being *Practicing Eternity* (1996). *St. Nadie in Winter: Zen Encounters with Loneliness* was published in the summer of 2001 and was one of only four finalists for the national NAPRA Nautilus Award. His poems have appeared in seven anthologies, with other poems and reviews in various journals, including *Ironwood* and the *Georgia Review*. He was cofounder of the Arts and Crafts Society of Central New York, dedicated to preserving the work and philosophy of the movement started by William Morris. He was a member at large of the Board of Trustees of Schola Cantorum of Syracuse. He has served as president and head monk of the Zen Center of Syracuse Hoen-ji, secretary to the Executive Committee of the Board of Directors of the Interreligious Council of Central New York (IRC), IRC liaison to the Southeast Asian Center, a member of the mayor's task force on the Asian Community, and a member of the IRC's Native American Task Force for Peace.

In the summer of 2001, he moved to rural Maryland. In 2005 he was appointed adjunct Buddhist chaplain in the pastoral care program at Johns Hopkins Hospital.

All paths are vague partings in the grasses.
It's not for what the leaved grave said
utmosts grow lost, the moment to choose passes,

but for the cluttered beliefs one amasses,
and for the blinding grey of dread
all paths are vague partings in the grasses.

Cleared by faith, eyes entertain what surpasses
day's simple sights, but in our dim twilight spread
utmosts grow lost, the moment to choose passes.

No wistful glance through the lying glasses
of hope will help put right an aimless tread.
All paths are vague partings in the grasses.

Hope is a fear of what now passes.
In time all traces of life are left by the dead.
Utmosts grow lost, the moment to choose passes.

There is no comfort in ends love encompasses,
or peace in wishing or refusing to be led.
Utmosts grow lost. The moment to choose passes.
All paths are vague partings in the grasses.

  —Terrance Keenan, "What the Wind Said"

Contents

Illustrations *xi*

Acknowledgments *xiii*

Introduction *xv*

1. The Beginning of Silence *5*
2. The Character of David Collin Sr. *10*
3. The Family Story *16*
4. Miriam *47*
5. What We Are Reminded to Remember *66*
6. Life on the Farm *94*
7. Miriam's Questions *131*
8. The Civil War *154*
9. Business as Usual *212*
10. The Romance *239*
11. Wherefore One Hundred Years of Silence *269*

Conclusion *300*

Afterword *303*

Source Notes *309*

Illustrations

Family tree of David Collin III   *2*
David Collin III   *15*
Anna Smith Collin   *46*
Miriam Collin Armstrong   *52*
Part of the 1869 will of David Collin III   *53*
Map of New York State   *57*
John Collin's bill of sale for a slave, 1810   *73*
David Collin IV   *83*
Clara Park Collin   *85*
The Collin home farm, ca. 1895   *104*
"Sweet Map" of Manlius and environs, including Collin lands, 1874   *132*
Map and drawing of the siege of Washington, N.C., 1863   *203*
Roswell Park Collin   *240*
Cardera Collin   *266*

Acknowledgments

First, Jane MacLeod Keenan, my wife and true companion. Her creation of the complex family tree and New York State map helped enormously. What can be said beyond expressing limitless gratitude for her patience, grace, and trust that I would some day finish this work?

Second, Antje B. Lemke, my mentor and friend, who has encouraged and supported each difficult step and who opened the door to this opportunity so many years ago.

Third, Barbara Rivette, Manlius town historian, and Hamilton Armstrong, who gave freely of their valuable time, meeting my enthusiasm and curiosity with their own. Both also shared with me their knowledge of and expertise in local history (making me aware of details I would never have uncovered on my own), their wry views of the human condition, and their joy in preserving the natural world.

Fourth, the research staff at the Onondaga Historical Association, who opened their doors to my needs and efficiently and courteously helped me from afar with my endless queries.

Fifth, Curtis Seay, my brother-in-law, whose knowledge of the Civil War was invaluable. He gave me his time, interest, and a series of significant connections, both personal and bibliographical, that made all the difference in my ability to report certain situations in the war accurately.

Sixth, the Presbyterian Historical Association, for allowing me to see their microfiche records regarding the history of the church in Fayetteville.

Seventh, Amy Dauphin, clerk at the Onondaga County Court House, who went out of her way to help me find copies of the wills and records I needed.

Eighth, Conor Keenan, my son, whose technical assistance with the New York State map and with innumerable computer problems saw me through the most difficult times.

Terrance Keenan
Monkton, Maryland
November 2006

Introduction

This book is a story about one branch of the Collin family, a family that is by many lights typical of those who formed the now somewhat strained backbone of nineteenth-century America, leading it from wilderness to the modern age in a few generations. This is not an entirely misguided view, but it is not the only view.

    I began writing it or, more frankly, pulling it together to honor a promise I made in 1992 to Betsy Knapp, who owned the family papers and with whom I worked for some years to organize them into a coherent collection: the Collin-Park-Knapp Archive at the Onondaga Historical Association. Yet the book is not a conventional history, a systematic laying out of facts to build a narrative of past events. While I allow, by and large, the family individuals to tell the story upon which I have focused through the use of documents from the archive, and while I cite other sources that filled out some historical details or influenced or clarified my thinking, it remains one story of many possible stories that could be drawn from the thousands of patchwork pieces that make up the archive. It is a story-quilt pieced together with an eye to the drama I discovered running like a dark thread through the lives of bright, noble people. I do not follow the conventions of scholarly historical writing, nor do I take the liberties of historical fiction. There are a few places where I suggest what might be going on in the minds of certain characters. It is a kind of artistic license to ascribe thoughts and emotions that we cannot actually know, but these moments are based upon my knowledge of the diaries and correspondence of many, even those not included in the narrative. It is merely an attempt to create a living picture of a family community and the individuals composing it.

John Fowles has written in *The Tree* that "Behind every path and any form of expression one does finally choose lie the ghosts of all those that one did not. There is a knowledge you can't explore and every path there, upon which you cannot walk, is filled with a sense of loss. You don't know exactly where you are going . . . (you are guided by feelings . . . very loosely)—you cannot know what a [person] experiences nor what will happen if you choose this path over that, real uncertainty." My motives stem from my understanding that being is not linear, although narrative is. As Fowles again puts it, "You don't begin to understand ordinary history until you have at least some sense of this staggering, perpetual, yet evanescent nowness."

Facts do not speak for themselves; they are merely tools we use—regardless of our purpose or desire right now in the midst of, as we cannot help but be, the muddled and complex human situation. This kind of family biography is only a network of resources and methods available. The materials I used to create this book are all original, aside from a few reference books, my own poorly kept commonplace book, and the records of the Presbyterian Historical Association in Philadelphia. As in all collections of historical documents, some parts of the archive in the Onondaga Historical Association are more nearly complete than others. The larger collection includes painted portraits, clothing, furniture, and many household artifacts. The documents vary from fragile, fading letters and newspaper clippings to bound diaries and farm records. They are organized overall by generation and within generations by both subject and document type. Within those categories they are arranged chronologically. There is a complete finding aid that is simple to master.

Although I am familiar with most of the documents, for the purposes of this book I found it useful to search for ones that supported, on the one hand, a broad story of the scope and range of the family endeavor and, on the other hand, the *King Lear*–like story of greed and betrayal that weaves together, in the manner of a fugue, with one of love and heartbreak. The David Collin branch of the widespread extended Collin family acquired its initial wealth from its homesteading roots in Columbia County, New York, near the Massachusetts line, going back well before the American

Revolution. By the second generation after the Revolution most of the men and many of the women went on to obtain both secondary and college education, usually at fine schools such as Yale or Williams or Smith, at a time when only 2 percent of the population did so. They were not just off the boat and into the woods. One side of the family descended from passengers on the *Mayflower* and the main branch traced its roots to late-seventeenth-century Huguenot immigrants. It may help to understand that most people of such a heritage recognized, in a far more literal sense that their twentieth-century counterparts would, the underlying order of things as a way of becoming close to God, and this understanding informs all they did and wrote.

The text is structured in such a way to create a natural flow, a sense of a continuing story. Yet one has to be patient to see all the forms and colors come into the final shape of the tale. I spend as much time as I do on the Civil War, when it was not central to the story, because each of the young men I discuss who served bore some important connection to the central family. They shared a world view, a romance of self, a plodding determination to do what must be done, and a remarkable stoicism in the face of death that was informed only in part by that romance of self and a sense of duty. These were traits shared across the generations and branches of this unique, stalwart tribe. So the extended records of Civil War activity move the family traits onto a larger stage, in a drama that has the usual denouement of the soldier returning to an uncaring world and yet demonstrates how the events of the world at large had begun to affect life at home as much as the weather or the immediate circumstances of the wilderness and farm life.

Also, there is a family tradition regarding a romance between Roswell and Cardera Collin, which I accept. The documentary evidence is slim, but the oral tradition seems a powerful one. I believe both types of evidence sufficient to support the tradition. I first heard the story from Betsy Knapp, who pointed out that Ruth Collin Stong, in her family genealogy, also mentions the tradition. The pact Roswell and Cardera made to marry neither one another (because they were too close as double cousins) nor anyone else was clearly an oral one. Aside from the changing tones of their letters to one another over the years and the sheer number of letters they exchanged compared with the number they wrote to others, there are Cardera's steady refusals of the many proposals of marriage made to her by the cousins' mutual friend, Charles May. In several letters from 1889 onward Roswell alludes to a need to talk with Cardera "face-to-face," after which presumed encounter Cardera finally accepts Charles May's proposal. There is a change of tone in the cousinly banter and family news of the letters as the two of them mature, a new tone of regret and of something rooted more deeply. Finally, Cardera and Charles named their first son after Roswell.

All these people faced death in a way we do not. They once lived, strove, suffered, felt joy, and experienced rewards and failures as we all do. And certainly we share their mortality and will vanish as surely as they have. But the way in which they had to face death was different in their lifetimes. On one hand there was the Divine Will, an absolute truth to those experiencing the world as it was then understood by them. On the other hand were the appalling diseases, the sources of which were unknown or misunderstood and which were largely incurable, that snatched child and adult away from the family center with grim regularity: smallpox, measles, typhoid, pneumonia.

There have been some technical problems in presenting the documents from the archive. Court reports and newspapers aside, the diaries and letters are replete with variations—now seen as errors—of grammar or spelling. There is little consistency. Mind you, these were, in the early days, people of little education, for whom paper and ink were treasured commodities linking them to family and to a world from which they were far removed. That was especially so for the women, who were so often confined to the home by endless hard labor. Where possible, I have kept the original spelling and grammar or punctuation. Very occasionally I have had to modify it to keep the sense of what was being written. I do not think it helps the reader of such a narrative to be encumbered by endless brackets—there are enough as it is—footnotes, or [sic]s, so I have avoided them unless the change I had to make was utter guesswork.

Two other awkward problems are worth mentioning. The first concerns the shift in monetary values over time. Obviously a dollar in 1790 did not have the same value as a dollar today. And of course that value shifted down as the years went by. I have, therefore, indicated present-day equivalents in brackets after the amount being given in the story, as in $100 [$1,600]. Where there are many figures close together in the narrative, as in the later chapters, I indicate only the significant amounts, allowing the reader to approximate the rest. The second problem concerns the need to differentiate the many David Collins from various generations. In an effort to simplify and be consistent, where possible confusion makes it necessary, I have referred to David Collin III (the settler) as David Collin Sr. and his son, who managed family affairs into the twentieth century, as David Collin Jr. Any other Davids mentioned are identified in direct relation to these two.

This is a story. The people in this story are all dead. They have gone the way of dust everywhere. The landscape they lived upon has changed. Second- and third-growth trees stand where pasture and crops once spread, looking for all the world as though they've been there forever. Few of the houses, built with such pride from the trees cleared to make room for those pastures and crops, remain, and where new trees do not grow there are subdivisions, some of which have been in place for a generation or more already. The plank-and-dirt road that ran in front of the Collin homestead is now a busy commuter artery into Syracuse, itself a struggling blue-collar, rust-belt city like so many other once-prosperous communities in the northeast, suffering middle-class flight and a crippling industrial exodus that have been bleeding the place for decades. Even the family names are largely forgotten: one small street, a largish plot in Fayetteville's old village cemetery, and a former bed-and-breakfast bear the family name. A sprawling unit of condominiums with the unlikely name of Signal Hill sits on the site of the original main farmhouse.

It is not death that troubles us. It is change. The distant past cannot give us our present. We must make our own meaning in our own present, and it will also vanish among all the winds that turn the world. Isaiah Berlin suggests that the most important test of the history of ideas is to be able to explain, but we always do so in our own context.

History, as we usually conceive it, is a myth not unlike other myths (Greek, Christian, Rational, Modern) by which we organize and believe we recognize our experience of life. The stories change because we change. What, then, when the story ends, or worse, fails? Do we leave ourselves nothing? Looking at the past, especially from personal documents, does tell us a story, and all true stories are about change. In *Metaphysics as a Guide to Morals,* Iris Murdoch points out that "The story of Christ is the story which we want to hear: that suffering can be redemptive, and that death is not the end." We want to hear that suffering need not be pointless, it need not be wasted, that it has meaning, that it can even be the way. But history always takes place everywhere. It is not postponed time. We write it today because we will die tomorrow. We throw our sense of a permanent self against change, create stories that wall us in against it. Yet we suffer and know suffering is true. Can we, however, as Barry Lopez said in *Resistance,* "believe in the divinity of life ... that everything can be remembered in time, that anyone may be redeemed, that no hierarchy is worth figuring out, that no flower or animal or body of water or star is common, that poetry is the key to a lock worth springing, that what is called for is not subjugation [of things] but genuflection"? To me this possibility of belief means gratitude, grace, and humility.

Desire determines all choices, muses a character in Linda Tatelbaum's 2004 novel *Yes and No* (I paraphrase). The demand for "text" mutes the past so that we become solitary facing the big issues. Solitude lets us wander through this wordless past. What do we hear in the silence of time, wavering and exhausted as we are by prolonged grief? How can words resurrect the time, space, and matter that was once a life? When we commit what we hear from the past to words, what have we committed? A fiction? A truth? An echo? Echoes of desire and the loss of it? Is it the teller who survives through the tale or the tale through the teller? "But why do scholars insist," Tatelbaum writes, "that whatever doesn't reach words is lost? What they call 'history' can't be all that's left. There must be something more. Something known with the heart.... [W]ords leave a trace of something never finally found in words."

No matter what I have done or what anyone else may do with these records, the precarious balance between the facts of the documents and the truth of the story, or the story as I have chosen to tell it, remains, as always, delicate. Some may feel this is a never-ending story, but it is also a wayward, ever-changing one. What we observe uses us for its own being.

If Our Lives Be Spared

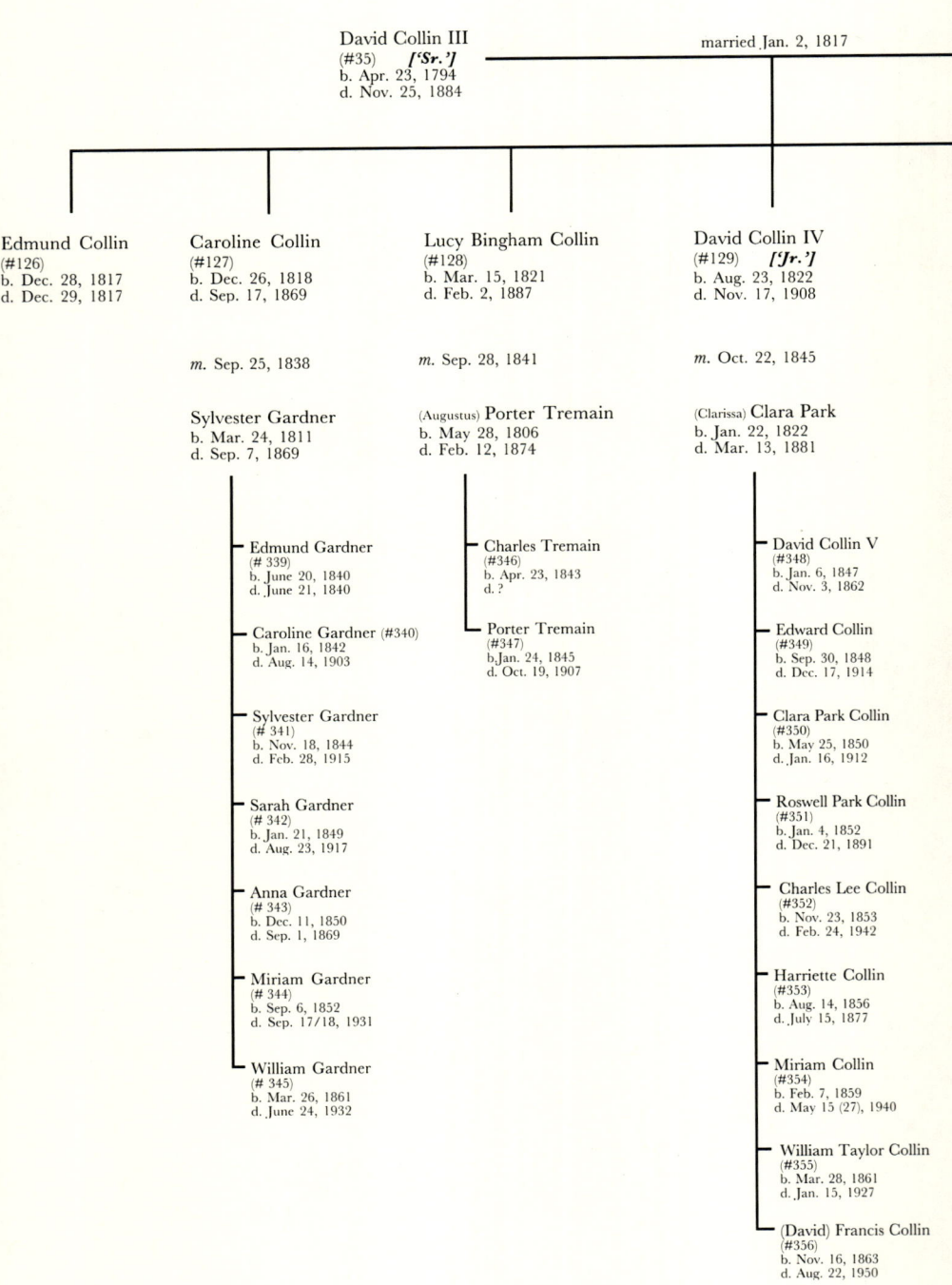

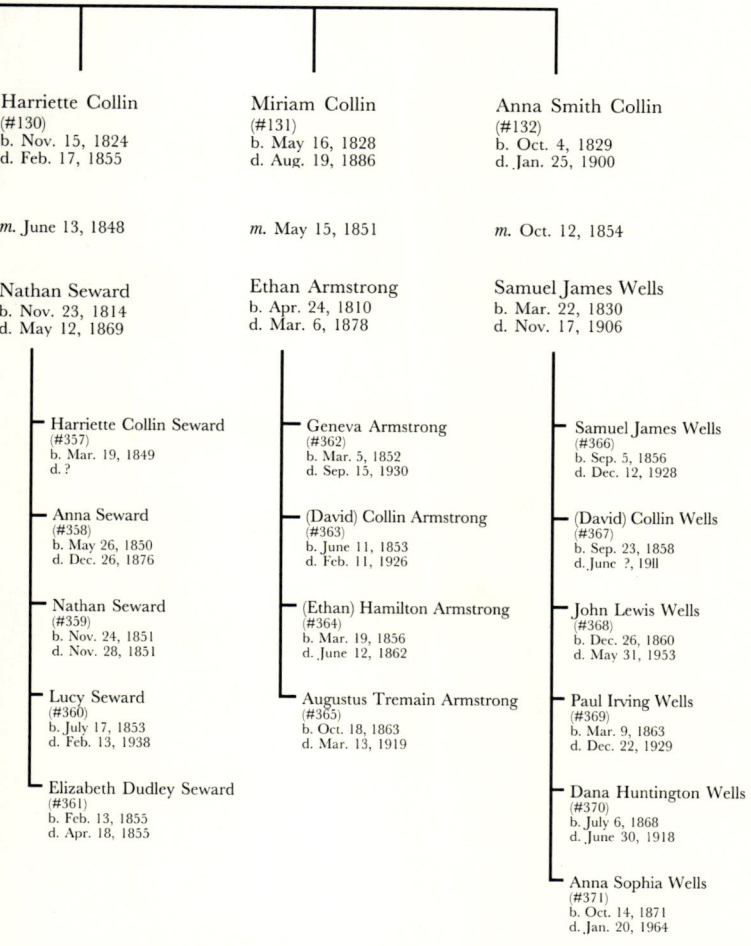

Notes: (#) identifies the descendant in the genealogy *John Collin: Stems and Branches,* by Ruth Collin Stong, Elmira, N.Y.: Elmira Quality Printers, 1981. ['Sr.'] or ['Jr.'] corresponds to usage in the text for David Collin III or David Collin IV respectively. Courtesy of Jane MacLeod Keenan.

1

The Beginning of Silence

> Which of you shall we say doth love us most?
> —Shakespeare, *King Lear,* 1.1.52

One warm Tuesday afternoon in May 1877, David Collin jumped into his carriage, flicked the whip smartly, took the two handsome horses out of the picket gates of the stately family homestead, and headed east along the old road then called the Genesee Turnpike. What he was about to do would change the course of his family forever, yet by his own lights there was nothing else he could do. He was in a state. What had been done to him had already changed him irrevocably, though he did not know that. He did not notice the new leaves on the tall arching elms, nor the old wolf maples casting shadows across his way. The cedar swamp in the dell to his right sent up a slight blue haze across the hills rising on the southern side of this pretty green valley. But neither the haze nor the sweet scent of lilacs from nearby dooryards touched him. He was thinking, not sightseeing. He did not like the thoughts he was having. Something was up, and from the little he knew, it was as bad as anything he could imagine.

He had been away from the farm on an errand all morning. Coming home, he'd been looking forward to a late midday meal with his beloved wife, Clara, before heading out to check on the hands and the stock. He was met instead by Frank Glover. Frank hadn't been too well of late and had come out to the farm to do some light labor to help regain his health. It was the sort of thing the Collin farm had been offering for as long as anyone cared to remember.

Frank told David he'd been visited by Wilbur Brown, who, with Frank, worked for a Collin cousin's law firm, Noxon and Cowles, in the village a couple of miles away. After hearing the message Wilbur had to deliver, David mumbled something about it being too late in the day to make the fifteen-mile journey into the growing town of Syracuse to attend to that particular business. He didn't much like Wilbur anyway, but as he moved to go into the house, Frank took his arm and spoke more closely.

It seemed that on the Sunday just past, after the regular church service in Fayetteville, young Charlie Tremain, David's impetuous nephew, had spoken to Wilbur of a Collin family gathering at his, David's, late sister's farm off Pierson Road near Green Lake. Clearly David hadn't been invited, and that could only mean that his niece Caroline, who now had her mother's farm, and, more especially, his bitter, testy sister Miriam were involved.

While Frank was mentioning the purpose of the meeting to David, it was clear, though he got the details somewhat garbled, that he was speaking as an employee of Noxon and Cowles, who handled so many of the Collin family's complex affairs. He made it clear that something was afoot to sabotage—a new word at the time—David's father's attempts to settle his affairs in an appropriate manner. David heard him out, spun around, and jumped back into his carriage, ordering Frank to explain to Clara.

As the fine horses moved briskly down the road, David barely noticed that the worst of the ruts from the mud season were gone. He could hardly even think of what had brought things to this unhappy place. All he knew was that his elderly father was with the others and that he was there under false pretenses or against his will. David smiled grimly at that thought. There was little his father did against his will. He found it impossible to imagine anyone trying to lie to the old man. But it had to be duplicity of some sort. His father may have been in his eighties and getting frail after a lifetime of hard farm labor, but he remained nobody's fool.

David thought about young Caroline. Well, at thirty-five perhaps she wasn't so young anymore, but he still thought of her that way. She'd had a tough go of it. It had been about ten years since both her mother, David's sister Caroline, and her father, as well as her sister Anne, had all died within three days of one another from typhoid. The family had pulled together then to help, as it always did, but that didn't seem to matter now.

Then there was nephew Charlie, son of David's sister Lucy Tremain. The cousins were close. Charlie was about Caroline's age but was still looking for his main chance. He claimed to have started out on Wall Street in distant New York City, but it wasn't too long before he was back home. He was a charmer, to be sure, and had, David had to admit, a wonderful singing voice. He was now part owner of a paper mill down in Manlius, a few miles further off than Fayetteville from the farm, and he had set up his so-called Tremain-Park right down by the lakes, with a dance hall, docks, boats, picnic tables, and so on. Everyone seemed to like him. Perhaps he was too likable.

And what about Miriam? How had she become so sour? She used to write wonderful letters: "a letter timely writ is a rivet in the chain of affection." He recalled her writing well. Clearly those continuing "reverses" remained a burden. Her husband Ethan's drinking had driven her to the Temperance Union and reinforced her intemperate frame of mind. Ethan Armstrong's massive debts still hung between Miriam and her siblings. Some of the largest were to her father, and he had not forgiven the debts. They were simply too huge, and it wasn't as though Ethan wasn't around to do something about them—though what David really meant, as he thought about it, was that Ethan was still alive, although he spent most of his time off in the Albany area with his dry-goods export business, which the family generally called the "Grocery Store."

David was sure Miriam was the prime mover behind this family meeting, and if Charlie's tongue hadn't been so loose (the high stakes must have made him want to crow a little), he, David, might never have heard of it. The thought set his face even more determinedly.

The wind tugged at his hat, but he didn't slow the pace. He was a handsome man, tall, with dark hair graying a little now that he was over fifty. Yet in the community he was still referred to as "young David," or "David Jr." or "Mr. David," even though he had managed the farm for years and had an army of his own children. "Mr. Collin," always meant his father. David (the IV) was well educated for a farmer of that time. His father had seen to that—his son graduated from the technical college in Rensselaer (now called RPI). But "Mr. David" wore that lightly, save in his own expectations for his eight surviving children, most of whom, including the women, went on to college in their turn. Smith, Williams, and Yale were among the main beneficiaries. David had a lot of his father's single-minded toughness. He was fair in business, but he didn't bend much. He was active as a community leader, but that was his self-perceived duty (received as a kind of heritage from his father)—which he sensed was his by right. He was at heart a kind man who loved his family deeply and who, in that family tradition, did not tolerate fools lightly.

To his mind, his sister Miriam had become foolish. His father had misjudged things—that is, he had misjudged the people involved when he'd reexamined the substantial legacy he intended to leave behind some years ago—but that didn't make him wrong. If much of that reexamination was to the younger David's advantage, he, David, saw it only as his due, since he had borne the main responsibility for the homestead for so long. And that was what this was about, or so he guessed. From what little Frank had told him, Miriam needed those debts cleared, and Charlie was sure to be making a case on behalf of the cousins to bring in their support, too.

The Collin family had been on this land for sixty years, a long time when all that had stood before was wilderness, at least in white men's eyes. When his father came, it had been indeed raw wilderness, virgin forest. By this time, the place was approaching fifteen hundred acres of good cleared farm land, and that above the three farms David Sr. had given his daughters and the several tenant farms he owned around the area and in adjacent counties. Young David was sure his father hadn't been told why he was invited out to the Pierson-Gardner farm, and he guessed the implications would never occur to the old man.

David Collin pulled his carriage into the front yard of his niece's farmhouse and just sat there. He knew those inside knew he'd come, and he knew they wouldn't come out to greet him. What could they be thinking now that their secret plan had been discovered? When a farm hand came by, David sent him in with a message to bring out his father. When the old man, dignified with his white hair, dark suit, and rugged features, emerged, David asked him if he was willing to ride back to the homestead with him. He was careful not to sound too forceful or demanding (an easy slip for such traditionally forceful folk). When his father said he was willing, David helped him up into the carriage, flicked his whip again, and road out of the farmyard toward home. No one had come out of the house. David knew they wouldn't have the courage.

From that day forward the Collins and the Armstrongs did not speak to one another. It was not until more than one hundred years later, during an annual Christmas party in 1989, that the silence was broken, the gray skeleton emerged from the closet, and a kind of reconciliation took place, but by then the world itself had changed completely, and things did not mean what they once had, and what they once had meant was almost wholly forgotten.

❧ 2 ❧

The Character of David Collin Sr.

> Our potency made good, take thy reward.
> —Shakespeare, *King Lear,* 1.1.75

There was a hearing before George R. Cook at the Surrogate Court in Syracuse, New York, on the morning of April 4, 1885. The case was a suit brought by Miriam Armstrong against her brother, David Collin Jr. Miriam was contesting her recently deceased father's will, from which David Jr. did quite well and she did not. Brought as witnesses to the hearing were the cosigners or witnesses to the will. The cosigning was an event that had taken place nine years prior to the hearing, and while memories were a bit foggy as to the specific details, even after close questioning, the character of David Collin Sr., who had settled the land seventy years prior to the hearing, emerged quite distinctly. There also develops a sense of community drawing protectively around one of its own. David Collin Sr. had lived for some years at Oak Grove, a home he had built for his father and mother (ca. 1845), just north of the village, when they had moved west in retirement from Hillsdale in Columbia County. His son David Jr. lived at the original main homestead (built ca. 1826) with his wife, Clara, and his large family.

The witnesses to the will present at the hearing were a Mr. Stearns, a Mr. Peck, and a Mr. Clark, neighbors of the Collin homestead. The counsel for the proponent, Miriam Armstrong, was Martin A. Knapp (no relation to the Knapps who later married into the Collin family). The selections I have made of the courtroom exchanges are taken directly and verbatim from the official hearing transcript in the family archive. They appear in chronological order. The archive copy contains primarily the questions by the counsel for Miriam Armstrong. The exchanges contain a good deal of redundancy as counsel picks through details of the testimonies. Where it has been possible once the point has been made, I elide some of this material.

Here Mr. Knapp is questioning Mr. Peck.

> Q: At this time of his life he was a man of cheerful disposition. Apparently a man who enjoyed life—lived happily or otherwise?
>
> A: Well, I couldn't say as to that. I remember hearing him tell once about the woman who took care of him keeping him nice and comfortable. His daughters would like to have him come and live with them, but he preferred to stay at the old homestead.
>
> Q: Did he seem to be a man of cheerful and happy temperament?
>
> A: He was always cheerful, not hilarious, but he was always equal in his temperament.
>
> Q: Well, he continued to live there about how long Mr. Peck?
>
> A: I couldn't say exactly; perhaps, say, a few years.
>
> Q: And did this same woman remain there during that time?
>
> A: Well, sir, I think she left not long after, but how long I couldn't say. I don't pay much attention to my neighbor's business.

This seemingly innocuous reference was at the heart of an earlier near scandal in the village, but here Mr. Peck rallies with the appropriate defense of silence on behalf of his neighbor.

At another point in the hearing the following exchange took place between Mr. Knapp and Mr. Peck:

> Q: Did you know how old he was at that time?
>
> A: No, sir, I don't think I did. In the neighborhood of eighty years old. I don't know exactly, merely from hearsay.
>
> Q: Well, did he appear to be a person of very great age?
>
> A: I don't think he did. He was of a good deal of vigor, walked off quite smart to church about that time I noticed.
>
> Q: Do you recollect his walking to church about this time?
>
> A: That or a little before.

Q: That same summer?

A: I couldn't say positively, but it was about that time. He used to occasionally go.

Q: Well then, he was not very infirm for a man of his years?

A: I didn't think he was. He was around seeing to his business. He didn't do any hard labor himself, but around seeing to business. He rode out frequently.

Q: You knew his son, the present David Collin, all that time of course?

A: Yes, sir.

Q: Quite well?

A: Yes, sir, as well as I would any neighbor.

Q: Where did you live at this time?

A: On Genesee Street, east of Fayetteville a mile and a half, or a mile or so, [near] where he lives now.

Q: In going from his place to his father's would he pass your place?

A: No sir.

Q: Did you see him frequently with his father?

A: I saw him occasionally riding with his father. He had a farm down north and I used to suppose they went down there to see to that. I didn't know anything about it. They had property in Sullivan. They some times used to ride down north together.

Q: So that you not infrequently saw them together?

A: I saw them occasionally together.

Q: At the time you signed this paper did you know that there had been some contention in the family in respect to the old gentleman's property?

A: I had heard rumors to that effect.

Q: You understood that about that time or before that time he had conveyed a large amount of property to his son?

A: It was rumored.

Q: It was current report?

A: Yes, sir, that was the rumor. I knew nothing further about it than neighborhood talk.

Q: You knew his other children I suppose?
A: Old Mr. Collin's?
Q: Yes.
A: I think I did, yes, sir.
Q: And you were aware that the transfer of that property had caused some unpleasant feeling in the Collin family?
A: That was the rumor.
Q: You understood that the property had been transferred without consideration, did you not? ...
A: Oh, I don't know anything about it.
Q: Did you ever hear the old gentleman say anything before this Will was made about the disposition he had made, or intended to make of his property?
A: I don't recollect that I did hear him say anything about that.
Q: He had never then, in any conversation with you, stated his intention?
A: No, I was never intimate with him at all in any of his family plans or business.
Q: You were not accustomed to talking over his business matters with him at all?
A: No, sir.
Q: Your acquaintance was of the ordinary character, living so nearly together you would see him frequently?
A: Yes, sir. He was an old man when I come there; pass along the road or on his own premises.
Q: Now, on the day that this paper was signed, did he say much at all as you recollect?
A: Why he talked. He was quite a hand for conversation and would talk of social subjects.
Q: Well, you are quite certain about that?
A: Yes, I think he spoke about having paid out considerable for his sons-in-law, and such talk as that.
Q: Well, let me see about that. About when did that occur?
A: Well, I think it was after the Will was signed.
Q: After the Will was signed?

A: Yes, sir, I think so.

Q: What did he say about that?

A: Well, he spoke about having paid out a good deal of money for them and had a right, I think he said, to do as he chose with his property.

Q: Did he mention or intimate what amount of money he had paid out for his sons-in-law?

A: No, sir.

Q: Did he call any of them by name?

A: No, sir, not as I remember.

Q: You don't pretend to remember his exact language about that?

A: No, sir.

Q: Well, from the substance of it did he convey the idea that he had paid out a large sum of money?

A: I think he conveyed the idea that he had paid out considerable money for the other members of the family. He said he had given the girls a good farm apiece, and that they ought to be content. Something of that kind. That was in the conversation, I think, after the Will was executed.

Q: When he made statements to that effect was there anything said by his son?

A: I don't recollect that there was.

A bit later in the questioning, Mr. Knapp is speaking to Mr. Stearns:

Q: Had you occasion at any time to ask favors of him in a business character or otherwise? The ordinary neighborly accommodations of one neighbor to another?

A: No, sir.

Q: Did you observe about his disposition, whether he yielded readily to the requests of others who made their requests in a pleasant and friendly way?

A: Well, I had the impression that he would befriend me if I wanted it. I could tell you the circumstances if it was necessary, but it is not necessary in this case. He was very friendly with me. There

David Collin III, known as David Collin Sr.

was times that I am satisfied that I could have got favors of him if I wished to.

Q: I mean more particularly with reference to the temperament?

A: Well, I always thought that he would have to be pretty well satisfied it was for his interest. He was considered one of the shrewdest men in the County.

Q: He was a man of singular shrewdness and promptness?
A: Yes, sir.

3

The Family Story

1

> Thy truth then be thy dower...
> —Shakespeare, *King Lear,* 1.1.110

Why would anyone be interested in this family squabble? As the local town historian put it, "Hardly any Will regarding land ever went uncontested in this town!" Although some members of each generation of Collin children seemed to keep diaries, all wrote to one another almost obsessively, *and* they held on to much of this documentation, or at least a fair bit of it, their own opinion of themselves as "good stock" hasn't outlasted them. They are largely forgotten in the community they helped to create.

There is a deeper story here. It unfolds in the personalities of certain family members. It is a story about faith, courage, strength, and betrayal. It is a story about what lasts and why certain things do not last. It is about values and morals and the legacy we have received from these vivid people who lived their lives as best they could. In order to understand the individuals involved in this drama, which reflects so tellingly on our own times, to give them a context for the roles they will play, it will be necessary to go back in time to find their roots and to learn how they told their own story. For only those from the past create what is knowable about the past.

In 1916, on the occasion of the hundredth anniversary of David and Anna Collin's marriage, there was a big family gathering, and a "Family

Chronicle" was printed, containing contributions from several generations. Ironically, that was about the time the central hold of the mere concept of "family" was beginning to unravel, and the wilderness that David and Anna had faced was fast becoming the suburbia it is now. The "Family Chronicle" was an attempt to capture the past and thus give to the present of 1916 a sense of grounding and permanence. But by then the world itself had changed irrevocably, and what was past could not make the present better, since it was the foundation of the shambled present, save perhaps in the lessons it might offer in the human condition of mortal fallibility. Because the coming of white men to the great forests of North America marks one of the most poignant and significant examples of the rapid change humans can bring to an environment and is fraught with all the problems the dynamics of change bring to any place, the story of the Collin family has yet another layer of unexpected mystery and teaching to offer us.

As luck would have it (though one could hardly call it luck in this family of congenital documenters), one of the central figures in the drama, Miriam Collin Armstrong, second youngest of the five daughters of David and Anna Collin, wrote an account of the family past for the occasion of their fiftieth anniversary, 1866. It was placed in the chronicle fifty years later by Anna's granddaughter Geneva, with some emendations to fill out the details. As Geneva wrote, "Grandmother knew, but could not remember who of our ancestors came in the Mayflower. Time and notes proved it to be Elder Brewster." Miriam's style is florid and very different from Geneva's. I have not made serious distinctions between them, since they are self-evident and say quite a bit themselves of the changes taking place already in the society that fostered these two strong women, inasmuch as the words we choose to express ourselves reflect our sense of who we are. From time to time I insert in brackets details to extend Geneva's notes a little further or to clarify subjects, the understanding of which was taken for granted in 1916, but which may no longer be clear today, almost a century later.

A Sketch Prepared for the Golden Wedding of David and Anna Smith Collin, January 2, 1866, by their daughter, Miriam Collin Armstrong

The pilgrim in a strange land having gained the summit of a dividing eminence, with a heart filled with varied memories and experiences, and exercised by soul-filling and subduing emotions—the promptings of nature suggest a pause to define his position and bearings, to note aught that may be of interest or profit to those who may journey after, and from this period of restful reflection to gain strength and cheerful courage for the remaining pilgrimage.

It is even thus in the life-journey of man. With our dear parents this journey is completed to the allotted span of three score years and ten. Fifty years ago today their paths converged, and, in obeyance to divine covenant, the twain were made one.... Looking into the past from this eminence in time, several generations distant, we discern the Pilgrim Fathers [passengers on the *Mayflower*] approaching their future and ours. The Elder of the little company lifted his voice in thanksgiving for the safe journey to the new-found home. His wife and some accompanied him, but Patience, his daughter, came later to the colony, on the ship "Ann" in July, 1623. On August 5, 1624, she was married to Thomas Prence, afterward third governor of the colony.... And there was a Smith in those days, Ralph by name, who came later and settled on Cape Cod with his growing family. In 1724 his grandson Jesse, son of Thomas, married Sarah Higgins, daughter of Benjamin Higgins and Sarah Freeman, granddaughter of Major John Freeman and Mercy Prence, who was daughter of Gov. Thomas Prence and Patience Brewster, daughter of the Elder of the Plymouth Colony. In 1715 Jesse Smith and his family journeyed to Windham, Conn., and a few years later records find them in the Far West, Dutchess County, New York.

Nine daughters and three sons gathered about his table in the primeval forest. Many were the brave self-denials encountered for the sake of posterity, such hope brightening labors which to us might bring despair. To supply their food, a hard maple stump was hollowed out to pestle corn in; while most of the necessary utensils were manufactured by themselves, and what could not be produced in this way, was cheerfully concluded upon with, "we can do without it." The rolling-pin of birds-eye maple, fashioned by the hands of our great grandfather, is still in the family, an humble but much prized relic.

When this family moved from the East into New York, it was by wagon over trail, where much roadway had to be cleared. Many family treasures were broken, among such mishaps was the broken back of the old Bible brought from England. Therein was kept the family records; and the woodcuts were a source of wonder and suggestion to the young and eager minds. The remains of that Bible came down to the childhood of Anna Smith in 1800, and in reverence for what it had stood for in the developing of past generations, she cherished the last leaf, which was the title page; proving it to be a Geneva Bible, of 1660.

This is a curious date because the Geneva Bible ceased publication around 1640. While not the first Bible in English, it was originally published in Geneva in 1560, during the reign of Elizabeth in England. It proved to be enormously popular, especially among Puritans and other Calvinists, for its many annotations and marginalia based on strict Calvinistic interpretations of the text; it remained so even after the publication in 1611 of the great King James Bible, which attempted to bring together a text uniting Separatist or Puritan ideals and those of the historic Church after its break with Rome. Given the tone of pride with which this family treasure is mentioned, it is clear that the Calvinist/Huguenot roots still ran deep.

The brothers Ephraim and James ... inherited and occupied together, with most exceptional harmony and affection, the ample homestead, until each family numbered eight children. The family of Ephraim and Miriam Smith (married April 19, 1783) was complete with six daughters and two sons. Their sixth child, Anna, concerns us very intimately. As her sisters, Polly and Eunice, have told us, she was ever full of good cheer, the life and wit of the home circle. Hers was the keen view of things as they are; with a clear sense of justice and right and wrong. More like her father than her mother, they were most companionable. She was with him in farm and town transactions, interested in his business and public affairs. Her brothers were not strong and both died in early manhood. And at her father's going, at the age of fifty-four, Anna was the daughter best fitted and most capable of settling the affairs of his estate. This meant much physical as well as mental work; including journeying to St. Albans on horseback, and numerous short trips by same conveyance to Poughkeepsie, the county seat some twenty miles away.

The order of the household life divided the general work among the sisters, and each was expected to spin the wool and flax for her personal use. This was an irksome task for Anna, although a fine spinner, she preferring double the amount of work in the open air, and someone "had to see to things out and around." So it came about that her special big sister Rachel ... undertook much of her indoor tasks, leaving her free to superintend the general work of the place. Books were rare enough in her day to be of real value, and Anna made the most of what came her way; often standing in the doorway she would read to the enlightenment of busy workers in the room and out on the sun-warm grass. Always ready with a wit and a helping hand, she was fulfilling her young life the better to fulfill her future—and ours.

Now we will turn to our parental ancestors who emigrated at a later period. Collin—"a hill that rises by degrees." [T]he family tradition has been for generations to this effect. They were of the Huguenots of France.

She paraphrases the following from Charles Baird's *History of the Huguenot Emigration to America*:

Off the coast of Aunis, and nearly opposite the city of Le [La] Rochelle, lies the Isle of Ré, a spot that may be said to rival that city in its claim upon the attention of Americans of Huguenot descent, for it was the native place or place of refuge of many families that ultimately found their way to the New World. The Isle of Ré is but sixteen miles long, with an average breadth of three miles. Its principal towns are St. Martin, La Floeto, and Ars-en-Ré. At the time of the revolution the population was almost wholly Protestant. The fishermen, seamen, and salters of the region had been among the earliest converts to the Evangelical faith, a century and a half before, and their seclusion and obscurity had shielded them in a measure from molestation on account of their belief. . . .

Nicholas Filoux and Paul Collin, ancestors of families that settled in Connecticut, were inhabitants of the isle of Ré. Paul Collin and his wife fled from Ré, in 1683, to Dublin, Ireland. Paul Collin [was] one of the settlers of Narragansett in 1686.... Paul appears to have removed to Milford, Conn., after the breaking up of the Narragansett Colony [suspected by the Puritans of being papist because they were French] and was probably the father of John Collin, 1706, ancestor of the Hillsdale Collins. The tradition that represents this family of Huguenot descent is confirmed by documentary evidence. The name is that of an ancient Rochelese family in which the name of Jean Collin frequently occurs.

There seems to be a jump or gap in Miriam's contribution to the chronicle connecting the aforementioned Paul and the John Collin that follows here.

Just before the opening of the French war, John Collin was attracted to try a home in the New World. In his own ship, *The Pilgrim,* he transported his family to America, locating them in a Dutch colony. He returned to settle his holdings, and lading the remainder of his effects, weighed anchor for another voyage, new homeward bound. This is the last that is known of him. His ship is supposed to have been captured by British cruisers. His widow and two sons, David [David I, grandfather to David III, of our main story] and John, were now left to themselves, with greatly curtailed resources. They were an industrious family, and with no father to culture thrifty habits in the young boys, their mother "bound them out," one to a carpenter, the other to a tanner. Their apprenticeship was of short duration. A press-gang covertly impressed them into service against the French in Canada. At the close of the war, after seven years of service, they were discharged....

[David] returned to the homestead, took himself a helpmate, one Lucy Smith, a woman whose pious influence would have been a boon to his posterity, but she was taken early, leaving motherless a little daughter, Hannah, and an infant son, David [II]. The second wife, Esther Gillet, was the mother of three other children....

The Revolution occurred while his family were growing up. War with all its horrors and terrors, both of uncertainty and insecurity, was a reality, familiar about every hearthstone. A civil foe is the direst of all foes. . . . Tories were in every neighborhood, in 1777, making prey of loyal men and their property. One could hardly tell who of his neighbors were his friends, for openly they were friends, but painted and disguised as Indians, they were foes.

A band of these hypocrites surrounded the home of our David the first one Sunday night and forced an entrance. All were sleeping but Hannah, who was sitting up with her beau according to old-time custom. The household was aroused, forbidden to flee or raise an alarm. They shaved part of the head of the young lover, and demanded of his sweetheart the gold beads seen upon her in the church that day. At the first alarm of the robbers, however, she had unclasped them, letting them fall down her bosom, so she replied, and truthfully, that they were not hers, but were borrowed. They were given her after, because of her prompt thought that saved them.

The Tories made a search lest any of the family had escaped, and finding one warm bed, with no one belonging to it, looked more diligently, and behind a chimney in the back chamber found David, a lad of ten, trembling in terror. From the father they would extort $7000 [$71,000], of which he declared ignorance. They threatened his life by three times hanging him from the rafters, till life hung by a thread. It was a fruitless search for the gold, but they gathered all the household treasure, heirlooms, silver, fine linen, silks and cherished possessions from England and France. The house was stripped of all these and the family left desolate and exhausted by the reaction of terror.

With morning light spread the tidings of the outrage committed on the good man, and forth went bands to discover the bandits. In the woods, just west of the house, was discovered the place of their midnight bivouac by fragments of food, and among other things the precious family Bible, stripped of its heavy gold clasps and mountings.

Poor mistaken souls, taking the setting and leaving the pearl. His brother John living near, came with the multitude to express sympathy, and to say it was himself had received the seven thousand the day before, in payment for wheat and corn furnished to the army. [See chapter 4 for further details on John Collin's earnings.] A thousand dollars offered for robbers or booty was never claimed.

David, our grandfather, the boy behind the chimney, grew to manhood cultured by a father of the "strictest sort." Notwithstanding his was a most kindly heart.... Early in life he formed an interested acquaintance with Lucy Bingham.... The young man at the time of their meeting was a sergeant, and with two officers of higher rank was entertained at Uncle Lee's [at Salisbury]. Lucy was called to go to the cellar for cider, and the young man did the gallant and took the candle for her. A mutual admiration and regard were apparent, and at sweet sixteen she became his bride. After a year in Dutchess County, they settled in Columbia County, where the work of their hands was well rewarded, and they had the satisfaction of seeing the five sons and four daughters grow into useful man- and womanhood, an honor and assurance to parental hopes.

Harry and David were their eldest sons, lads of steady habits, a little experience in the War of 1812 as volunteers, and enough experience with the world to awaken the spirit of ambition, they were champing at the bit "to go." Their father proposed they search out his land in the great West [of New York State], or if more favorable to their inclination, he would give them a deed on a farm at home, or a check for a few thousand as a "nest egg."

The boys decided for the great West—away to western New York! On foot and almost without effects, they started to spy out their Canaan. The first day's walk of 35 miles took them to Albany, footsore and weary enough. They learned that to begin with moderation is speed at last, and overcame the distance accordingly. The turnpike from Albany to Fort Niagara was the only thoroughfare, and it thronged with teaming government wagons, enginery of war, returning soldiers from the victory of Commodore Perry and the Oswego Guards. Going west was the interminable train of covered moving wagons. But our travelers walked all the way through a land in its native glory of noble forest growth. A land of promise—promising much timber, eventually much harvest, and above all much hard labor.... From [Yates County] David returned home. Harry went on ... sight seeing.

The story which today's anniversary makes memorable to us ... was on this wise: The Collin families, in Columbia and Dutchess counties, in their exchange of visits, came to Hillsdale to see David and Lucy. In the good old-fashioned visit, each recounted freely of their welfare and interests. Uncle Clark, inadvertently speaking of his good neighbors, mentioned particularly Captain Smith's family, and spoke of his smart daughters, especially of one Anna. Of course, it was but a passing tribute, and none would care to listen but the elder people. But what young man was ever caught napping when smart girls were being talked about? Surely not our father. He caught an idea which was unsuspectedly accomplished. The Clark cousins suddenly became very interesting, also their neighbors, the Smiths. The sleigh was often at the door, in the style befitting one and twenty, and away they go, David and his sister Harriet, "a-cousining!"

But they only call on the Clarks; as they are out for a ride, a call at the Smiths' was different—an evening gone before they knew it. A social winter it was—the journey West, and plans for a second in the spring were themes for two of the company at least. To Onondaga County David came again, hired five acres cleared, and built a future home on a purchase of land adjoining the "State's Hundred" that came to him as bounty for service in the war of 1812—on this very spot where we are celebrating this fiftieth anniversary....

The Autumn found a comfortable home [see the later description for just how comfortable!] in the heart of the forest, and the woods resounded to the ring of the woodsman's ax. On January 2, 1817, David Collin, 3rd, and Anna Smith were married at Northeast, Dutchess County, New York. Her sister, Polly, and Orin Clark officiated as bridesmaid and groomsman. Until February 10th thoughts and hands were busy in the mother's home providing all that prudent ones could devise or suggest. On the 13th they left

Hillsdale, accompanied by one man and a little boy, Benson Brazee, aged six. It was a weary nine days' journey of toil and plunge—now mud, now snow, in wagon or sleigh as roads permitted; a foot stove and soap stone were comforts by the way. Arriving at their own door, the carpenters bench was cleared of shavings and spread for their first meal in the heart of the winter-covered forest—the one best enjoyed in all their lives.

Geneva Armstrong added this entry fifty years later:

> They soon settled down to real life, boarding the help, cooking over the fireplace and baking in the brick oven or the tin oven before the fire. In time they kept a blacksmith and carpenter all the time, a shop being built for their purposes. A tailor and a cobbler came once a year and fitted up the family. Visitors were miles away, and holidays farther apart. Thanksgiving dinner was served to large numbers, friends coming in long, low box sleighs, with no lack of straw or buffalo robes. Long, heavy cloaks, high-crowned bonnets, full skirted gowns that would last for years and years without any change, thick topped boots for winter, a long camelot cloak, saddlebag—pockets tied round the waist, capacious in the extreme—and a cloth riding habit were some of the articles of apparel worn by the mistress of the new house.
>
> Butter, cheese, lard, soap, maple-sugar, candles, ropes, baskets, harness, etc., were all home made. The first boy, Edmond, was choked on catnip tea, which the helpful neighbor forgot to strain for the newborn baby. The six others were at the village school till advanced enough to be away—Harriet and Miriam at Mrs. Willard's Seminary for Girls in Troy, David at the Polytechnic in the same city, Anna at Homer Academy. Education, progress and helpfulness were strong points in the mother's influence over her children and her husband. As it is, or was, the man had the credit of helping largely in the building of church, school, mills, waterpower for manufacturing purposes, but in reality the wife was the progressive power behind the throne that helped, and persisted in bringing about these improvements.

2

> "Allow not nature more than nature needs..."
> —*King Lear*, 2.4.269

In 1916, descendants of Anna Collin Wells, daughter of David Collin III, on the occasion of the one hundredth anniversary of David and Anna Collin's wedding, added the following extracts from her memoirs to the family chronicle, which I have abridged a very little. There is some redundancy with her older sister Miriam's account of fifty years earlier, especially regarding the early days, but Anna's has richer detail and character and elements deserve retelling, if only to fix in our own minds how the family saw themselves.

When Grandfather David [David Sr.'s father], attained his majority he, with his brother James, son of Esther Gillett [David II's second wife], so half-brother, divided their inheritance, David most generously giving James the large landed estate, taking only $10,000 [$110,000+] as his portion, going to Hillsdale, Columbia County, to begin anew. Having a practical mind for application to "whatever his hand came to" with energy and perseverance, slowly wrought his own fortune, purchased a farm by the "sweat of his brow," toiled, labored unceasingly for success, with one true, honest purpose to deal justly by all....

The marriage of David Collin and Lucy Bingham proved as full of happiness as of care for fifty-three years. Nine children were given them, born and thriftily cared for in the old homestead in Hillsdale. Lived to see them all married was the history. Every energy was brought to secure the wherewithal. The stalwart, strong, practical man had little of the more sensitive, tender nature that the small, delicate ladywife was given. The imagination of rose-tinted cloud land, vistas never opening to the austere, decided man of business, she subdued inherited longings for the more gentle phases of life. But with the income from harvests from fertile farms, multiplied by the interest accruing from safe investments, was added the selling to New York markets the herd of fattened beeves. Each year all income, small expenditure.

The sons, as my father often told his children, at least the older ones, were allowed only occasional days in the Winter at school. So David's whole course was covered by three months of schooling, his educational equipment for life's responsibilities. Of the younger sons, one, at least, found his way to Hudson, entered a course without leave of authorities, who at last paid the bills of the seeker for knowledge without murmuring. The mother, keeping the confidence, loved of the children, stood as a barrier to the stern, inflexible law-maker of the head of the house, slipping quietly into ever-willing hands, when baking was completed, little turnovers for lunch, delighting hungry children, testifying to mother-love in this satisfying, sustaining way. When old, the remembrance of this treat, savory, spicy, was a welcome subject as a testimony "to mother," as she sat in her straight-backed chair in her corner of the broad fireplace by the oven door.

As majority was reached, Harry and David [David III, or David Sr., of Fayetteville] were told of Revolutionary soldier rights, lands purchased in the Far West, two and three hundred acre pieces. The boys could take horses for conveyance and each take as his own, one of the sections. The journey beyond civilization in 1813 through the forest, often by blazed trees, sleeping under haystacks, over footpaths or corduroy roads [logs laid transversely], found them first at Manlius, one mile east of [what would become] Fayetteville on the Black section [possibly named for a former owner], where were five acres of clearing. Stopped at the tavern just east, kept by one Jones. Manlius Four Corners [as Fayetteville was then known] had but a few houses. Inhabitants [were] Breeds, Kinneys and others. Each with their quiver full of a good dozen heirs. . . .

The brothers lingered only for a rest, then rode on to Benton, Yates County, which location Harry selected. [Harry] [w]ishing to see Niagara Falls, the brothers parted, Harry going westward to view the wonderful Falls, David returning to Jones tavern, engaged help for erecting a house. Leaving the work to be completed, he returned home to report the journey. Meantime work had not been all-engrossing. The young people had gathered for merry times now and then in society, dancing being the favorite pastime.... Report reached the young business man through James Collin, half-brother of his father, living at Northeast, that one Anna Smith was the smartest, most capable girl in Dutchess County. Common sense directed the [wish?] to an introduction to said Anne. Her home, that of Ephraim and Miriam Smith, at Northeast, Dutchess County, NY, was upon a farm. The story and a half house still [stood] [ca. 1890] as at the time in 1783, when they established a new home. This roof covered two households, brothers James and Ephraim Smith, until each numbered eight children, James occupying the basement . . . Anna, the dexterous spinner of wool and flax, reigned in the large basement workroom, where a great fireplace occupies its due share of the room.... In this lower room it was where each season Anna Smith spun yarn sufficient for five hundred yards of woolen and linen cloth; it was woven by some weaver who made a weaving business. As the rolls came home, she divided each piece into three equal parts; each of the sisters who did the housework had her third with the spinner of warp and woof. They always had patience. When finding a cup creamy from the pan set down upon their snow-white shelves—"Oh, Anna's been here!" were the words heard at the wheel. There too, many a long poem or chapters were learned that were as fresh in memory at threescore and ten as when learned quickly, as "the book or papers could be retained but for a little—must be returned." Education was the one unsatisfied hunger of the soul; schools were rare opportunities. Only the most common branches were taught by Miss Susan Goodrich in the District School. But the wonderful gift of memory, clear quick judgment, that was given Anna Smith as a special talent, grew stronger with added years, even in to old age. Her father, appreciating her gifts so transparent to all, coming in contact with her, looked to her as a leader, guide and took his daughter into his confidence in business as a helper. Thus, in legal knowledge her education was wrought out by insight into complications, where avarice and greed were not in harmony with truth and the right. Human nature is unchanged. Each generation evinces selfishness....

Then came the goodly young man from Columbia County, introduced by his uncle, James Collin, wooed and won his bride. The wedding trousseau was mostly of homemade material, the bride's own spinning, as were dozens of linen sheets and woolen artistically woven patterns of tablecloths—the whole outfit for a well-to-do bride. Then came the trip to Poughkeepsie for house-furnishing; she must prepare the sidesaddle, nests of brass kettles from one holding eight pails or more down to a tiny pattern, the brass warming-pan, footstove, innumerable necessary kitchen conveniences for cooking. In this department Anna invested $700 [nearly $6000 today]. What bride of this generation has a single thought for this practical need! Then the broadcloth pelisse, belted down with gold clasps, broadcloth cloak and store cloth dresses, made in town. All imperative.

The wedding dinner, which, with real Dutchess County hospitality, must include all kinds of meats, fowls, delicacies in generous, loaded tables, around which those bidden to the marriage must sit for a substantial meal, with cakes and pies baked in the great brick oven days before, so there was no lack at the feast, neither lack of kindest wishes for the favorite daughter of the house, who, with much trembling of heart, was given to a new life in the wildwood, where Indians dwelt and wild beasts roamed—Central New York....

The boxes containing the wherewithal to furnish with every comfort the new home in the wilderness were loaded upon sleighs, the many items loving, thoughtful ones in this Smith home could add to surprise in the unpacking. Three teams, two sleighs drawn by horses, one by yoke of cattle, started with the bride and groom next day [January 3, 1817] for Hillsdale, the home of David Collin, remaining there for a little visit and adding other necessary articles; the groom had provided outfit for farming. The day before leaving, a poor man, Mr. Brazee, came bringing his little son, Benson, as a gift to the young people. The feeble condition of his wife, his own days nearly numbered by consumption, induced him to secure homes for his little children. This boy of five years he earnestly urged they would take. The Smith nature, ever compassionate, accepted the charge; the boy accepted the father's tearful blessing as they parted forever on the following wintry morning.

The romance of the nine days' journey was more of weariness, slow travel, toward the last corduroy roads through dense forests at Hartsville [just a bit east of what is now the Fayetteville area]. The high hills either side of the way in the gloaming cast heavy shadows over the weary travelers. "Almost home," said the young husband; "how do you like the prospect?" Unworded loneliness brought the old homestead with its loving faces before the mind's eye, though the response was cheery, but the picture then reflected upon memory's halls never faded.

At twilight of a cold winter's day the real home was reached, roughly furnished by the jobbers. The story and a half house, with its large kitchen, open fireplace that received great, whole logs, smaller topstick, forestick upon iron andirons, with many split sticks piled over shavings, etc., making a genuine woodpile and generous fire; the door opened upon a stoop at the east; two windows, either side lighting the living-room. By the north one was the chamber door leading to one large room, which held four beds in my childhood. Upon the west side of the kitchen was a bedroom, one window, then the pantry. This was "the home" for eight years.

The first impressions were not of a house swept and garnished. A carpenter's bench was the furniture. Upon this the bride spread the evening meal from the stores, while the young husband helped by brushing off the shavings, kindling a cheerful fire. The teamsters were sent to neighbor Jones' tavern. Dry-goods boxes furnished seats for the first meal. The hired teams, after a little rest, were sent back to their distant home. Thus was established, in 1817, a new home in central New York. The chief employment was laborious—felling giant trees the day long, logging or burning great heaps of these magnificent lords of the forest until 11 o'clock at night. These days I've often heard my father number "as the happiest of his life." The trees and stumps must needs be removed that the ground could be plowed for seed-time and harvest.

In the lot north of the house an apple orchard was soon set, the trees bought of a Mr. Bliss, the nurseryman of this locality, who himself owned and set out acres of orcharding upon a farm on High Bridge Street. The little trees were placed among the stumps, growing to produce superior apples—every year Spitzenbergs, Seek-no-furthers, Alfred Sweets, Gilliflowers, Greenings, Harvest Boughs, Fall Pippins, Golden Sweets, Russets and other grafted varieties—large, perfect, each of them, in flavor, size, soundness, excelling any seen since. This provision for future health and table supplies was most timely, wise, providing abundance of wholesome, toothsome fruit to many families aside from their own, and large hogsheads of cider for vinegar and drinking.

My mother had a terror, fear, of Indians, reading of the Wyoming [in northeastern Pennsylvania] massacre. [In July 1778, Iroquois and British troops destroyed the settlement. By the time David and Anna had settled in Manlius Four Corners, the Iroquois had come through a period of terrible cultural dissolution to a new revival and revision of the traditional ways under the teaching of the prophet Handsome Lake, ca. 1750–1815.] This first winter, I think, just at evening-time, a band of young Indians, eighteen in number, came to the door asking for lodging for the night. Father dared not refuse, knowing the memory of a kindness never fades with these children of the forest. Quickly they saw the young wife's fear, or felt it in the atmosphere, their quick occult faculties reading clearly. At once they walked up to my father, handing him their guns, having returned from a long hunt. He opened the door of the bedroom, which would not close, and put the guns in a corner of the little room. The warriors at once lay themselves upon the floor, with their feet to the fire, falling peacefully asleep. Early my parents awoke to find the guns and their owners had folded their blankets, like the Arabs, and as quietly stolen away.

Thereafter there was never a heart-beat of fear, but most kindly welcome to the Indians and squaws, with their papooses bound straight upon a board, which had its carved arch over the head to carry the child by, some very artistically done. These natives of the soil were at home in the wood. North of the house upon the hill, east, was a rocky ledge—a square long oven—which they told my mother they baked bread in years ago [whence the name of Betsy Knapp's farm, Indian Oven]. Often in my childhood a band of fifteen or twenty would occupy our kitchen floor at night at one time. [The Collin farm was a good halfway mark between the Oneida and Onondaga nations, and the present Route 5 was the main route between the reservations.] Three bands, not friends, were, unknown to each other, lodged, one in the large weaving and washing room, one in the kitchen, another in the barn. Every one was addressed by name, as my mother remembered faces. I recall one "Margaret" one evening taught Miriam and me to sew beads upon knitting sheaves' bags made of buckskin or the pretty moccasins. Of woven baskets, in every form, many were purchased— "hand baskets," in all sizes, with covers.

The remnants of the family dinner were passed along, for their appetites were not fastidious, save in the matter of bread; light "white bread was all cheat," holes not sustaining. Their own bread, great brown round loaves, was solid with beans [which, along with corn and squash, made up the "three sisters," both spiritual and vegetable staples of their diet]. One summer day a band of ten or fifteen, counting children of all sizes, from little papoose lashed upon a board, after sundry cooking in the kitchen, assembled in the front yard, now enclosed by a white picket fence with three gates, east, west, south to the road. Miriam and I, with children's inquisitive disposition to take in knowledge quietly through the eye source, went to see the party dine. For the elders was a grass seat circling the repast. From a bag was rolled out one of the solid bread loaves; upon this a two-year brave was seated, another for yet an older heir, while the papoose was leaned against the fence, satisfied in watching the diners. As bread was called for, a child was lifted from a loaf, a thick slice cut, the little one reseated, content in ministering to the course; the babies kept bound with no tossing, trotting or rocking, save as tied to the limb of a swaying tree, whence tradition says originated the "Rock-a-by baby on the tree top,/When the wind blows the cradle will rock...."

A crooked baby of the aborigines was never seen; for nine months the tender frame was kept straight as an Indian should grow. So the bones were not bent to a nurse's comfort in position to induce weak, tender, pliable framework for the living to contend with through a longer or shorter period, when, after "enduring all things," comes rest. . . .

Workmen were employed to help in the clearing, boarded and lodged in the spacious chamber. Early one morning, while preparing breakfast for the family, [my mother noticed] five wolves walked slowing by the open door, tired after a long tramp, seating themselves where the cowhouse afterward stood, to rest, but as the men were called together they had gone, so at later times a sharpshooter was in demand. Word came that the next neighbor, Mr. Jones, was accidentally killed in felling a tree near the present school house. He kept the inn, afterward the stage hostelry for travelers on the turnpike. Elder Breed's family owned a farm southeast upon the hillside adjoining my father's three hundred acres. Mr. "Elder," following in the steps of his father, "Gershon" Breed, one of the first settlers, was a Baptist preacher officiating in various hamlets, school houses serving for sanctuaries on Sabbath days. The cares of the farm were delegated to his alert, energetic "Teall" wife who was equal to the ingathering at harvest time, caring for the large flocks of geese and her fourteen children. They were excellent neighbors, true friends.

December 28, 1817, was born to David and Anna Smith Collin a son, Edmund, a strong, healthy baby boy. Quiet was established for a restful night, after the anxiety and unworded experiences where joy and thanksgiving song filled the hearts of the young parents. The good physician had gone upon horseback over the hill to his Manlius home. The child awoke to cry. A kind neighbor on attendance prepared a caraway seed tea, giving it without straining. A seed somehow stopped the breath, and the child was not, for God took it to join the innumerable infant choral above. The sorrow, fulfilling the best intentions, could not recall life, while bereavement, disappointment and grief of the parents only ended with their lives.

In Bible times of patriarchs, wealth was counted by wells; "and Isaac digged a well," is recorded as an event worthy of his effort. Water, pure, clear, refreshing, is never so prized as in a dry and thirsty land where no water is.... So for the dwellers in the new home a well must be dug. The earth twenty feet to the plaster rock, thirty through it and twenty below was found to reach pure flowing water. The usual peach limb, its two branches held each in a hand of the locator of water, was found to gradually incline toward the said spot where digging began. Whether wind controlled the twig, or the judgment of man the decision, is not recorded. The deep well was north of the kitchen, between that and the woodhouse; a large cylinder wheel above for strong rope and chain to wind upon hung high over the well curb; a large stone was suspended by chain; northeast of the curb was the balance power (inclosed). No need of ice to cool the water from the depths. A cistern in the woodhouse furnished a supply of soft water.

A barn was the first building erected south of the road across the corduroy, made by felling trees laid side by side closely, covered with earth, opposite to the house. There stood giant forest trees which, when felled, furnished heavy timbers for the foundation and framework of the great building; the stumps thereof, left standing in the barn [as a kind of flooring], where when we were children [we] jumped upon the hay.

A stranger from the East [David Collin Sr.] was an object of neighborly interest, as the maidens about had thought the young man who came to build and establish a home somewhat superior. As mother's house-furnishing was so generous in supply, many comforts unusual, the friendly caller found topic wherewith to interest her friends. Their children partook of the spirit. As a little girl came in, socially inclined, she observed a hair-covered trunk with brass-headed nails, used to decorate and hold the affair. The initials of my grandfather upon the top she spied at once, airing her knowledge by saying, "E. for David, and S. for Collin; Mr. Collin has all of his things marked."

Another, as wise, saw a long black bottle hung high above the mantel tree, in the cork a goose quill for the ink to flow through when pouring and questioned Mrs. Collin, "Who sucks there?" she doubtless helping care for the home baby. The little boy, Benson, proved company in the lonely hours; he could gather chips for the fire. One day, utilizing his Bible lessons, he came in with a question and this thought evolved, "Who picks up chips for God and the Lord in Heaven?"

Benson, ever faithful, loyal, was a "bound boy," but never knew the meaning of the legal term; ever kind, willing. At twenty-one, as the papers read, he had two suits of new clothes and $100 [$1,600], but remained until twenty-four for wages, when, with little gifts to little Miriam and Anna, mine a sugar dollie, still extant, with a tender, sad parting, he bade us all good-by. He never again saw any of his relatives, his parents both dying soon after they gave him away, the brothers being placed with other families. Benson went to Wisconsin, investing his money in a farm near Milwaukee, which proved wise. Afterward he wrote my father he could purchase for him, at Waukesha, a good investment, as afterward that was sold for cash at $25,000 [$460,000]. The ratio of increase wonderfully multiplied, part now of the thriving city of Waukesha. Benson married a school teacher who came from the east. His sons grew to be active business men. One, a lawyer, came to see us years ago. The family have passed away mostly. . . .

December 26, 1818, Caroline was born, the very welcome little stranger from a far country, coming as sunshine, joy, light to the hearts for the young parents . . . March 15, 1821, another daughter, Lucy Bingham, was added to the group. . . . The days were full of duties; besides the care of the household and children, the spinning was essential, for garments must be renewed—not like the Israelites' in warp and woof that never failed during forty years of wilderness life. Would that such fabric could now be found!

Then, August 22, 1822, was born unto them a son, David [David Jr.], and on November 15, 1824, Henriette, that dark-haired maiden. When she was eight months old the preparations for a more roomy dwelling were complete. Work began. The erection of the present front now standing, gave a hall, stairway into chambers three, with a baggage room for supplies with presses, and a fireplace in the east and west larger rooms; below at the right the sitting room with its china cupboard, two tiers of shelves above, below for the pretty pink and chocolate colored dishes and a set of all sizes of plates, etc., representing the great fire in the city of New York in 1835....

This cupboard was between the door that opened into the old kitchen, family room and a clothes-press east that held father's and mother's best garments, a blue chest of Dutchess County linen, shelves with always generous supplies of mother's raised doughnuts, honey that with all the children's appetites went together, maple sugar, the great white sugar loaf for the company and my parents' tea; its wrapping used to color stockings a fine dark chocolate shade. In the northwest corner of the sitting-room stood the high-post curtained bed-stead with its gracefully hung curtains, fine pictures of dogs, horses, etc., with environment of flowers upon the cambric. A double box plaiting, of which 3/4 of a yard deep about the top, and other long hangings on either side, looped back, with a valance of the same material, curtained the bottom box, plaited as above.

The high feather bed, well shook up and covered with a double carpet coverlet of artistic pattern in the blue and white weaving, was my parents' resting place. A bed was considered a part of the furnishing of a complete sitting-room; a mantel above a large fireplace between the two east windows, with brass andirons, shovel, tongs and their rests, holding them at either side, with a bellows essential to start the blaze. The same outfit was in the parlor upon the west side. This room was also more attractive for its two alcoves, either side of the fireplace, with cupboards, close wood doors below and glass above. Here were convenient locked places for choice sweetmeats, best bonnets, hats, papers, books. At the end of the hall a door entered under the stairs to the cellar-way, from whence came fragrant smells of toothsome apples and cider. Upon the platform in the corner, in the season, stood a barrel of cider-apple sauce, served three times a day upon the long table, a dish at each end.

In the building of the house skilled workmen were employed. One, "Keefe," a carpenter, applied to have fine work in charge, as blinds, fancy carved mantels in the parlor, corner woodwork finished with gilt-covered stars set in a blue ground, all of the extra decoration hand-wrought.

This man, John Van Zandt, associated from this time, 1825, until 1853, with the family as one of its members, a gentleman in all the etiquette of refinement, deserving a place in this record.... His parents were Albany Van Zandts, who held positions social and business among its first-class people. His mother died when John was three or four years of age. Two maiden sisters cared for his early instruction....

Society had its charms; as he attained manhood, gaiety in dancing, etc., was heartily enjoyed. Singing in the Presbyterian church choir was a religious pleasure, as one of the sweet singers of soprano had promised to be his chosen bride.... A fever prevalent (typhoid) prostrated her. The devoted lover prayerfully watched beside her when the fever ran high ... [but] death came to claim the dear Martha.

With multiplied years her lover grew more and more absorbed in her, loving the memory of every word; grace idealized.... The shock to the young man when the end came was more than endurance could meet.

Van Zandt fled from friends, home, country, boarding as ship's carpenter on a man-of-war vessel, seeking in activity equilibrium for tired brain, in labor forgetfulness. Several years a wanderer upon the waves of the ocean, to still the restless waves, billows of sorrow, bereavement, he visited many lands;... While Napoleon Bonaparte "slept his last sleep" on the isle of St. Helena, the vessel twice circled it. None were allowed to land. Shipwrecked upon the Canada coast, exhausted, he was taken to a nunnery hospital. He refused to take the last unction from the priests, ... and rallied with unceasing gratitude to those who ministered to him.

He came to Fayetteville and was employed by my father, who twice paid him $75 [$1,200] at a time. Going with a full purse, he would return with an empty one in a few days. First, taste established in the home where wine was common, then stronger drink to drown trouble, forged the chains to wreck the possibilities of a grand future for one of nature's true generous-hearted noblemen.... After the second payment was gone, Van Zandt returned to say to my father he wished to remain with him in any capacity—carpenter, gardner [sic], or man of all work with no pay, save occasionally a new suit and some change. When the impulse overpowered him, he would ask for money, be gone to Fayetteville or Manlius Center a day or two.

When crossing the bridge over the creek he would say, "Uncle John, you've too much sail on; get down," and so would creep over. Instinct. Van Zandt was most reverent in his regard for my mother, who always treated him with kindness and sympathy. 'Twas for this he chose to remain.... When work was waiting for the effects of dazed brain to clear in harvest-time, some implement needing mending, and Van Zandt refused all calls to meals, sitting on the end of the bench upon the stoop, the word, "Anna, go bring Van Zandt to dinner," was a command always effectual. Softly whistling to himself the echo of the strain still in the air, I could not have been over four years, when, with emphasis [I said,] "Van Zandt, come right in to dinner!" he would, as if the evil was exorcized, smilingly take my hand, to be led to his usual seat at my father's left, the calm of weeks following.... Van Zandt must have been more than ninety years of age when he bade us the last good-by....

To return to the completed house with its extension: Beyond the first habitation was a milk and sink room a step up, next the first pantry, with one window west, a door east, a step down to the well platform, then a step up again to the large woodhouse with its cistern at the southwest side, a door west, a platform direct from well house to the large, one step up, workroom where spinning-wheels for the wool, flax, reels, quillwheels, warping-swifts, bars and all the various needful cloth-making implements were in use, with the great loom for weaving; an iron kettle set in an arch used for washing-day, lard-trying, souse-making, etc.; by the open under fire arch was a door into the carriage room, harness and fine family sleigh. The workroom also had a large fireplace, a sink and a corner cupboard.

'Twas in this room business in results was achieved. Kersey blankets, plaid, blue and white, black and white, were woven; crash towels, wooled clothes spun and made into great webs rolled on the beam.... Now one woman can attend many spindles in the great factories. The age of single-handed carding, dyeing in the round dye tubs always standing in a corner of the kitchen fireplace as a seat, is past.

The town or country had at this time few poor dependent upon charity, no poorhouse. My father was poormaster about 1826. People about would take, for a small consideration, one or more of the needy, helpless to board. There were no insane asylums [though Utica was to have one in a couple of decades]. Among the suffering was a refined, polished Frenchman, insane, that no one would receive. My father assumed the care, placing him in the west chamber, my mother often taking him his meals. The one constant refrain, repeated continually, was, "I never killed anybody." His name was La Farge, I believe. One day he thrust his fork into his side, without serious injury. Another time he followed the one who took his meal through the door; quickly slipping by, he jumped over the banister. The imprint of the fall remained ever after upon the baseboard. Then he was removed to the wash or workroom, the neighbors dropping in to cheer and chat with the unfortunate exile. He had doubtless observed the well curb in passing. Without a word, one day slipping by the incomer, he took three long jumps over the walk and leaped the fatal seventy-five feet to the bottom of the well. No trace of his friends was ever found. The shock to my mother's nervous system induced prostration, indeed, never left her....

One by one the neighboring farmers were attacked by the western fever, as every day [prairie] schooners carrying movers westward passed on the road. These long wagons with arched tops covered with white cloth contained the earthly possessions and family of the sturdy farmer. Kettles were suspended underneath and all implements possible were attached to the moving caravan, sometime two extra horses and cows accompanying. Later in my childhood finished houses with windows, doors, stove, cupboards, etc., complete, were drawn; the wagon wheels at either end were on long reaches containing most convenient, useful things for a home in the wilds.

As the owners of farms about desired to sell, my father purchased one by one, adding acres to his own, the Jones', Black, Gregory, land proprietors, with others, selling for $40 or so an acre [$650]. My father cultivated the farms, the produce, at good prices, paying for the investment. Then he was sure of his father's ready help, in Hillsdale, he having money to place....

The stage route on the Genesee Turnpike [now Route 5] from Albany to Buffalo, each city throughout the State still having its Genesee Street, was the only way of travel westward, save by the family wagons, the four horses often having all they could manage in pulling the coach through the Spring and Autumn road ruts, twelve or more passengers inside the swaying box and others with the skilled driver, who handled the reins as if interests of government in the state all depended on him alone. The stage coming away over the hill was an event, breaking the monotony of the day by the clarion note of the bugle horn, the children's joy.... [T]he Mecca of all inns, noted and sought by all stage travelers was Mrs. Neeley's.... Mrs. Neeley's skill as a cook, giving a generous, savory, appetizing meal, was well known. The weary would tighten girdles, Indian fashion, fasting without murmuring until they should reach the wholesome, satisfying table.

In times of special political events, as presidential or State elections, as in [the] Harrison and Tyler "Tippecanoe and Tyler too" convention, twelve coaches would take politicians through the State, often with string bands, As my father's was one of the historic country places in the new State, music and songs of serenade were there given in going and returning.

There was no church at Manlius Four Corners, so in the early days my father and mother rode on horseback over the hills to Trinity Presbyterian, Manlius [about three miles over the hills along Duiguid Road] taking their lunch or accepting cordial invitations with their friends. As their visiting circle included Pompey people [another eight to ten miles further south], so the few scattering, congenial ones were drawn together in close sympathy. The dinners and teas were genuine visits of hours, the meals sustaining, not dainty, transparent sandwiches or crackers with a baby cup of tea, as now meet social obligations, with a crowd rushing, exchanging frosty conventional nothings in cold critical greetings, more to the wardrobe than individuals.

Rev. Cushman supplied the pulpit in Manlius; his wife and daughters, most agreeable, often visited my mother. I recall she presented Mrs. Cushman my first cheese, made when I was ten years of age. In 1829 the Fayetteville Presbyterian Church was built, dedicated with suitable services, after which, in July, a grand feast was spread on tables upon the grass in front of the edifice. The structure was of wood, the gallery extending on east, south and west sides; many windows with small glass. The pulpit with its eight or ten ascent steps, was at the north, a half-circular railing closing pillars beneath to support it. Each contributor bought, at varied prices, the pew desired and was given a deed of the same.... My father owned a pew for his tenants to occupy. Later the Baptists erected their sanctuary. He secured a pew in that; had one in Manlius Church, I believe.

The District School was, as now, at the corner of Genesee Turnpike and Manlius Road. In 1828 Sylvester Gardner, of Eagle Village, was the teacher in the school, Caroline, a maiden of ten, his pupil. The Winter lesson he learned was to wait for her as his bride, so returned to his father's farm with resolve. They met when ten years more had gone. Busy years they were, my father's business growing, with never a vacation time in the building of large barns to secure hay and grain, a saw mill and plaster mill by the mill pond ... with lime kilns for farms supply of material as buildings were put up, a blacksmith shop and skilled smith by the year to keep tools in repair, Philander Smith for many years, Van Zandt, the gardner [sic] and carpenter, plaster bed to work upon the banks of Upper Green Lake, with all the farm work, seven tenant houses occupied, while always single hands were lodged by the year. All the workers boarded at my father's table, in summer eighteen, in Winter six or eight, to chop, hew, and, in Springtime, work in the sugar bush.

There is a family legend about daily morning prayers at this period, too, depicting the family on their knees in the kitchen and the many hands, with hats in hand, still and silent in the barnyard, while Mr. Collin's voice boomed the word of the Lord across the landscape.

This all involved unworded toil within; not strange that my mother, after the nervous shock, should have been physically overworked. The early breakfast cooking was done by and over a great kitchen fire and in the brick oven and open tin baker before the blazing heat; yet never were there such sweet-cream breakfast biscuits eaten or so light, toothsome, raised fried cakes, pies innumerable, bread kneaded in the great bread trough to its capacity, filling the mouth of the deep oven, so tender, sweet and tasty. Then the great iron dinner pot upon the crane, holding four or five pales full, with its chicken pot pie, tossing, bubbling up to lift the cover, well seasoned with a generous 2/3 of a roll of golden butter. The cooking for the multitude involved constant labor under the sun and by candle light far into the night. [Indeed the women of the family and the female help often did not leave the fireplace or workroom for days on end.]

Hours were not limited by laborers to eight, ten or twelve a day. Fifty cents a day [$8+], or the same in food supplies, was the normal wage; sometimes a pork from the packing of eighteen or twenty pigs, all fatted on corn. Van Zandt had charge of feeding—he used to say, "with a spoon," at last, when they could not rise to eat. Smoked hams or shoulders, beef, lamb, mutton, wheat or corn flour, etc. There was no market [in those early days]; there were the herds, fresh, fat, to draw from. In summer, besides the three full meals, there were morning and afternoon luncheon to set out. Often dinner and lunch were packed for [?] of center farm hands, Henry Hiltz, Joseph Zea, Joseph Esmond among the leaders, to march through wheat fields with cradles swinging, six or eight following in a row, among the hayfields.

The shoemaker came once a year, as father had bench and tools, into the workroom to peg away or sew with bristle and waxed end the family supply of boots and shoes. Tailoresses and dress makers, Arvilla and Euphrasia Cook, often came for months, with goose and patterns.... Often two helpers were in the kitchen department; competent spinners they must be, to give several hours to spinning the wool. The "leach" tub for soap making was an institution standing west of the house by the smokehouse and milking-yard. Always the soap in the great barrels in the cellar must be a year or two old before using, age improving the light mahogany-colored mass you could cut into quivering pieces, superior to any compound that now has for its body "talc" from South Carolina at $7.00 a ton [$120], or rosin to hold the unspeakable scented compound in cake form with a foreign name applied.

Candle dipping was another variety of labor. For days before the wick must be cut the right length, twisted evenly about a long cedar stick, upon which eight wicks were placed. In the morning the great kettle with clear tallow, a proportion of beeswax added, was heated over the washroom fire, long poles laid upon two chairs, the sticks with wicks placed at regular intervals, laid across the kettle of grease, in the middle of the way rough boards placed under to catch the drops, and two people seated, one upon either side, put two sticks at a time over the tallow, so the wicks would be thoroughly wetted, then placed at the chair end, so repeating until the stiff candles were of sufficient size. I think the wicks were first wet with vinegar and dried to prevent sputtering as they burned. The kettle was kept full to the brim by hot water added as the grease lowered. Next morning, when hardened, the candles were slipped off into boxes for a year's use. Only the very aged wore spectacles, dim, clear, one candle being sufficient; it did not injure the delicate organ as gas, electric or kerosene light of today.

At the north end of the garden, just below the cornhouse, stood the long rows of beehives, square boxes, smaller ones, a foot square, placed upon the top at a certain time for whiter cap honey storing. In the Autumn my father had the charge of taking up the honey. Small pits were digged 1/2 foot deep, pine sticks with rags tied at one end dipped in sulfur being placed in the bottom wigwam style, the sulfur ends converging to the top. A hive of bees was carefully brought as the sulfur was lighted and set over the pit, the whole covered with a cloth, the bees dropping dead in the pit. These hives were brought to the workroom, the perfectly filled comb taken carefully out into the pans, the broken pieces put into a strong linen strainer suspended before the blazing fire to drain for days. When all was finished, the hives were carefully scraped, the honeycomb was put into an iron kettle to melt and be strained for beeswax.

Every year some of the small broken pieces that [had] drained were put into a new tub filled with clear well water made so thick with honey when you tested by an egg put into the mixture it would show the size of a shilling. This was then strained, put into a half barrel, working, was drawn off into another half barrel, tightly corked or closed. This was "Meitheglein" tonic for invalids, particularly those with lung weakness.

My mother was a noted healer of physical ailments, having from her mother many remedies, more from the squaws, who gave her the various roots and herbs used by the tribes. The west side and south side of the garden were her medical herb quarters—southernwood, wormwood, rue, tansy, archangel, King Solomon's seal, black cohosh, Burnet, sage, Summer savory and many other varieties, interspersed with lavender, balm, white-water grapevine, asparagus bed and choice flowers, pansies, lilies, etc., for brightness. And pits of superior peaches, plums, etc., were always put into the ground, tree-growing being her specialty.

My mother's cheerful, social nature, with gifts conversational, always interspersed with pat anecdote in illustration, with keen insight into human nature, brought her constant guests to entertain. The wives of the workmen, either as a duty or pleasure, almost daily happened in for the day or afternoon with some of their children. Having no occasion for much home work, their husbands boarding at my father's, they had no haste or occupation, save easy going round. Some would take sewing to do, others spinning. Old Mrs. Zea, who lived in the log house on the lake farm, now Armstrong, I recall as a little, short, jolly mother of sixteen, "yet never sick in my life," she told Dr. Shipman, who was called at the last.... But with all her responsibilities as home mother, nurse, cook, wash woman, and all combined in the upbringing of a large family, her flax-spinning of fine thread for sewing was as even and smooth as any you can find....

The many times of butchering gave extra days' work for trying out lard by the barrel, sausage making and souse cooking to a turn. Butter and cheese required daily churning, setting of curd, turning, rubbing, greasing the shelves loaded with creamy cheese, here and there a sage one, decorated with leaves in figures of bouquets of green....

There is no royal road around, though we tread the world around to find it. God alone knows the end from the beginning. "As thy day thy strength will be." [Here ends Anna Collin Wells's contribution to the family chronicle.]

Author Graham Swift writes in his novel *Waterland,* "only animals live entirely in the Here and Now. Only nature knows neither memory nor history. But man—let me offer you a definition—is the story-telling animal. Wherever he goes he wants to leave behind not a chaotic wake, not an empty space, but the comforting marker-buoys and trail-signs of stories.... He has to keep on making them up. As long as there's a story, it's all right."

It is also said that stories become legend. Legend becomes myth. In its simplest form a story is a narrative of events. This story of the Collin clan as told by Collin family members has had many things quietly elided from the narrative. Thus they began to create an incompletely verifiable story that was commonly taken at face value as complete and historical. As those who knew the omissions died away, the story became more of a legend. Noble deeds, Herculean labors, wisdom, faith, weakness, and betrayal—all truly

Anna Smith Collin, wife of David Collin III

if selectively part of the story, even as it was told by the people who lived it—over time were no longer the day-to-day activities of real people but the stuff of a past so different from the present that its impact is more popular tradition than historical fact. And as those who kept this *legend* alive began themselves to die away, the legend became myth.

Myth is commonly thought of, these days, as any invented story rumored to have some link to a real past, and sometimes even a fanciful past, making it a kind of idealized fiction. Myth is also, more seriously, what is remembered when meaning is forgotten. So the legend of the time of the Collin family has quickly become a kind of myth, an unproved collective belief in the people who conquered the wilderness.

But there *is* a story that is neither legend or myth, though the truth of it may have been forgotten. It is our work to remember.

4

Miriam

> How shall your houseless heads and unfed sides,
> Your loop'd and window'd raggedness, defend you
> from seasons such as these?
> —Shakespeare, *King Lear,* 3.4.30

Miriam Armstrong stood in her late sister's front parlor. She was not a pacer, but at the moment she had to force herself not to pace the room. The little strained conversation that went on had come to a halt some time ago. An old man, her father, sat in a large chair by the fire in his good suit. He had come at Charlie's invitation, yet he had several questions when he found his troublesome daughter there. All she would say is that she was expecting some guests who wanted to meet her father. The old man watched his grandniece and grandnephew come and go or sit uncomfortably in his presence. He was no fool, but he decided to wait out events in silence. When Miriam heard the carriage pull up, she hoped it was the one bringing the visitors, as she was wont to call them, who had taken the train all the way from Utica, some fifty miles to the east. They were running a bit late. But the carriage wasn't carrying them. It held her brother.

 Miriam was a presence. The old man in the chair was a greater presence, a figure with the strength and solidity of one cut from stone, and she really did not know what to say once she saw David's carriage pull up outside the farmstead. This was the last moment when what was to follow could change. She did not move. A nervous silence swept the room. Eyes flashed back and forth. They all, save the old man, had plans, and it looked as though they were all at just this moment dashed. Old Mr. Collin, her father, indicated that it looked like David's carriage. No one spoke. Her nephew and niece were there, but for once Charlie was speechless. She wanted to think it was someone's fault, maybe Charlie's for all his scheming. But if David was here, that meant this was the worst. Maybe he wouldn't get out of the carriage. She couldn't imagine facing him, not if he had figured out this much of her plan.

One of the hands poked his head in the door and asked for Mr. Collin. The old man rose with some difficulty, but you could see from his face that he had already understood that something was amiss. None of the others in the room would face him. If Miriam presented a large grim presence, which she did easily, her father, even in his frail last years, presented such an iron contrast that she quailed before it. The old man stood, moved with his walking stick, hat in hand, and with difficulty stepped toward the door. He was hale, but over eighty, and a life of hard farm labor had left its toll. Miriam watched from the window, being careful to keep herself out of sight. What would she tell the visitors once they arrived? She could hardly afford to pay them as it was, and she assumed they would want something for their time and effort. Another bitter expense to face. She felt hers was a story in which everything happened too late.

She could hear the voices of the two Davids in the farmyard, but not what was said. Charlie made some motion to go out to them, but Miriam gestured him to stay. She watched David help her father up into the carriage, and she noted the smart clip at which the horses stepped out of the drive.

How had it come to this? For so long it had been between her husband and the family. Part of her was bitter about the poor reception he had received. And now there was her beloved brother taking her father away. She would probably never be able to talk with either of them again. And yet, she had her rights, as she saw them. It was not a good day, and she was glad that the events did not take place at her own home, the farm she had been given by her father.

By that time of year Miriam had moved back onto the farmstead from one of the houses in the village that the family maintained. Winters were tough, and traffic between the village and outlying homes was minimal, unless you lived, as the main Collin family did, on the turnpike that led into the village. But in the spring it was not at all uncommon for families to move back into the country, and that is what Miriam did, despite the continuing absence of her husband. No doubt there were many in the village who wondered about his long absences. David Collin, her father, made it clear to any who asked that he was in business with Ethan Armstrong and that his son, David, would continue the relationship. That all sounded pretty good. But Ethan was rumored to be in hock for a lot. Indeed, some years before this incident, he had been declared a bankrupt, and he had never really caught up. Miriam had never really caught up with the shame. She had hoped for so much those years ago, but it had even begun badly. There is a note among the family papers in the hand of Harriet Beebee Collin Knapp, Miriam's grandniece, stating that just after his marriage to Miriam, Ethan Armstrong had handed his new father-in-law a note saying he owed several thousand dollars, and he expected David Collin Sr. to cover it. In the note Harriet states emphatically that David Collin "did not do business in that way!" Indeed, the family stories suggest Ethan had lost so much by the end of his life that he returned home to Fayetteville to retire and die in the hope that his father-in-law would cover his astronomical losses. Miriam was weary of putting a good face on it all. She was her father's daughter, and she was tired of the crowded family stage that left so little room for her to stand. She knew that he would never see it, but her father just took up too much room and in doing so took away all her choices. She had resolved to make some of her own, and one was to unmoor her father's weighty presence in her life. But he, of course, never questioned his own motives, as she was forced to do, nor did he wonder what others made of him, as she felt she was doomed to do. He seemed to feed his own strength without taking stock of himself, while she did so too much.

If you stand out in the lane to the west of the main house on the Armstrong Farm and look north, you'll have an unexcelled view of the vast flood plain of Lake Ontario. The plain stretches north fifty or more miles, as well as east and west as far as the eye can see, which, from that height, is perhaps as much as forty or fifty miles.

There are perhaps fewer trees now, but the cut made by the Erie Canal, just below, and those made by the railway lines built only slightly later are still clearly visible. It is like a vast Bruegel landscape, filtering off into the blue north (where, on a clear day, you can see the cooling tower of the Nine Mile Point nuclear power station), where you cannot quite—but can almost—imagine seeing the great lake itself, or into the Tug Hill Plateau and the foothills of the Adirondacks to the northeast.

From the lane, the main house of the Armstrong Farm seems unprepossessing, but it is larger than it appears, with unexpected rooms and turns and many interesting nooks and crannies. In the front parlor is a very large portrait of Miriam Armstrong by Francis Bicknell Carpenter. She is clearly a woman to be reckoned with. Handsome, in a solid sort of way, as Collin women often were, but not as beautiful as her sister-in-law, Clara. David, her beloved brother, managed to be very handsome. It was unfair, really, but what could one do? She had a husband full of promise. Family records about why she spent so much time in Fayetteville while her husband was in Troy or New York or other places of business are a bit thin. The beauty of the vista is perhaps only the least part of the story.

Miriam was born in May 1828 and was the first of David and Anna Collin's children to grow up entirely in the new "big house" built across the road from the original dwelling. It was a lively and busy household, and Miriam's deep attachment to it can be seen in her reminiscences of it, written as she approached middle age. She was, as all the Collin children were, well educated for the time, having been sent away to Troy to attend the Troy Female Academy, where she later met her future husband, Ethan Armstrong. The account of their affairs in the official family history, *John Collin: Roots and Branches,* by Ruth Collin Stong, runs as follows:

> Ethan came to Troy, NY, in 1845 and set up a wholesale grocery business with a partner under the name of Armstrong and Squires. They also had an interest in three freighters. The firm dealt mainly in grain, buying around the country and selling in Europe, and had been in business for ten years when one of the freighters sank and the partner absconded with the firm's funds. Ethan reorganized his business with the help of his father-in-law. His brother Jerome became his partner under the firm name of E. Armstrong & Co.

Ethan and Miriam had homes in both Troy and Fayetteville [roughly 150 miles apart, no small distance then]. Since she declined to live in Troy and his business was not in Fayetteville, they were apart a good deal of the time. They lived on a farm near Fayetteville, inherited by Miriam from her father, since called the Armstrong Farm, as well as in various winter residences in the village.

Ethan was a deacon in the Second Presbyterian Church in Troy, later an elder in the Troy First Presbyterian Church....

Miriam was active in the Presbyterian Church Sunday School in Fayetteville and served as president of the Women's Temperance Union. Her concern for temperance is shown by her articles in the weekly newspaper on the evils of alcohol and her speeches before the Temperance Union.

What this account does not relate is that Ethan filed for bankruptcy in 1868, some dozen years after his father-in-law helped him out of his first financial difficulties. Of the many thousands owed to more than fifty individuals and businesses, he owed his father-in-law more than $12,000 [$148,000+] as well as $500 to Miriam herself [$6,000+]. The official record also fails to mention that in his will of 1869, David Collin Sr. wrote that he would not bequeath to his daughter Miriam various lands and properties unless the following condition—one of several—was met: "First if Ethan Armstrong pays up the Liabilities whereon I am holden with E. Armstrong, to the amount of Nine Thousand five hundred dollars or some over including the Principal and Interest to May the first, 1869—with the Interest that will accumulate thereon."

The troubles had earlier roots, however, as Miriam, a young mother with some barely concealed concerns and a deep homesickness, wrote to her brother in early 1858 from what she called her "Trojan Home," where she lived early in her marriage, a reluctant Helen with no rescuers:

"A letter timely writ is a rivet in the chain of affection," applies emphatically to the one you so kindly sent us. I cannot well express to you the emotions its contents enkindled save they were the earnest fresh gushings of a *sister's love*. Not only to know, but to *realize* that *my* brother *is still* my own dear brother is more than the treasures of a mine!

Miriam Collin Armstrong, daughter of David Collin III

That ought should have originated in *us* or our *life allotments* to shadow the beautiful sunlight of family harmony and love, has been and is to both my dear husband and myself a source of unfeigned and bitter regret. We could choose to, and cheerfully bear reverses alone, but that others—even those we hold so dear—should feel my unhappy influence from them, adds an ingredient to our cup that we would force it from our lips. But this may not be. The draught is mingled by a hand that is *wise* and *kind* and given us for our good. Our Friend *to whom* we would *commit all our ways,* is divine, and hath love and pity far more tender than an earthly parent

Part of the 1869 will of David Collin III

and withal, *unerring* wisdom. He knoweth His children, and we are assured, will withhold no good thing from those who *trust in Him*.

Miriam was not some frail thing given to distress over domestic duties. Indeed, in the same letter just quoted, she appends a note to her sister-in-law that is full of the pleasure she takes in domestic activity. The life on her parents' farm became comfortable, but it became that way through very hard work, and she had been deeply inculcated with the value of that experience by sharing in it all through her childhood.

Yet Ethan was often away, even from Troy. She mentions in a letter to her brother in the next year that Ethan was in New York City again. She must have felt very cut off from her family and the network of sharing and support it represented. She turned her thoughts to her God when she could not explain what felt like an inexplicable injustice.

And there was a certain unconscious shame over Ethan Armstrong's business dealings. He was a businessman for whom money was a tool. You used it, worked it, lost it, remade it. It was not shameful in his mind for him to be in trade, nor to make use of the fruits of another's labor. But for the Collin family it was different. As devout Presbyterians with deep Calvinist/Huguenot roots, they saw money as both a family right and a sign from God that they were among the elect. It informed their entire worldview. Money had to be earned, but prosperity was more a sign than a result. The Geneva Bible was, family notes indicate, the source of inspiration. In it Saint Peter said, "But ye are a chosen generation, a royal priesthood, an holy nation, a peculiar people, that ye should show forth the praises of him, who hath called you out of darkness into his marvelous light."

Calvin himself said, in a Commentary on Genesis 1.6, "The defection of our first parents ... proved to be the destruction of the whole race ... consequently no part of us is sound." He adds at a later point, in his Commentary on Philippians 2.13, "God anticipates us by His grace, and also calls us to Himself.... We do not turn through our own will or efforts, but it is the spirit's work.... This is the engine for bringing down all haughtiness, this the sword for putting an end to all pride, when we are taught that we are utterly nothing and can do nothing except through the grace of God alone. I mean supernatural grace, which comes from the spirit of regeneration.... There are in any action two principal departments—the inclination, and the power to carry it into effect. Both of these he ascribes wholly to God. What more remains to us as a ground of glorying?"

Judging from her letters, these words were a reality to Miriam. Calvin also says, "The foundation and first cause, both of our calling and of all the benefits which we receive from God, is here declared to be His eternal election.... This leads us to conclude that holiness, purity and every excellence that is found among men are the fruit of election" (Commentary on Ephesians 1.4).

In another place he adds, "God knew before the world was created whom He had elected for salvation. Hence, when Peter calls them elect, according to the precognition of God, he intimates that the cause of it depends on nothing else but on God alone, for He of His own free will has chosen us" (Commentary on 1 Peter). The Puritan Paul Bayne, also commenting on Ephesians 1.4, says, "We see what is a blessing worthy [of] all thankfulness, even ... our election. This is the root out of which all these blessings grow.... God doth not choose because of faith, and holiness, and perseverance foreseen, seeing He Chooseth us to these things, [which] follow by force of His election, and therefore [they] cannot be the cause of that which is before them."

How must Miriam, as deeply rooted as she was in this faith, have felt about her circumstances? What kind of Divine statement was being made here? But these roots informed only a part of her consciousness. As David Ellis points out in his little-known book *Landlords and Farmers in the Hudson-Mohawk Region, 1790–1850*:

> When the country was new, there was a great demand for labor to clear and fence the land, erect buildings, build roads, and construct churches. Once these improvements had been made there was less need for labor except among those actually employed in cultivation. Furthermore, the sheep industry getting under way required a larger farm unit which in turn tended to displace population.
>
> It would be uncharitable as well as untrue to leave the impression that farm life was one unbroken succession of misfortunes and a hopeless struggle against unkind nature. Serious evils did exist, evils which contemporary observers were quite frank in admitting. These evils, whether the excessive drinking prevailing among the people or the lack of interest in agricultural improvements, complicated the general problem of readjusting agriculture to meet new conditions. On the credit side, many farmers displayed a willingness to support innovations such as Merino sheep and the county fair.

The Collin family was certainly involved in raising sheep and in enlarging and stabilizing their holdings. But there was more going on as well in this dynamic time that we tend to want to see as stable and sure. Ellis continues,

"The effects of our agrarian life were revolutionary. By 1850 all but the most isolated farmers in the hill country were raising foodstuffs for sale. Conversely, the old life of self-sufficiency was rapidly vanishing. Turnpike, canal, and railroad were linking market and farm closer together. Not without reason, therefore, do historians refer to this period as the agricultural revolution." Elsewhere Ellis cites William Cobbett, "[he] could say in 1819, 'A farmer here depends on nobody but himself and on his own proper means; and, if he be not at his ease, and even rich, it must be his own fault.'"

Miriam saw herself as missing both this farming revolution and the edge to the trade side of things, as Ethan's enterprises continued to rise and fall and fail. She was unable to make her farm produce to the standards her father had created, relying often on family support. It is true that the extended family always helped one another. She was well aware, however, that the family did not start entirely from scratch, and it is not unreasonable to guess that she felt some right, both legal and spiritual, to that heritage. There was also a heritage of self-satisfaction among family members, who were often unaware of the judgment of others. Miriam could feel she saw all of them as they could not see themselves. Did she then become a kind of unconscious rationalist needing to abandon her theological fantasies and yearnings for romantic independence in order to gain some sort of acceptance? On that fateful afternoon she had played her best card in what had seemed such a rational way. It had failed her. Now she was even further outside that fold of the seemingly elect.

How did the larger Collin family become so well situated? Clearly it was largely through plain hard work, but there was money involved, too, recalling the legacy her grandfather had been given. For generations no one really knew where the family money had come from until the time in the early 1980s a cache of documents was deposited at the Onondaga Historical Association (OHA).

These documents take us back to the great-uncle of David Collin Sr., Captain John Collin, the nominal head of the prosperous and tightly knit extended family, and to his grandson, John Francis Collin. John Collin III, the son of Captain Collin, died in December 1833. Sometime in the year before his death, probably in late 1832, his second son, John Francis Collin, drew up a memorandum for himself of some items he wanted settled concerning his father's land holdings in the western part of the state. John

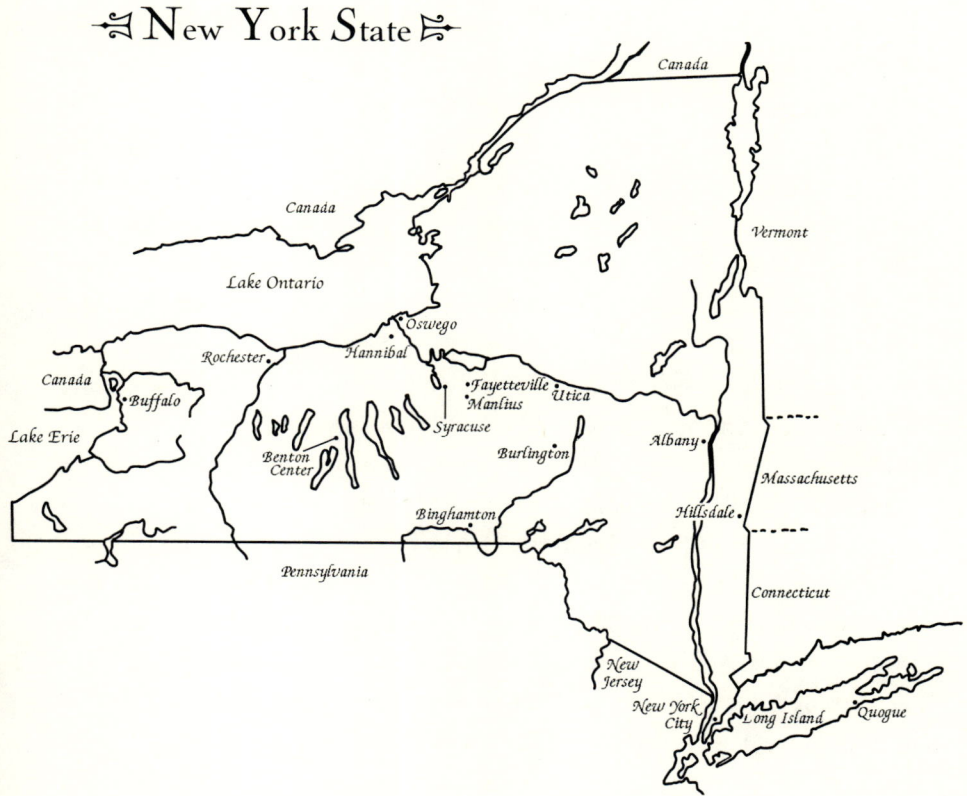

Map of New York State; courtesy of Jane MacLeod Keenan

Collin III was now in frail health, and John Francis had taken up not only the running of the successful farm in Hillsdale (in Columbia County near the Massachusetts border), but also the management of most of his father's affairs across the state. The date of the undated memo can be surmised because it refers to the need to find deeds and to conduct deed searches for lots in Herkimer, Onondaga, Madison, Cayuga, and Tomkins counties. There are letters from lawyers and county clerks dated March and May 1833, in apparent response to John Francis's own inquiries. John Francis also mentions in the memo that he wants to go to Ithaca to talk with lawyers and that he will take with him $152 [$2,600] in cash.

One must remember that in the 1830s this part of New York was still considered the frontier, if not actually wilderness; that travel was arduous (aside from that provided by the Erie Canal, completed in 1825); and that $152 was a considerable sum. How large were the holdings that would have taken a man, barely thirty, away from his ailing father and busy farm for what must have been a dangerous journey of several weeks on horseback? It is difficult to be exact, for the evidence is fragmentary and the documents overlap in irregular ways, but there is no doubt that the various holdings were in excess of 10,000 acres and probably closer to 15,000 acres of land. Perhaps a mere drop in the vast wooded wilderness, but a substantial investment in an agrarian society where land meant wealth.

For general evidence one need not itemize or trace all the deeds and bonds that are collected in the archives. Two or three documents belonging to Captain John Collin, grandfather to John Francis, will be enough to suggest the extent of the holdings. A deed dated September 10, 1795, shows that Henry Platner sold John Collin the "whole" of lot 83 in the town of Locke for four hundred pounds. Locke was part of western Onondaga County contained in the Military Tract. The whole lot amounted to more than two thousand acres. Another deed, dated August 3, 1798, shows Anthony Maxwell selling John Collin four thousand acres for $2,000 [$20,000]. Also, in a kind of journal and sporadically kept account book, running from 1792 to around 1806, John Collin had a list entitled *My Genesee Lands* that mentions a variety of smaller holdings in the western regions of the state, totaling more than four thousand acres.

How did a wilderness farmer's holdings become so substantial? To understand it, one must look at a curious combination of factors: hard work and quick thinking, the chances of larger historical events, being in the right place at the right time, and a certain amount of ruthlessness. When Captain John Collin moved to the Hillsdale area in 1788, he was already a man of maturity and substance. He was born in Connecticut in 1732. He had begun land speculation as early as 1760, when he bought half rights to land purchased from the Delawares. In 1773 he received a commission as captain in the colonial militia of Dutchess County, and in 1777 he joined the patriotic cause as a captain in the Continental Army.

Legend has it that Captain John Collin was physically imposing and immensely strong. Clearly he was admired as a man of authority, for he became an important mediator between tenants holding land under the

English Massachusetts grants and those doing so under the Dutch Manor Title where the lands and claims overlapped in the area east and south of Albany. This responsibility put him in a good position to know the major landholders of the area, such as the Schuylers and the Rensselaers. Indeed, he seems to have been on particularly friendly terms with both of these families, for there are several documents bearing their signatures. His standing also put John Collin in a position to pick up any loose property that came his way. At least some of the capital for his speculations came from returns on stocks he owned in area turnpikes, such as the Hudson and the Susquehanna. If the number of bonds and leases in the archive is any indication, he also acted as a sort of local banker for farmers and townspeople (when safe and reliable banking had not yet reached to rural and frontier regions). Often a bonded individual was unable to make good on his agreement and John Collin would take over the land. There are some letters from sheriffs detailing evictions, including in one case a widow. Most of the lands purchased before 1790 were in Hillsdale, near his farm or adjacent to the turnpikes.

When John Collin began purchasing "western lands" in the late 1790s, he was buying land primarily in the Military Tract. The Military Tract was a huge piece of wilderness (1,500,000 acres) set aside by the financially strapped New York State to pay the soldiers who had fought in the Continental Army. In order to keep the land, however, the owner had to improve it in some way, such as clearing and planting portions or putting up a building. Meeting this requirement was often impossible for those to whom the land was given (imagine a soldier from nicely settled Hudson Valley having to travel hundreds of miles to the seemingly godforsaken wilderness of what we now call Upstate New York, to clear primeval forest), and it was sold at bargain prices to other interested parties, such as John Collin, who saw the flood of migration out of New England beginning.

By the time John Francis was planning his trip, some of the lands had already been given to other branches of the family, especially the Truesdells. An undated list, probably from the 1830s, mentions nearly fifteen hundred acres in the Fingerlakes region divided between Collin and Truesdell children. But overall management seems to have remained with the head of the family, and John Francis was being groomed for the role. Though he was the second son, he was given the farm in Hillsdale in his father's will of

1833 because he was stronger and more able than his older brother, James. Indeed he was so able he helped James with the merchandising business their father had set him up in at Egremont, near Hillsdale. A daybook for 1826 through 1828 belonging to John Francis shows the carefully noted sales made in his brother's business.

Thomas Jefferson once remarked that man would never have the chance to grow and create the democratic experiment on such a scale again. None of those in the so-called "heart of the experiment" saw themselves in the heart of anything, but instead as striving and playing their beliefs against the realities they encountered.

Here we take a somewhat dyspeptic aside from our already roughly digested narrative to note just how hard it was to create the life of pastoral bliss we assume, as a national heritage, came as a right to those who experienced it. Fortunately for us, the women of the Collin clan wrote to one another, and we can learn that it was not only the so-called noble efforts of the men who made the transformation of the wilderness possible. There are, of course, many stories of women who also struggled and won out, but what of those who just managed, for whom the effort brought them to the edge of failure and destitution? What of those who had to face death each day through the illness of children or the demise of neighbors? What of those who missed desperately the support of their extended families, from whom they were separated by distances that would entail weeks of travel?

In the family archives there is a long note by Betsy Knapp, the last "hero of the legacy" (and Betsy would have appreciated that ambivalent gender). She wrote:

> Nancy McAlpine Collin [the wife of Henry, brother to David Collin Sr., who went further "west" and settled in Benson, in what became Yates County, in the Fingerlakes region] wrote that her Henry was thinking of looking over the Ohio country. She thanked her sister-in-law Harriet for the letter she wrote to discourage him from that idea. I have ten letters that Nancy wrote home between 1814 and 1826. The almost exclusive theme was, "I cannot tell you how much I want to come to Hillsdale and see you all. I hope if it is possible for any of you to come and see us you will." [There is a sense in Betsy's notes and in the letters that Nancy won't live long enough

to make it to her former home.] At one point she pushed her idea of her father selling his home farm and settling near her new home and tells her sister to advise him to do so. She adds that her husband appeared anxious for his father-in-law to do just this lest he be forced " ... to carry Nancy back again for a visit ... " After a trip home, Nancy writes, "It appears as though I never can be reconciled to live such a distance from you." Apart from the loneliness, her sense of isolation was aggravated by lack of help, poor health, ailing babies, and what she refers to as the dying time in the neighborhood, "Eleven deaths within a mile east and west of us in about two years." One of the killers was measles, which she was momentarily expecting to hit her children. It really was an affecting time, she tells us. Her tone changes somewhat in 1826 [after a "mere" ten years more of all this continuing stuff!] when she writes: "The best news I can tell you is the Lord has not forgotten our land but is dealing graciously to the inhabitants of this western country." She then describes the results of what I assume must have been a successful revival. Her conclusion was to "feel more reconciled to this country than I ever have before. I sometimes think my lot is cast in a happy land. Life is uncertain with us all, but I hope we may all be prepared to meet a better world. I think religion to be of the greatest importance to all, so that when we are done with the things of this transitory world we may have a treasure in heaven. I hope it will be the happy lot of us all."

 Her lot turned out to be death in the birth of her 4th child at the age of 39. Her husband Henry followed three years later and the three children were divided among Fayetteville and Hillsdale relatives until the seventeen year old son was able to take over the farm.

Here are a couple of the letters themselves, which sound more like pleas made by Etty Hillesum from her ghetto in Amsterdam in the 1940s than from a noble spouse breaking the wilderness, and as her spirit almost breaks down, so does her writing, making it difficult to decipher:

Dear Parents,
 Having an opportunity of sending you a letter, I thought I must not fail of it as it is seldom I have (even put by the mail) I

have enjoyed a verry poor state of health since I wrote to you last . . . I[?] but I am much better now than I have been . . . my babe is not verry healthy but is a smart little boy when he is well. Harriet Am[y] is well, and talks about granmammy.

Thomas [unreadable?] is here today he moved a family here and staid last night at our nearest neighbors and knew not that wee lived here he says his family is well and [Alfine?] herself likewise I was quite pleased to see him and here from my cousins the woman that he moved out lived near them. Polly F[irepher?] lives with me this summer she came in the spring to make us a visit and was verry anxious to live with me again and I was unable to do my work at that time and she staid and I expect will as long as I want her but I have got so smart now that I do my work and keep her at spinning. One of Henry Heefers' boys lives with us this summer. I feel verry anxious to come down to Hillsdale in the fall but I fear I shall not. Harry talks quite indifferent about it but I mean to persuade him if I can to come for I think that he can if he has a mind to he has not much of a notion of comming back to Hillsdale to live. I really wish he had I think it would bee better for him. He has said he thought he should be better of[f] if he had a good farm there but he don't like the name of going back. It is some time since I began my letter as I missed of the opportunity of sending it so I thought I would finish writing and put it in the post office.

I know you are desirous to herre from me oftener than I write but you must excuse me as I have two troublesome children a crying about me. I hope it will not discourage any of you from writing as often as you can. I have received several letters since I wrote to you last and it is a great satisfaction to here from you if I cannot see you. I often feel Harry his father's family will think he has entirely forgotten them he is so neglectful about writing to them. wee expect father Collin and Harriet out in the fall. I have about giving up coming this fall. Harry says he shall come a years from next fall if we nothing happens. I cannot tell you how much I want to come to Hillsdale and see you all. I hope if it is possible for any of you to come and see us you will tell Aunt [Terizell?] I think of her every day and want to here how she enjoys her health and Abigail I often think how much satisfaction wee should take if wee was near each other. I wish that Anna or Abby could come and stay some time and make a long visit. I want you to write often and when you send by the mail direct to Penn Yan post office. Give my love to Ann[. . . ?] and all of the family and I must close wishing you all health and prosperity.

       Nancy Collin
       Benton, July 12/29, 1819

The following two letters were posted together.

 Dear sisters,

  I must write a line to you and tell you I have not forgot you through all the cares and love of my family my thoughts often wing to you. I think I can never be [become?] wholly reconciled to think wee must spend our lives so far from each other. I anticipate great happiness visiting Hillsdale next fall. Harry says he shall come . . . in the fall if we are well. I hope we shall not be disappointed. I often count the months to come before wee shall see each other and converse together, but alas how fleeting is this life wee may some of us bee laid low in the dust before that time. I felt an anxious desire that wee may all live to [see] each other again. I shall omit writing lengthy thinking, the time will not be long before wee shall see on another my pen is so poor I must stop if you read this you will do well. I calculate to take both of my children with me when i come. Give my love to father Collin and family. Harriet Ann talks a great deal about Granmammy Collin, you must write soon,

      I close,
      Nancy, Abigail and Ann [?]
      Benton, May 10, 1821

 Dear Brother,

  I once more take pen in hand to write to you to let you know that I and my family are enjoying tolerable health at present and I think we have reason to be thankful for it has been a dying time about this neighborhood. There has been eleven deaths within a mile east and west of us in about too years.... Cole died last week and the week before a young man on the hill this side of Mr. Cole's with the measles. I have attended his father and mother['s] funeral[s] and his. It was real an affecting time he died happy it was thought he said he was a going to heavin to his father and mother. The measles have been verry thick about here and go verry hard, my children have not had them yet I expect they will wee have not heard any thing from you since father Collin was here. I want to here from you all verry much, uncle Keepper [?] lives with Henry, he lives on our place yet walter lives six miles from here. They are all well I believe.

I shall write short I expect if wee are spared with life and health to see you next fall and then I can tell you more than I can write. Give my love to father and mother and aunt Grizell and all ... friends,

Nancy Collin Andrew McAlpine
[May 10, 1821]

As Miriam watched her father and brother ride away she bore the burden of this history of longing. Though these were the words of her aunt, they could easily have been those of her mother or indeed of herself as she was torn from the family fold. She could hear the white-throated sparrows and see the trees move in the spring breezes, but what she saw or heard did not measure her inner passion. Suddenly nature was without passion or romance. Neither it nor God paid any attention to who was just and who was sinful. Nature was no longer a home. Victory did not always come to the good. It always came to the strong, and she did not feel very strong at that moment. Faith. Passion. Righteousness. It was neither who she was nor how she was in the world. Something had ended. A door closed. The stories would remain but who would remain to remember their meaning or what was left out of their telling?

In *The World as Will and Idea,* Arthur Schopenhauer has written, "The demand for poetical justice rests on entire misconception of the nature of tragedy, and, indeed of the nature of the world itself. It boldly appears ... [in] the dull optimistic Protestant nationalistic view of life ... will makes the demand for poetic justice and finds satisfaction in it. The true sense of tragedy is the deeper insight, that it is not his own individual sins that the hero atones for, but original sin, i.e., the crime of existence itself."

The story of David Collin's and his family's experience of the world, and the story of the world going about its business indifferent to David and Miriam and all the others were the realities unfolding simultaneously. Miriam had responded to the, to her, already fading myth of her father and of religion and the eternity of the promised land. Miriam was poised to act, and the bitter wheels were ready to turn. She saw with her heart if not her mind that her father's self-regard and sense of right had precipitated catastrophe.

Loss and unhappiness were teaching her patience, however. Within two years her husband would be dead and her diatribes against the evils of drink would be appearing in the local paper. Within five years of her husband's death, her father would also finally die at the age of ninety. Then she would take her once-beloved brother to court and force the hand she felt she had been wrongly dealt. She would stand before the gates and not be denied entry. Our Lear does not die of grief for he cannot see the betrayal of his daughter with unreasoning passion. There is little passion at all save the passion of silence.

The irony is the daughter's passion. She loved. She hoped. She longed. An object lesson in how relationships fail and a prophecy of an impending family disintegration. God is the word around which everything fails.

> ... we are not ourselves
> when nature, being oppress'd, commands the mind
> to suffer with the body.
> —Shakespeare, *King Lear,* 2.4.108–10

5

What We Are Reminded to Remember

> You have begot me, bred me, loved me: I
> Return those duties back as are right fit,
> Obey you, love you, and most honour you.
> —Shakespeare, *King Lear,* 1.1.98–100

What we choose to remember is not the same as what we must remember. Our selective memorials to the past are our unconscious way of finding and defining ourselves on the map of the present.

Among the smattering of letters and documents below are obituaries of three persons central to this story: David Collin Sr.; his wife, Anna; and their one surviving son, David Jr. These versions of the larger story are what the community has chosen to remember of them. And they are models of the way the community pats itself on the back for having such good and noble progenitors. Already the community is preparing the ground for its own idealized memorial over the pragmatic stones laid by others.

On a cold mid-December day in 1874, a year after the death of his wife, his companion and helpmeet of fifty-six years, David Collin left his Oak Grove home and rode out the three miles to the home farm. Oak Grove was a large house he had built for his own father and mother, much closer to the village, so that in their old age they could come west from Columbia County. But his mother had been dead twenty years and his father thirty. He himself was now eighty, and with Anna gone he lived alone in the big house with just a housekeeper. He had decided to make official what had in any case been the de facto situation for a long time. David Jr. had lived on and managed the home farm for many years, raising his own large family there and continuing to extend the family interests across the region and especially in the village of Fayetteville. It has often been written in family accounts that the entire home farm was willed to David Jr., but what David Collin wanted to do was sell to his son much of what he had designated for him in his will of 1869. He had asked that both his son and his much-loved daughter-in-law, Clara, be present when he arrived.

> This Indenture, Made this seventeenth day of December in the year of our Lord one thousand eight hundred and seventy-four, between David Collin of the town of Manlius, county of Onondaga and state of New York, of the first part, and David Collin Junior of the same place, of the second part, Witnesseth, That the said party of the first part, in consideration of the natural love and affection which he bears his son David Collin Jr., and for *one dollar* to him duly paid, has sold, and by these Presents does grant and convey to the said party of the second part, his heirs and assigns, All that tract or parcel of Land situate in the town of Manlius, County of Onondaga, on lot No. 56 lying between the Green Lakes being all the land east and north of land heretofore deeded to my daughters Caroline, Miriam and Anna, adjoining Smith on the north containing twenty acres of land more or less. Also in the same lot No. 56 on the west bank of the upper Green Lake containing six acres of land more or less. Also in original lot No. 55 in Manlius about 25 acres to be laid off from the south side of the states hundred acres, a parallel line from lot No. 56 to Waniers or Owens lot west. Also about ten acres of timber land lying between Miriam's and David's land, to include all the land which I have not deeded or willed to my daughter Miriam or my son David on lot No. 55. Also the farm on which I now live [Oak Grove] on lot No. 65 in Manlius of about 40 acres of land, all of which I have not heretofore willed or deeded to my daughters Harriette, Miriam, Lucy or Anna or their children. Also on regional lots Nos. 45 and 54 about ten acres of land lying west and adjoining the highway from Manlius Center to the Depot. Also on Original lot

No. 46 in the town of Manlius 123 3/8 acres of land, except 23 acres off the east end deeded to my daughters Lucy and Anna and my Grandchildren, the children of my daughter Caroline. Also a strip of land on the canal feeder in original lot No. 65 in Manlius lying between strips of land deeded to my daughters Lucy and Anna reserved in a deed to my daughter Harriette. Also about one half acre of land reserved in said deed lying on the west side of the Kinial [?] road (so called) in Fayetteville. Also one and one fourth acres of land in original lot No. 77 in Manlius being a lime stone quarry which I purchased of Lieve Snell.

This sale of more than 230 acres for a dollar David Collin wrote out in his own hand. Over his long and busy life, despite only a handful of months of formal education, he had written many such. He needed no lawyer to tell him how to phrase the terms of the agreement. One can see him sitting at the table in Oak Grove by a window in his front parlor (where he also kept his bed—a custom we often forget or neglect because it doesn't suit our sensibility of the past) marking out the details, knowing his son, the one who most shared and practiced his ideals, would sign the document without hesitation. He knew the choices were his to make, and at this late stage in his life the situation had gone beyond familial affection and even beyond mere business concerns. There was a need to fix a legacy, and old David Collin was wise enough to know that relying only on the strength of individuals would fix nothing. We might feel the subject of his devotion was other than we would choose, but he had put his heart and life into it, nevertheless.

Fragments of life, fragments without context. Out of each accidental moment we try to create a context to provide solace, as though our self-created meaning came from somewhere else larger and more purposeful. Iris Murdoch writes:

> [I]n real life there occur what one might call "pieces of tragic utterance." But then who hears them, who repeats them, and when, for what purpose? ... There are stories which we hesitate to repeat lest we seem to be gloating over horrors or trying to gratify unworthy emotions in ourselves or our hearers.... Of course

pieces of historical data constantly detach themselves as repeatable stories, and the same is true of memorable words, like Vanzetti's last speech in the law court. "If it had not been for these thing I might have live out my life talking at street corners to scorning men. I might have died unmarked, unknown, a failure. This is our career and our triumph. Never in our full life can we hope to do such work for tolerance, for justice, for man's understanding of man, as we do now by accident."

David Collin did not believe in accident nor in leaving things to chance. In a world where change is ubiquitous, this attitude is called hubris. It is a word some have suggested belongs to a discussion of tragedy. But the Collin history is not *tragic,* though we might make a tragic tale of it. If the characters of the Collin story (and they often saw themselves as part of a story) were to rescue themselves from triviality and obscurity in the face of the dark truth of change, their reward and consolation had to be the willed purposefulness of their lives. Their work was God's work, work against the threat of godlessness, like the threat of the godless wilderness that must be conquered by the Elect. Against this threat David Collin wished to fix his legacy and to give his life's purpose meaning, as he saw it.

David Collin was born in April 1794. When he was only eighteen, he served and saw conflict in the War of 1812. He settled on and developed wilderness land. Just as we today cannot explain or describe away the experience of those who went through the Great Depression or who fought in World War II (usually the same people, our parents and grandparents), those generations immediately succeeding David Collin's really had no idea what made him who he was. When he was born it was into frontier conditions. He grew to manhood not far from Hillsdale, in Columbia County, near the Massachusetts border. His parents' farm was two miles from Hillsdale. During the war of 1812 he volunteered for the state militia, becoming a 4th Sergeant in a company of light infantry engaged in expelling an invasion of the state by way of Plattsburgh (well north of Hillsdale, above the Adirondacks, near the Canadian border), in September 1814.

As has been recorded earlier, David and his brother Henry went west in 1813 to inspect their father's holdings in the Military Tract and the Phelps and Gorham Purchase. David Ellis writes in his *History of New York State:*

The homestead idea, that is, the granting of land in small parcels to actual settlers rather than to absentee speculators, won little support in New York until well along in the nineteenth century. The major exception to the policy of sale was the grant of approximately 1,500,000 acres to veterans of the Revolution, who were given the right to select land within the Military Tract of central New York.... Massachusetts officials also adopted the policy of selling their huge tract of 6,000,000 acres west of Seneca Lake to land jobbers. Oliver Phelps and Nathaniel Gorham headed a syndicate of capitalists and politicians who agreed to pay the state approximately $175,000 [$1,898,418] in gold for the land. Phelps hastened west to clear the Indian title and to run surveys. The sachems [now more properly called the *Todedaho,* the primary spiritual leaders and *Rememberers* selected by the clan mothers in this matriarchal society] and chiefs of the Iroquois assembled about the council fire at Buffalo Creek in July 1788 and sold about 2,500,000 acres lying east of the Genesee River for $5,000 [$54,000] and an annuity of $500 [$5,400]. Phelps laid off townships six miles square and opened one of the first land offices in the United States at Canandaigua.

Financial troubles soon caught up with Phelps and Gorham. They could get little hard cash out of the settlers, and some of their fellow capitalists backed out of the venture. Most disheartening of all was the upsurge in the price of Massachusetts securities, which they had expected to buy at depreciated levels and to turn over to the state at par. In 1790 they turned back the western two-thirds of the tract in order to retain full title to the eastern section.

Their ill luck did not deter Robert Morris from buying 1,000,000 acres from Phelps and Gorham in the region between Seneca Lake and the Genesee River. A few months later Morris paid Massachusetts $333,333 [$3,614,338] for approximately 4,000,000 acres west of the Genesee River. Morris was basically a wholesaler who expected that his reputation as secretary of finance during the Revolution would enable him to unload his holdings on bankers in Amsterdam, London, and Paris....

What effect did the entrance of European capitalists have upon the development of New York apart from sprinkling the countryside with Old World place names? The permanent effect was negligible, although the immediate result was the acceleration of settlement. The London and Amsterdam bankers had ample capital to improve their holdings by adding buildings, roads, taverns, gristmills, and sawmills. In general, foreign investors found it necessary to abandon preconceived ideas of developing their holdings and found it wise to follow rather closely the practices of native Americans in disposing of their tracts.

Most people have long forgotten that slaves were not illegal in New York State, and they were indeed a part of the labor system until toward the end of the eighteenth century. There was a slave revolt in 1712 in New York City, harshly suppressed by the (British) military. David Ellis writes:

> During the second half of the century, relations between whites and blacks improved, largely because of the arrival of many new white immigrants. Proportionately reduced in number, the blacks seemed less menacing. Furthermore, the slaves became less defiant as they adjusted to white customs through their contacts as house servants and farm laborers. Humanitarian impulses generated by the Quakers resulted in better treatment and education for the slave. A few bold spirits began to advocate emancipation, and by 1777 one-third of the legislators were willing to free the slaves. Opposition was strong, however, among conservatives, property holders, and white laborers, and local emancipation was not to come for another half century....
>
> The presence of slavery and the absence of guilds were two circumstances in New York contrasting most sharply with those in Britain. There were four categories of labor: free labor, apprenticeship, indentured servitude, and slavery. In general, the trend was toward the use of free labor. Apprenticeship, indentured servitude, and slavery gradually lost ground because New Yorkers found free labor more efficient, reliable and flexible.... Negro slaves performed most unskilled and menial tasks. Many substantial farmers

had one or two slaves, and the aristocracy used Negroes as household servants. A large proportion of slaves were highly skilled and had as great a command of technical skills as that of white workingmen. Their masters granted them varying degrees of freedom. A slave code evolved which defined the limits of slavery as a labor system. The laws protected the owner's property and gave him the power to punish unruly slaves. Slavery, however, was losing ground during the last half of the eighteenth century. People found it generally cheaper to hire free laborers than to maintain slaves during periods of idleness as well as usefulness.

We do not know how many of the branches of the Collin family dealt in slavery, but Captain John Collin, David Collin's great-uncle (the one who began to build the family fortune), was one of those "substantial farmers," and there is a bill of sale with his name on it buying "one certain Negro Slave or boy about sixteen years old named 'James'" from a Michael Ham for the "consideration of the sum of two hundred and fifty Dollars [$2,950] to me in hand paid by John Collin . . . this 23rd Day of April 1810." There is also among the family papers a manumission statement, part of the codicil to John Collin's will, which one might expect to ameliorate some of the awfulness of this bill of sale. But it is dated less than a year *before* the sale of the boy James. It says in part:

> I John Collin of Hillsdale in the County of Columbia . . . order and direct that all my Slaves should be manumitted from and immediately after my decease. Now I do hereby revoke so much of the clause as relates to the period or time of their manumission and in lieu thereof, will order and direct, that my Negro man Slave named Robin serve my Son John as his servant till he shall arrive at the age of thirty years. And I will order and direct that my Negro girl Slave Flora shall faithfully serve my daughter Hannah till the said Flora shall attain the age of twenty eight if the said Hannah should live so long, but if not then I will order and direct that she shall serve the Children of my said Daughter Hannah during the residue of the said term or until she shall arrive at the age of twenty eight years. Provided however that during the life time of my said

John Collin's bill of sale for a slave, 1810

daughter Hannah the said Flora shall not be subject or liable to any sale without her consent and if sold without her consent I will order and direct that she shall thenceforth immediately be free and I do order and direct this codicil to be annexed to my said will.

The codicil was witnessed by his brother, David, and Rutsen Van Rensselaer, as well as David Carshove. This manumission document was prominently displayed in an exhibition at OHA in the late 1980s. It was thought at that time to mark the nobility of the Collin prerogatives and to give credibility to the idea of "good stock," of hard-working pioneers who forged this country of ours. Well, be that as it may, John Collin still bought and sold humans well after his noble codicil, and even within that codicil he restricted the freedom of at least two of them until the "white" needs were met in some way more important than the freedom of the "black" needs. I realize this is laying present standards over the past when those standards could not have been understood. It is nevertheless the heritage of David Collin and his son, which clarifies somewhat their attitude toward farm labor, tenants, and so forth. Morals cannot, however, be merely relative if they are to bear any weight or mean anything at all. This confusion with the truth and mere belief becomes central to the unraveling of the clan and all that they stood for.

David Sr.'s father gave him 550 acres, of which David contracted to have five cleared and a cabin built. Meanwhile he married, as is related elsewhere, Anna Smith, whose family was close to the Collin family in Hillsdale. On February 13, 1817, they set out with three wagonloads of household goods and farm equipment over the frozen roads and trails. Contrary to common modern belief, the winter was actually an easier time to travel than spring or summer, for streams and roads, where there were any, tended to be frozen so that wagons and sledges could be dragged over them instead of being mired in mud on undrained paths. The journey took nine days. They lived for eight years in the cabin, adding a second story at one point, until a new, much larger and grander place was built in 1825.

Ruth Stong's official family genealogical account says:

> David [Sr.] also acted as his father's agent by watching over the elder David's other property in the Military Tract. This was a rigorous and time consuming task because he had to keep tenants on the land as well as settle disputes and guard against theft [see below].
>
> In 1845 when David IV [that is, David Jr.], was married, David and Anna gave him the homestead and moved into Oak Grove to care for Lucy Bingham Collin [David Sr.'s mother], recently widowed. After Anna's death in 1873, David Sr. soon moved from Oak Grove back to the homestead with David Jr., and Clara, dying there at age 90. He bequeathed a farm to each of his six children....
>
> David Sr. was one of the pioneers of Central New York State and one of the first settlers of Fayetteville. In 1829 his name appears among six original trustees of the Presbyterian Church in

Fayetteville. He contributed generously toward the first church building and academy. He was one of the founders of the National Bank of Fayetteville and a founder of the Farmer's Bank. When the Ledyard Canal and Dyke was proposed, he was one of the four original promoters and one of its largest owners. The canal furnished water power to the town and contributed much to its prosperity. [Tradition has it that the Ledyard Dyke system was supposed to raise Fayetteville above Syracuse as a center of manufacture and electrical power.]

More important than all of his business acumen were the warmth and love he and Anna provided for their children. Although their own education had been necessarily short, David and Anna thought that education was important and saw that each of their children received as much as they could provide—a rarity in that time. Of their large family, the first son Edmund is said to have choked to death on a seed in some unstrained caraway-seed tea which a well meaning neighbor gave him. The other son, David IV, must have felt himself overwhelmed by is five sisters, three of whom the family affectionately called "the Amazons." They were remarkable women, strong of mind and body, purposeful and determined.

One of them was Miriam.

Despite a life of hard labor David Collin lived to be ninety, dying on November 25, 1884. General small dairy farming remains among the hardest physical labor one can engage in, requiring one to be a veterinarian, a botanist, a mechanic, a geologist, a meteorologist, a chemist, an accountant, able to go without sleep for long periods, able to do hard physical work—from spreading manure by hand to felling and splitting wood, to calving or lambing at all sorts of ungodly hours. Barry Lopez notes, "Regimes and ideologies . . . whatever their horrors, whatever afflictions they deliver, pass away. What endures is simple devotion to the question of having been alive." The obituary from the *Syracuse Evening Herald* reads, in part:

> Another historic figure is gone, one which towered among us out of a past generation like a rugged tree of the primeval forest. Such

lives possess more than a personal interest, for by them we measure our political and social development. . . .

Perhaps no one better deserved the title of "pioneer" than Mr. Collin, for he loved to subdue nature—to fit the rich land for cultivation, and call broad acres his own. By an industry that never flagged from daylight until dark, year after year, these days rarely witness, he became the owner of thousands of acres in Onondaga and neighboring counties, Michigan, Wisconsin, Indiana, and Illinois. The hospitality of his house was never refused anyone and Mrs. Collin never allowed guests to leave without some substantial token of their old-time generosity. Several friendless boys found a home with them for years and are now prosperous men who bless their memory. Mr. and Mrs. Collin celebrated their golden wedding in 1867, and Mrs. Collin died in 1873, aged eighty years.

Up to his very end Mr. Collin read the newspapers and loved to pore over the crumpled pages of his Bible. His end was peaceful and painless, almost his last words being: "Lord, take me home to my mother." . . .

Children and grandchildren and great-grandchildren were there to lay at rest the truly remarkable man—remarkable not merely for his great age, or as representative of the pioneer stage of the developments in Onondaga County, or for his eminent service in bringing hundreds and even thousands of acres into cultivation, but as well for his heroic qualities, inflexible purpose, indomitable will, calm self-repose and deep conscientiousness in all the duties of his long and eventful career.

A noble, heroic life has ended, a life which was nourished in the atmosphere of the Washington and Jefferson era, and witnessed changes more rapid and momentous than those great men had dreamed of, or any other life may hope to span.

Unlike much of his family, David Collin did not keep extensive journals, though he did keep accurate farm records. Nor is there much correspondence. What does survive expresses the purpose and directness of the man clearly. In February 1819, as a young father, having lost his firstborn in an apparent accident, with unforgiving hard labor facing him each day, he wrote home to his father and mother (he used little punctuation and the spelling is his own):

> Manlius
> February the 8th, 1819
>
> Father and Mother I have delay wrighting to you as long as I could with out embarassment till this present time We are now all enjoying good health we have a Daughter born the twenty six of December she grows like the weeds in June we have not name d her yet we both of calling her Caroline, I come to water in my well the 14 of January we Dug Down two feete after we come to the water and struck on a hard Slate rock the water two feete Deeper the water came in as fast a we could Drain it out with a half barel the debth of the well is 70 feete we dug through 40 feete of solid rock of plaster and slate the slate was mixed some with plaster that was more slatty, the pure plaster lay in solid bodies Between the slate in [?] we had to Blast the hole 40 feet I got out about twelve tons of pure plaster I have now got it [?] up I had a very smart and faithful man who under stood this kind Business Mr. WB Swift from Genesee County to assist me we have been to work at it two months & a half most all in the winter season It is not likely that the water will ever fail the stream at the time that i came to the water was as low as they were ever known in this county since that time there has been Rain to Raise the streams some when the streams comes to rise I think it will stand 6 or 8 fee in high water proberly 20 or 30 feet we found two holes almost twenty ...
>
> I have paid your taxes in Suliven which was $19.74 cents I under stand they have laid a tax for Draining the big stream from $15 to 50 on each lot it is talked of cutting a damn [?] around the swamp and then to the lake they have not begun to work yet Lot no. 88 i think must be a good lot it was taxet $4 that man that I wrote to about has not gone on to the [?] The man that ough Mr. Jacob's of sack Romao Bayster [?] Came here last week and paid up the Interest on the obligation he said he would be very glad if you would waite on him two or three years after the obligation is out ... he will pay the interest yearly and some of the principle if you

can wait he would like a new obligation: he would be glad to know soon I think he will be able to pay for his with a little Chance the other two are Desirous to know on the same grounds And am answered to me and i will send the same to them ... Anna joins with me is sending her respects ... Anna requests to tell Mrs. Mager [?] that she has a fine little girl to take care and like wise Lucy and [?] tell them I should be glad if they could come out west and make us a visit....

I Remain yours [??]
David Collin Jr.

Caroline, the baby, and her mother, Anna, fit in there somewhere. Eight years later, well established in his much larger home, with the farm rapidly expanding (sawmill, smithy, lime quarry) he writes again to Hillsdale. This is not to suggest he didn't communicate during the intervening years, but rather to model the tone of his writing even after such a span.

January 28, 1833

I was notified last week that they were cutting timber on lot 88 and I went down and was there three days. They have cut all the oak on the lot. 20 trees—most of this was done last winter and worked into staves and carried off but I am in hopes to save about 2,000 staves on lot 88. They have taken all the white wood [white pine] and ash. The lot is completely stript of the valuable timber. I agreed with one Elwood that uncle James sold to—to see that there was no timber cut on the lot and on Uncle James, but he proved to be villain. he goes right on getting timber off both lots and I know nothing of it until I went down. now [he] frequently told me there was no timber cut on the lot. He has left the country. the men that cut the oak and some ash and white wood live near to the lot that can be proved against them they are a poor set of fellows they ought not to go unpunished this lot is injured between 2 and 3 thousand dollars (between $35,000 and $52,000 today). I went on to lot 102003 [?] the oak timber on those two lots is almost all cut these are the handsomest oaks I ever see some are four feet across at the butt. Principally done last winter I am in hopes to save about 2,000 staves here, hogshead staves these were all sold to merchants and justice of the peace for $15 (approx. $250 today) per thousand, they advanced pay to those thieves ... They have gone about 3 miles up the creek cut all on one of the Kirkland lots which is as far upcreek as they have gone—stript it clean—last winter got out about $2000 worth of staves. I have checked them in their career this winter They appear to feel rather bad about—there appears to be a combination of them I am in hope to find them out that cut on the creek lots Some of them have property Judge Watson tells me

There has been men seen cutting pine on Wm Burtons lot 27. he had better send power of attorney to someone Wm. Jones lot 82 thay have taken off several hundred cedar posts—he had better send his deeds. Before I commence with them it is necessary that I should have the deeds (being not resident).

Making a success of a farm was more than planting crops, and there was more than one kind of thief nosing around the edges of settlements. To see his various lands—sometimes farms bought up from those who had farmed out the land and headed west or, as in the above letter, simply lots for timber or minerals—meant David Collin often traveled through empty country and faced unsavory, desperate men alone. It was another kind of courage than that required to face the wilderness with a new family, and it was his sense of who he was and his purpose in the world that must have made him an intimidating presence when he rode up to your place in the vast woods asking after his timber. But timber cutting in the quantities he mentions in his letter to Hillsdale required organized theft, and he was not afraid to turn to larger legal recourse for help. Since family records show that his father and uncles did not hesitate to call in sheriffs when some tenant reneged on rent in the western territories, it is fair to assume he did the same when so much money was at stake on his timber lands.

What about his wife at home with a growing number of children and farm hands to feed, not to mention clothe and heal, and a hundred other things for which people came to her as the mistress of the "Big House"? It is true she rarely left the fireplace or workroom. While she would never be considered frail by our standards, after the incident of the "Mad Frenchman" jumping down the well to his death the family often wrote that she was "of a more delicate inclination" in her later years. Nevertheless, when she died at eighty, in October 1873, the local paper had this to say about her:

> Mrs. Anna Smith Collin, whose death recently occurred, was one of the oldest citizens, and with her husband, David Collin, Sen., was of the early settlers in the town of Manlius. To recount somewhat of her history may be an appropriate tribute to one of those to whose character and influence as mothers, that of our Nation may be safely traced and trusted, as, also, "In Memorium," pleasant to her friends.
>
> Anna Smith was born February 14, 1794, at North-East, Dutchess County. Her paternal ancestors were of English descent, and their emigration shortly succeeded those of the May Flower. Staunch and firm in faith—decided in every virtue and piety, as was shown in the command of their own household and example; also in their efficient aid in sustaining the Old Stone Church, which still remains and is the oldest church edifice in the State—located on a tract of land known as Phillips Patent, granted by Charles II, of England, to Fredrick Phillips—and was built by Mr. Phillips, whose wife was of the family of whom we are speaking. Her grandfather had *great regard for the Sabbath.* No trifling excuse was allowed to detain him and his three sons from regular attendance upon divine service, although they must often have walked the five miles. Two of these sons inherited and together occupied the ample homestead until each family numbered six children, and this in unexceptionable harmony! Of these two families, the deceased and Mr. Ambrose Smith, of this village, were the last representatives. Among pleasant reminiscences of their childhood were the visits of an Aunt and her "charge," a bright little boy who interested them with his sweet voice, particularly in singing with pathos, touching lines written by himself on the death of his mother. He is known to us as the good missionary "anointed of the lord," William Goodell. . . . [Goodell was one of the first American missionaries, going to the near East in the 1830s and establishing Congregationalist missions

in Beirut, Syria, as well as one for Armenians in Constantinople where he took twenty years to make an Armeno-Turkish translation of the Bible.]

In a new country neighborhood the young wife found a wide sphere for the exercise of her large, warm heart of sympathies and many claims for her kind offices in times of sickness and affliction. The recital of the experiences of these years has often delighted her children. Forest animals still roamed their native woods. Indian faces were as familiar as the "white-man's," and the Indians soon learned what warm friends they had in the new comers, whose hospitality was always open and free to these natural owners of the land, who often lay upon the floor of the one living-room for a night's lodging. Bands of erect, stalwart young "braves" going to and from their hunting grounds, would stack their arms in a small room adjoining and spend the night stretched around the large, open fireplace.

With time came changes. In the progress of improvements, particularly those of school and church, she was truly interested, and active so far as woman's influence admitted.... Of her seven children four are still living, and of her thirty-two grandchildren there are twenty-seven, and two great grandchildren. Of others brought up under her care and influence, five remain and are honorable citizens.

The deceased was not a passive character. Hers was a superior mind in power and scope. She was clear, positive, and self-reliant in her convictions. She was interested in whatever affected the good of the public, and deeply desired the patriotic to prevail over the partisan spirit. She was an admiring lover of nature, was fond of reading, and a close observer of character, principles and events. Gifted with sound judgment she made successful application of her knowledge to practical life. Her memory was largely stored, and her ready, apt quotations, and her recitation of poetry and scripture was something marvelous. Even when her faculties were well nigh oblivious to things of the present, she would draw things new and at length from this storehouse of the mind.

But love and cheerfulness were her crowning characteristics. And while the former was strong and self-sacrificing at its center, it knew no boundaries nor distinctions, all alike—high and lowly—shared her kindnesses, sympathies and hospitalities. For the orphaned and homeless there was tenderest regard and a ready place in her heart and home. She was never troubled with the pettiness of life, neither would she touch the inharmonious keys of the human heart.

Thus do our few remaining aged ones—these living links to the past—drop before us from life to death.

After death who will garden our memories? These were the parents of David Collin Jr. To be given the trust of a man such as David Collin Sr., his father, was no small thing, even if you were his only surviving son. Mr. David was given his father's complete trust, for they both understood that the success of the larger family enterprise required the larger view, the realization that tough business always applied so that both family and finance could prosper in God's will for those who were chosen.

Born in August 1822, David Jr. was five years older than his sister Miriam and lived his entire life (save for a couple of years at RPI, graduating in the class of 1843) on the family land. His was the first generation to receive a more complete education. It is interesting to note that he never flaunted it before his father, who had so little formal education, at least as far as available documentation shows. But his training gave him a thing or two his father couldn't have had, despite his father's fine mind, hard work, and extensive experience. It is also important to recall that what education was available to David Jr. simply did not exist for his father, as the institutions themselves had not yet been founded when he would have, traditionally, been of an age to attend them.

In a letter he writes home to his father about his courtship of and marriage to the beautiful Clarissa Park (called Clara) of Burlington, New York, with whom he had nine children. There is a certain staginess, a mild sort of posturing, as though to say—this is how one writes letters. But as time and life move on, the tone and quality change. Here, he is only twenty-two:

David Collin IV, known as David Collin Jr.

North-East
Oct. 2nd, 1845

Dear Father,

    I received yours of the twenty-fifth last evening and agreeable to your request I write a few lines in reply. When I came here I found Harry Clark had leisure time to go around with me to look for sheep. We rode from Wednesday morning till Saturday evening visiting all the finest flocks within fifteen or 20 miles around and inquiring of those farther off.

    We found that such sheep as I wanted could not be had less than from two to 8 dollars a head [that is, $37–$148 per head today]. I like Douglas Clark's sheep much better than any that we saw, so I took fifty ewes and 5 bucks off of him, and 48 ewes and 2 bucks of Harry Clark. I engaged a man [of?] D [?] Clark that he recommended to me to be very very trusty to drive the sheep home. He left yesterday morning with them. I went as far [as?] Pine Plain.

With regard to my engagement I trust that I acted upon such motives as you write and believe it to be so with regard to him. I have thought much upon the different young ladies of my acquaitance [sic] and think that none of them possess somary [sic] of those qualities desirable and every thing that is calculated to make life pleasant to me and my friends as the young lady of my choice [Clara]. . . .

Yours in haste, David Collin

What we cannot know, but what his father knew he was doing was that he had brought along on his journey his own minister, Richard F. Cleveland, father of President Grover Cleveland. It may also help to know that Clara was sister to Eliza and Maria Louisa Park, who were wives of David Jr.'s uncle and first cousin, respectively. It was a close-knit family.

It is difficult to get a grasp on this man who so well represented his father's dream, the dream of prosperity, which was the word and choice of the Lord manifest in what each man had accomplished. Just a couple of years after his marriage to Clara, we find him writing back to her relations in eastern upper New York, with a certain "educated" tone until he finds himself getting down to the business of farming:

Collin House
Jan. 20, '47

Dear Brother and Sister,

Your long expected letter of the 2nd was received Tuesday of last week and afforded us much pleasure. I can assure you to hear from you as we had not heard particularly from you since you left us last fall. I doubt not but our anxiety to hear from each other has been reciprocal and the only excuse we can plead is the want of time and even now while I am writing our little (David) is crying in the cradle by my side for me to rock him or mother to take

Clara Park Collin, wife of David Collin IV

him. He was born Wednesday Jan. 6th And is a fine musical fellow weighing seven pounds fourteen ounces.

Clara has been quite comfortable since with the exception of sore nipples. We have an excellent nurse and hope in a few weeks she will be about again as usual. She is much obliged for the patterns you have been so kind to send her, she has not needed them and should not have used them if they had been here before.

We were happy to hear that your journey to our place last fall has proved so beneficial to [Maria's?] health and think a similar visit if made in due time would not only restore her to perfect health but would materially improve Clara's or at least gladden our hearts to welcome you again with us. We may possibly come out to Benton next season though uncertain as yet do not wait for us if you can spare a few days from avocations at home, come and spend them with us.

And he goes on with family affairs about children in school and getting plaster from the quarry and the little bit of sleighing they did around Christmas. The penmanship is tidy and largely clear. He becomes quite philosophical when he writes about his sister Harriet's death in 1855:

[Feb. 20, 1855]
He that loveth son or daughter or brother or sister here her voice stoped and once more looked around upon us all then resting her eyes upon me until she sweetly fell asleep in Jesus, without struggle perfectly conscious to the last. Mr. Seward says she had a premonition some time before we went to your place that she was doing her last work that she should not live long. Not one of us supposed there was any thing serious the matter of her, whenever she spoke of not enjoying the society of her friends long we thought she alluded to Mr. Seward not herself and when he would try to cheer her up she would say you don't believe me but I am going soon and you will soon follow. She has gone to her rest a little before us. Though we mourn her loss deeply yet we cannot wish her here again in this world of sorrow, suffering and separations. She has gone to her Savior and our Savior a disembodied spirit to unite with loved ones that have gone before her forever and forever in celebrating that love that hath reclaimed them from the power of sin. May we live by faith and so adorn our profession that when we shall be called from earthly scenes we may join the precious company of departed loved ones in the [?] of the [?] before the throne of their Father and our Father. Our minister preached a most excelant sermon from her last words in Mathew 10, 34 verse. ["Think not that I am come to send peace on earth; I came not to send peace, but a sword."] We now think of having it printed and I will send you a copy of it.

Ever yours,
David Collin, Jr.

As a businessman and farmer, he seemed to think and behave much as his father did, straightforwardly, having spent his days at the side of the master. But his experience at Rensselaer Polytechnic Institute encouraged and opened his natural thoughtfulness when he wrote personal letters.

> Fayetteville
> Oct. 23rd, 1848
>
> Dear Brother and Sister,
>
> Clara has been asking me every day for three weeks to write to you but I like a naughty boy have not done it. Now I will tell you why she is so anxious and why I have not written before. Three weeks last Saturday Clara presented us with a fine little boy [who, as a teen, later ran away] weighing nine pounds and one ounce. She got along pretty well for a week and by over exertion in sitting up she was taken worse but is now quite smart. Sabbath morning she went into the kitchen to breakfast. Today she has been up all day. I did not like to write you until she was getting along pretty well, and having thrashers here for a week past—I have not had time to write.
>
> We heard by way of Mr. Tremain that you had given up coming down this fall or I should have written sooner.
>
> Clara says we have got so many boys now we shall want some help to name them and if you have any extra names please send down or what would please us much better—Father [his father-in-law] wrote us soon after their return from the East that they might possibly come out here this winter and make us a short visit, to have you come down and meet them now that we might visit together and find a good name for the boy.
>
> Aunt Farnham received a letter last week from Auburn Wager bearing the sad intelligence of the death of their youngest sister Harriette who died after a short illness of the inflamation of the brain. How great the berievement must be to them. How few remain of that large family. Truly mysterious are the ways of Providence. Elizabeth left here about the first of September with a cousin our Henry Wager of Western near Utica to spend a few days in his family there in company with him to return home. How little did she expect to so soon be again clothed in mourning and that for a near sister.

Though we may feel to sympathize with them yet how little compared with the loss they feel. It seems but another admonition to all of us to be prepared for the hour of our dissolution that we may rise in the likeness of our Saviour and be forever with the blest.

Judge Tremain has been out here a little more than a week. He took a severe cold on his way over here so that he has staid at Porter's [Porter Tremain, a cousin] all of the time. I have not had time to see him to inquire about our friends at the East, but I presume they are well—Mrs. Stanton Park and one of her sons made us a short visit in the fore part of September She was in rather feeble health. Henry Douglas had gone to Louisiana.

My crops have come in rather light except corn which I think will yield well. I have not sold my barly yet it is now 5 shillings How was the barly crop with you and the price

Have you disposed of your wool or do you want any more sheep if [you] do I can let you have some this fall quite low, as I have more of them than I want to winter. I have not had an offer for my wool yet I wish you would write to us soon, and come down this winter, and let us know what the prospect is of your going East next season.

Harriette has commenced housekeeping in Mrs. Flint's house next to Dr. Shipman's—it is a time of usual health with us—Is there much excitement in politics this campaign—for which of the candidates do you vote—It is all, or almost all free soil here [The Free Soil Party, which was opposed to slavery and for the Homestead law, was a short-lived political party that helped put Zachary Taylor in the White House.]

There is a warmth and ease in the way David Jr. mixes practical business with family news. It is not difficult to picture the author of this letter as a good neighbor.

[Sept. 26 1844?]

Dear brother [his brother-in-law],

Being absent from home attending the Grand Jury till last evening I did not get your letter as soon as I otherwise should. With regard to letting you have some of my sheep, I will sell you fifty ewes two years old and over for twenty shillings a head running them off from the flock and give you the privilege of throwing out 4 or 5 which you might think too old. [A shilling was roughly 15 cents of the contemporary dollar, which in today's values is equivalent to just under $20, so a shilling was worth about $3.00 in our terms.] I have seven bucks to spare, which if you take I will let you have them at $5.00 per head, or if you select but the best I should want from six to ten dollars. They are all excellent sheep—the yearling bucks shearing from six to 7 1/2 lbs. and the older bucks from 7 1/2 to 11 lbs of wool of first rate length and beautiful style. My sheep have been but very little lame this season and since I examined them I have not seen a lame one and I consider them now about as good as before they were taken lame. I think my flock will shear from 4 1/2 to 5 pounds a head and a very nice style of wool. If you should not conclude to take them nor attend the fair I wish you would write me soon after the receipt of this as I have now an opportunity to dispose of them. I assume you have received a catalogue of S. P. Chapmans sale on the first day of the fair, if you would like to attend I'd like to go with you to Canastota. I hope you will not fail to attend the fair and make us a good long visit and have Henry and Charlie come with you or some of the other children and Clara says tell Maria to come *by all means* for she has a great deal to say to her that she cannot by writing and she wants to see her *very much*. Lydia and Mary left here day before yesterday for Burlington. We had a very pleasant visit from L. Mary expects to be back on the week of the fair. Mr. Seward has been quite sick for 2 weeks but is now recovering. Lucy [his sister Lucy, who married Porter Tremain; they were the parents of Charlie Tremain] and Porter Jr. have been very sick for a few days but seem to be recovering—Anna has a young son and doing well. The rest of our friends are in usual health and those that are sick in all probability will be around in a few days. We had heard of Russell's sickness which is a sad misfortune, and add another to the many severe trials which it has been [. . . ? . . .] to endure. We feel to sympathize in the afflictions and Clara has felt very anxious to see them [and] comfort them if it was so that she could.

We forget that what to us is an ordinary and minor illness and discomfort could be fatal in 1844. Death and illness were so ever-present that they bore mention and regret, but not much more. The mail he received (or kept) was all business.

>
> Clayville
> Dec. 18, 1869
>
> David Collins
>
> De[ar] Sir if you now wish to sell that Wool and take the going price i think you can sell it her[e] I have bin talking with Parker to day hee Says after the first of january thay shall By some fin Wool hee says thay Shall Pay from 42 to 45d [cents?] for such Wool as thay want ... [?] ... if you want to sell you must come down and bring a fin sample of Both lotts By so doing we can arang[e] it and I Beliv you Can git More for it her than any Where Else.
>
> if you Can decid to do this Come on the receit of this or Wright By Return of Post. for parker sayes thay Shall go to New york after bisnes and by than I think this is a good Chance for you to Sell as Wool is vary [?] and harder to sell. we are all Well
>
> yours [? truly?]
> S. B. McBrady [?]

He answered queries from those seeking livelihood:

>
> Fayetteville
> Jan. 19th, 1877
>
> Squire M. Coon,
>
> I received yours of Jan. 13th last evening and in reply would say that I want one good man by the year. I spoke to N. McLyman to write if your health was so you come and work for me and I would do better by you than I am by my present help by the year. I would let you have the house and garden near the school house and dead hard wood for winter and soft wood the rest of the time in the woods and [a] team to draw the same and plough

the garden and bring a load of your things from the railroad dept. Also the use of a cow (one of the heifers coming in in the spring) to keep her as my cows are kept on grass and fodder and apples if I have any to spare and such as I shall direct and give you two hundred dollars for the year [$3,250] and you board yourself and work as I am accustomed to work my men. There may be some things I have not mentioned which if you come we can readily arrange. If you conclude to come, write me at once as there are several men ready to come. Hoping if you will come it will be satisfactory to both, I remain,

                        Respectfully, David Collin, Jr.

He was, perhaps, not always timely with his own debts, though regarding this request we will learn why a little later.

                 Syracuse
                 Jany. 25th, 1886

David Collin, Esq.
Dear Sir—

I have written you once heretofore concerning my bill in the case of contract over your father's will; I have obtained an order from the Surrogate Court for the payment of the amount which has been served on you, but I am still without any reply.

I need the money very much at once and write to ask if you will be good enough to remit the amount at once. It is now over two months since the case was closed and it is nearly if not quite a year since I commenced rendering services in the case.

I do not like to complain but I need the money, therefore ask for it.

                 Yours respectfully,
                 W. Carpenter

At his death in 1908 the *Manlius Eagle* said this about him:

He was one of the oldest and best known residents of our village. David Collin, whose death occurred on Tuesday (Nov. 19) at his late home near Fayetteville, was one of the oldest residents of eastern Onondaga County, having been born eighty six years ago on the farm where he died, and where his entire life was spent....

Mr. Collin was educated in the Fayetteville academy and the Rensselaer Polytechnic Institute of Troy, from which latter institution he was graduated in 1843 with the degree of C.E. In 1845 he married Clara Park, youngest daughter of Capt. Avery Park of Burlington Green, Otsego County. Traveling in those days was not the simple matter that it is now, and Mr. Collin drove the sixty-three miles to the home of his bride near Cooperstown, accompanied by his pastor, Rev. Richard F. Cleveland, father of the late Grover Cleveland, who performed the marriage ceremony. The home which was then established, has been famous through three generations for its warm hearted and generous hospitality, and to it a large circle of relatives and friends have ever made joyful pilgrimages.

Although Mr. Collin held many positions of trust, he never sought publicity or notoriety, his chief ambition being for his home.... He early in life identified himself with the Fayetteville Presbyterian Church where in the councils of the session and the Board of trustees, his judgment was always respected.

With enthusiastic interest furthering every public good, a man of strict integrity and uprightness, and of firm moral courage, he was one whose impress upon the community cannot be erased by the shifting sands of time. He was especially interested in young people and many successful business men of today owe their start in life to the help and encouragement received from Mr. Collin. While attending Troy Polytechnic he became much interested in the study of geology and the valuable collection of minerals which he made at that time he presented several years ago to the Fayetteville High School.

So we have the noble son of noble parents. Moral and stoic, obedient to the service of others. In observing the past we are inclined to think not of that awful suffering of the human race, but rather of how these figures ennobled their world and, by extrapolation and our own selfish inclination, ours. But this dehumanizes them and makes their work a false labor. It was hard, and save for their own documentation of it, so little is recalled.

David Jr. himself noted, regarding the death of his sister, "Though we mourn her loss deeply yet we cannot wish her here again in this world of sorrow, suffering and separations. She has gone to her Savior and our Savior, a disembodied spirit." How bitter the material world has proved to be. The suffering is true, but it is not ameliorated by our choosing to exclude it from what we wish to remember.

When David Jr. retrieved his father from the strange plans of his sister Miriam, he did what was necessary to avert what he saw as a tragedy in the making. The fantasy of the united family was breaking. Tragedy breaks the illusory vision of idealized unity, the vision of family, permanence, rightness, and certainty.

6

Life on the Farm

> For though she's as like this as a crab's like an apple,
> yet I can tell what I can tell . . .
> —Shakespeare, *King Lear,* 1.5.14–15

In the spring of 1844 word began to go out that Grandfather Collin, that is, the father whom David Sr. had brought out west to settle in Oak Grove, was failing. He was the one who had sent Henry and David Sr. into the "Western Territories" and with whom he laid out the plan for the development of the clan back in 1816. By 1844 things were well on their way toward that end, and the homestead in Fayetteville was fast becoming a local landmark. The eldest David Collin's granddaughter, Emeline, wrote from Oak Grove in March of 1844 to her Aunt Eliza:

> Grandfather requests me to fill this sheet—an invitation which I shall certainly not decline, although I have nothing of particular interest to write. Grandfather's health is quite poor, but rather better than it has been. He is getting very deaf, so much so that he cannot hear conversation carried on in an ordinary tone of voice. He seems to think himself failing, but wishes me to tell you that you may expect a visit from himself and Grandmother about the first of next Sept. if his health remains as good as present. Our little family circle remains unbroken yet, but David [that is David Jr., also grandchild to the subject of this letter, i.e., Emeline's cousin and favorite family candidate for her husband] will soon

leave us, and we shall miss him very much. I assure you I hardly know what I should have done without such a *second brother.* We have had fine sleighing most of the winter, and with us it was well improved. I have never known our young people so social as they have been this winter. Rides and parties followed each other in quick succession, and weekly we have had lectures or discussions before the Young Men's Association which have been a source of interest and amusement. The ladies are admitted as honorary members of this Association with the privilege of writing for it. Uncle Farnham [David Farnham had married a sister of David Collin III] is *the* orator. He is said to have made one of his best efforts a short time since at an abolition meeting. I was not present, but heard it much talked of. The meeting was got up by a few ultra, hot headed abolitionists and to gain an audience notices were given out, that a fine singer from Syracuse would be present, and the meeting addressed by a celebrated lecturer. The singer was not there and the speaker dealt only in slander. Uncle Farnham felt perfectly outraged, and being *challenged* to speak, he rose, as he says, choked with anger, and hurled such thunderbolts at the speaker that some of the ladies nearly fainted with fright. . . . We came near to losing Mr. Cleveland [father to the president] this Spring but thanks to the *ladies,* we can now keep him. The gentlemen, failing to make out his salary within fifty dollars [$1,000], referred the matter to the ladies. With characteristic zeal they immediately formed a society, the members of which are to pay annually a certain [hole in the paper] for the support of Mr. Cleveland. A president, secretary and treasurer, four solicitors and collectors were appointed as officers of the society. The plan has succeeded admirably—and the fifty dollars are already secured, proving the assertion that the influence of one lady is equal to that of *seven and a half men.*

Let no one suggest Collin women were afraid to make their mark. Who knows how Grover's future might have been without their support of his father?

96 | IF OUR LIVES BE SPARED

On May 4, 1844, Emeline wrote, again from Oak Grove (where she, as an unmarried woman, was expected to care for her elders) to her brother Henry and his wife, Maria:

> When I received your *very welcome* letter I promised myself that it should be answered at least in a few days.... I am going to commence by telling you all the news I can *think* of, and I suppose anything which has occurred since *last Fall* will be news to you.... You will not doubt that a great *noise* and *show* were produced when I tell you that it was got up entirely under "Fred's" direction, and I have never seen anything equal it, in heartless parade.

And from the same letter:

> It has also been not less positively reported that I was to have cousin David [she was the daughter of the senior David's brother, very close first cousins],—and the rumor has even reached Hillsdale, and Uncle Norton [David Collin II's brother, i.e., her great-uncle] seems inclined to believe it. I feel vexed whenever I hear anything about it; it is perfectly absurd. I fancy I can find somebody beside a cousin, and if some of the *property does get out of the family* I suspect it will not be so much regretted as some good people of Fayetteville imagine. Oh! it almost makes *my blood boil* to be suspected of such sordid motive. But time will prove how very easy it is to be mistaken....
>
> Grandfather's health is now very poor. He has had for several weeks a sore throat which almost prevents him from swallowing. You would be surprised to see how feeble he looks. There are one or two cases of *black tongue* in the village, but they will probably not prove fatal [this sounds like Weil's Disease, a kind of infectious jaundice. It is certainly NOT the plague, which also has "black tongue" as a distinguishing feature]. Mrs. Foote and Mrs. Ambrose Smith died some weeks since. Have you heard from Clara lately?

On May 9, 1844, she wrote the following to her uncle Norton, who lived back in Hillsdale:

Our friends have requested me to write to you particularly in regard to Grandfather's health. We have purposed writing for more than a week, but his symptoms at times appearing more favorable, we have delayed until now. Although he is apparently no worse at present than he has been, we still thought it proper to write knowing you were always anxious to hear when any change occurred.

I think I wrote you that Grandfather's health had been quite poor during the winter. It has since been sensibly failing, and for five or six weeks past he has suffered very much from a sore throat, which has made it very distressing for him to swallow. It has been thought to proceed from a canker, but is now decided to be the Quinsy [a kind of tonsillitis, what is called a suppurative inflammation of the tonsils]. He has seemed to be impressed with the idea that he would not recover, still as there seems to be nothing immediately alarming in his case, we are hoping that he will soon recover his usual strength. (The doctor has just come and I will wait until I hear his opinion before finishing this).

Friday 10th—Dr. Shipman seems to think Grandfather will soon recover—says his sore throat does not proceed from Quinsy, but is something similar. Perhaps you may think from what I have written that he is confined to the house. He is not, but walks about the yard. Grandmother's health is about as good as usual. She wished me to tell you that you night expect to see them in Hillsdale next Fall if Grandfather should recover. . . .

If Grandfather should be worse I will write again. If he gets better I will send you a paper. I would write more, but I have a violent tooth ache, and it being something new for me, I have not learned to bear it very *philosophically,* and perhaps you will believe me when I tell you that I feel *real cross.*

On August 16, 1844, Emeline wrote from Fayetteville to her brother Henry, back in Benton Center, where her own branch of the family took root.

I have waited long and *patiently* for a letter from you since you left Fayette. Notwithstanding your promise to write very soon. What *can* be the reason? I have nothing in particular to write as nothing has occurred which I think would very much interest you since you were here. Uncle Norton and Harriette [brother and sister to her grandfather; Norton was bequeathed the main farm in Hillsdale] left the next Wednesday after you did. We have not heard from them yet except by a paper. The celebration on the fourth passed off finely, even better than was anticipated. About *fourteen hundred children* are said to have been present. We had fine speaking, fine music, and "good cheer." The sabbath after the fourth Laura Rumsey spent with me. She had written to me that she was coming and I met her in Syracuse on Saturday. She only stayed till Monday noon, but I enjoyed the visit very much indeed. She was on her way to New Haven, where her sister was at school and her brother tutors in the college. I have received a long letter from her since she has been there telling me all about old schoolmates. David and Harriette [cousins; children of her uncle David Collin] were very much pleased with their jaunt—visited New York, New Haven and Boston. By the way, the report that I was going to have David has been *insisted* upon until within a week or two past. All sorts of ridiculous things have been said about it. Some said it depended upon a clause in Grandfather's will—others that this place [Oak Grove] was willed to David and myself. You can't think how it has vexed me. But it is all given up now as a "bad job".... Have you sold that wheat yet, and how much did you get for it? If you think it best you may sell that which is due from last year's rent after it is threshed. I should like the money.... I wish you would write as soon as you receive this, so that I may know how much I shall want of Uncle David.

A month later, her beloved grandfather died. By autumn she had gone on an extended visit back east to Hillsdale to be with cousins. She was courted most assiduously by the young Dr. Welch, to which she alludes only obliquely. Further, she also suggests, but only suggests, as though with some whimsy, that certain things were not talked about in family correspondence, especially since everyone should understand the allusions anyway. In October she writes from Hillsdale back to her brother Henry in the western Finger Lakes village of Benton Center.

I have been expecting to hear from you ever since I came to Hillsdale, but have now concluded you must be waiting to hear from me, and perhaps you have daily looked for a special invitation to appear here in *person*. My object in now writing is to *warn* of that invitation, and when it comes, which may be in three or four weeks, will you not accept it? It would be to me a source of great gratification, and were I to express my feelings fully I should say you *must* come. . . . Have you sold that wheat? I should very much like to have the money. You will please write as soon as you receive this so that I may know what to depend upon, but *bring* the money instead of sending it if you can.

I have written this in great haste as I expect to start for New York this morning in company with Uncle Norton, Aunt Eliza and Clara [the cousin being courted by her other cousin David, about whom everyone had been speaking]. Mr. Bidwell is also going. We are going to attend the fair of the American Institute, and I have some shopping to do which makes me particularly anxious to go.

I have been to Rhinebeck with Uncle N. and Aunt E. and attended the state fair where I saw David. He visited Dutchess County for something *particular* I suspect—from thence he came to Hillsdale and Grandmother returned to Fayette with him.

At the end of the month she writes again to Henry:

I now write you for the express purpose of inviting you to attend my wedding on the 7th of Nov. Will you not come? It has been deferred until after the election that you might have time to come. I feel as if you *must* come but I will not urge you against your convenience. My heart is full, but I can write no more. Oh! how I want to see you.

Your affectionate sister, Emeline

I received your letter containing the check—it was all right.

Both mail and persons had already begun to move about the state quickly with the advent of the railway system in the early 1840s. The pace of life and the rate of change began to increase exponentially. In his introduction to *The Oxford Book of Light Verse,* W. H. Auden wrote: "As long as society was united in its religious faith and its view of the universe, as long as the way in which people lived changed slowly, audience and artists alike tended to have much the same interests and to see much the same things." He adds that the upheavals of the Romantic period disrupted profoundly this sense of community so that, "the only true community was that of the family, the only real social bond that of parent and child." There were other social and political upheavals in the still-youthful America. Funding for and later expansion of the Erie Canal and other waterways, creating the railway infrastructure, taxes and trade, and larger national issues brought those concerns to the local level. They began dividing the northern states from the south. They also turned over the common ground of pioneer and early rural life with its broad shared needs and values. The Collin family turned to themselves for community, as fragile an entity as it came to be.

June 28, 1844, was a day that slipped by in people's journals. The usual assiduously kept notes about weather, crops, chores, neighbors are missing. David Collin [Sr.] was appearing before the Surrogate Court to have his father's will of 1837 confirmed. It set the stage for what was to happen later. Miriam was only sixteen, when this "affirmation" took place and so was grouped among the many grandchildren noted in the will. But the central role played by her father in what resulted placed the decisions about her heritage in other hands. It is worth noting that there is a lot of land distributed in the will, and what David Collin received is not spelled out in detail. He was the son who built Oak Grove for his parents' retirement. The original will was apparently from 1837, but David Collin's mother, Lucy Bingham, did not die until 1854, ten years after this court event. Clearly some family rumblings were beginning. This is the central portion of the document David Collin received from the Surrogate Court, "In the matter of proving the last will and testament of David Collin, deceased":

> *First* I give & bequeath to my wife Lucy so long as she shall continue my widow and no longer the interest of two thousand dollars [$37,720] which sum is to be loaned and secured by bond & mortgage upon real estate and the interest thereof paid to her

annually after my decease during her life and so long as she shall continue my widow and no longer by my executors hereinafter named and the principal to be distributed among my grand children by my said executors after her death in like manner and proportion as my other personal estate hereinafter given & bequeathed to my grand children—I also give and bequeath to my said wife Lucy during her natural life and so long as she shall remain my widow all my household furniture & goods of every description with power to the said Lucy to distribute the same among my daughters at her discretion while she shall continue my widow and such portion thereof as shall remain indisposed of by her at the time of her death to be distributed among my daughters by my executors so as to render their shares of the same as nearly equal as may be.

Second I give and bequeath to my daughter Hannah the wife of David L. Farnham the farm in Manlius, county of Onondaga, which I purchased of Stephen Herrick containing about one hundred and thirty or one hundred and forty acres to descend and go to heirs of her body begotten and if she dies without such heirs to be sold by my executors and the avails thereof distributed by them among my grand children in like manner and proportion with my other personal estate herein bequeathed to my grand children. I also give and bequeath to my said daughter Hannah the wife of David L. Farnham the sum of one thousand dollars to be paid to her by my executors.

Third I give & devise to my son Solomon B. Collin my West farm so called in Hillsdale aforesaid lying south of the farm now in possession of Frederick P. Stukle containing about one hundred and seventy five acres and also the lot of land called the side hill lot which lies on the east side of the road which runs past the house on said west farm beginning on the east side of the road at a stone wall which runs eastwardly until it intersects a fence running northerly, then along said fence to the road which runs from Samuel Truesdell's to the house on said West farm, then follows the fence to the place of beginning which last described lot contains about fifty acres.

Fourth I give & devise to my son Norton S. Collin the farm on which I now live [he didn't move to Fayetteville until the next year, 1838] and also my wood lot in Hillsdale aforesaid containing about sixty acres and his adjoining farm which was in possession of Eli Foster deceased at the time of his death.

Fifth I give & devise all the rest & residue of the real estate & land of which I may die seized & possessed and which is not otherwise herein devised and wherever the same may be to my son David Collin.

Sixth I give & bequeath to my daughter Lucy the wife of Barnet Wager the sum of one thousand dollars to be paid to her by my executors.

Seventh I give & bequeath to my daughter Amanda the wife of Porter Tremain the sum of one thousand dollars to be paid to her by my executors.

Eighth I give & bequeath all the rest & residue of my personal estate to all my grand children, to be distributed among and paid to them share & share alike by my executors in manner & form following, viz.: to be vested in good securities bearing interest and to be paid to them severally as they arrive at the age of twenty one years in equal shares estimating the whole amount of such residue of my personal estate at the time of each payment and thus making as equal distribution of the same among such grand children

Ninth It is also my will & intention that if my wife Lucy shall survive me and shall within one year after my death accept the Provisions made for her by this my last will and testament that such provision shall be in lieu of her dower at law.

Tenth I nominate & appoint my sons David Collin & Norton S. Collin and my friend Thomas K. Baker of Hillsdale aforesaid to be executors of this my last will and testament, hereby revoking and annulling all former and other wills by me heretofore made.

On June 2, 1844, David Collin, the grandfather of Miriam and our David Collin Jr., died. His son, now David Collin Sr., came into his full inheritance and became the head of his branch of the family. David Collin

Sr. and his wife, Anna, had a total of thirty-three grandchildren. Documentation is not complete on all of them, as some died shortly after birth, and the layers of intermarrying with various cousins is so baroque that it would shame European monarchs of the Renaissance.

David Collin's daughter Lucy, for example, married her aunt's widower, Porter Tremain, when her aunt died at age thirty-one, and gave birth to Charles, one of the grandchildren who was particularly close to his Gardner and Armstrong cousins (who were in turn close to their aunt Miriam, a sister of David Collin Jr.), and who was central in many ways to the family drama as it unfolded.

Each generation lost some children or had someone who died young. David Collin Sr. and Anna lost their first child, Edmund, in 1817. Their daughter Caroline lost her first child, also called, fatefully, Edmund, after he was born in 1840. Indeed Caroline, her husband, Sylvester Gardner, and their daughter Anna, then nineteen, all died within three weeks of each other from a typhoid epidemic that raced through the countryside.

David Collin Jr. and his wife, Clara, lost their first son, David Collin (V), to exposure when he went through a snow storm to attend to sheep in a distant outbuilding. Their daughter Harriet (one of the nine children born to them) was only twenty when she succumbed to tuberculosis.

Then there was Edward, the second son of David Collin Jr., who ran away as a teen, causing the whole clan great anxiety. The complex interlayering of affections and loyalties was enriched by the sense of family history, which everyone kept reciting to one another, and by the legacy of the land.

We have many stereotyped images sent along to us out of the past about what life was like in the midcentury after the wilderness had been beaten out of existence. Men seemed to rule the land. Did they indeed? While his youth was a bit after the crux period we are talking about, Roswell Park Collin, the fourth child of David Collin Jr. and one of the darlings of the clan along with his beloved cousin Cardera, steadily kept diaries all his life. In them he talks of school, the coming and going of friends, family and neighbors, weather, chores, stock, and life on the farm. Much that went on he has already come to take for granted, having no way to know what

The Collin home farm, ca. 1895

his grandparents had to do to make his own life possible. So rich are his diaries, an entire book could be drawn from them. What follows are some excerpts starting in 1859, when he was merely seven, living in the big house that was to stand for a hundred years—a time when life was settled, values were certain, the cousins many, and things were really good. Or so we'd like to remember.

A boy's Christmas

> Dec. 28, 1859
> David and Edward got Charley and I to go to bed and David put one cent in my stockings and I had a pair of mittens; in the afternoon we went up to Manlius at Smith Hall. We went in an old

room that looked as if it had been an old store. Then we went up three pair of stairs. Then we went into a large room where there was a large table with cakes, candies, apples, grapes, nuts and great many nice things. We had the Manlius Band real near us. When we was coming home the road was very bare and we had to go on the side of the road. It was very slanting and the most weight was on the lower side. The sleigh turned over. 18 in it. It was a bob sleigh. It had no reach to hold it together and the front part was drawn out from the box. It went over very slow and no one was hurt. We got the box on the 2 sleighs and got in again but Peter and John Rowe ran and got David's sleigh and we rode home. When we got home it was very nearly dark. I done my chores. I am so tired that I think I have wrote enough and so good night!

Dec. 29, 1859

We had a very nice time up to Manlius at Smith's Hall and I was so tired that I did not finish telling about what I was up to Manlius. First the band played. Then Mr. Little talked to us. Then the Malodian played and the people sang. At the same time there was a Christmas tree standing on a stand and there was a great many little red apples around it. I think it was the nicest time I ever had before. I am going to bed.

Playing (reflecting back on the Thanksgiving holiday)

Monday, Dec. 9–12, 1861

The night before Thanksgiving I had just come home from school and I went and got Eddie's little ax to split kindling wood and the stick was very narrow at the top and the ax missed the stick and hit my toe and cut the cord and cut my toe so bad that I can not step on it. Here is what they put in the Fayetteville Gazette about it: "Accident. A younger son of Mr. David Collin, Jr., met with a severe accident on Thanksgiving day. He was splitting some kindling wood when the ax glanced striking his foot making a terrible gash. We understand he is now quite comfortable though at first the wound was thought quite dangerous and might lead to amputation" [not so far-fetched in the days before antiseptics or antibiotics]. Monday Dr. Taylor came to see it and he thought it was nothing very bad. Grandmother came up Sunday and the Dr. came the next day. Cousin Arthur Park was here with his wife. They came two weeks ago last Friday and stayed three days and a half. Cousin Mary and Roswell Park [a cousin from his mother's side after whom he was named] came the night before Thanksgiving day and stayed till Thursday. Cousin Rosy gave me a little gun, 3 cents and a ball of string and a piece of sealing wax. We would take white paper and cut it up in strips and make figures on them and play it was money. As soon as we had enough of bills we done them up. I gave Rosy about ten packages. We had a very pleasant time and I was sorry to have him go away.

Thanksgiving

In the morning Charlie went down to uncle Seward's to see if the girls could come up here. Uncle Seward was married to Miss Hoag 2 weeks last Wednesday, 1861, and went to Albany on business. Hattie, Anna and Lucy Seward came up here. David went down after them. We had a turkey for dinner. In the evening we played blindfold and Cousin Mary taught us how to play malaga raisins and I purchased my [?]

Monday, Dec. 9

This morning Charlie and I tried on our new boots. Charlie's fitted and mine fitted me and Father said Mr. Edward's never done so well in his life. To day it is muddy and very much like Spring. David and Eddie go to school down to the village and their teacher is Mr. Kinney. Yesterday Grandma Neva and Collin came up here and spent the afternoon here. In a little while Aunt Corrie and Sylvester Gardner came here but they went home after a little while. We have got a stove up in our room and Collin and I went up there and played.

Tuesday

This morning I got up and put on my pance alone. Before the boys went to school Eddie gave me some cedar to whittle and I made a waterwheel and 2 watches and a scraper. The waterwheel I brought out in the kitchen and I set it in motion.

Wednesday

This morning I made five large watches and this afternoon I made 2 large [ones]. In the evening Mr. Edward Flint came in and took tea with us and after went down to the Concert with Mother, Mary and David, father, Clara and Eddie, Margret, Hattie, Charley, Miny, Willy and myself. We cut up little sticks (and) had them for sawlogs. We played that the waterwheel was a sawmill. I made a little sleigh, and in the morning I sold it to Hattie for 15 butternuts.

Thursday

This morning Clara wished me to make [one] and she bought it for Miny. In a little [?] I went to studying. But I had just got to going when Francis led Stub up and put a saddle and bridle on him and came in and told us that David Hildreth cut [his] foot almost off. He said that he split it from his toes up to his ankle. William Robison and David's father were there and they carried him a little way but he was so heavy that they could not carry him. His father there with him wished William came here to get a horse and wagon but Granpas was here and he took it. Francis took Stub and went after Dr. Byington and he said it was cut through cord, bone and all.

Christmas, 1861

December 23, Monday

This morning the snow was about 4 inches deep and it is now snowing. Tomorrow is the last day of school down to the village. David's and Clara's throats were so sour that they did not go to school. There is an "exaningation" today and tomorrow down to the boys school.

December 24, Tuesday

This morning we found the snow about 6 inches deep and it is very cold. Clara did not go to school. I bought a little dustpan for Clara. My toe is not well yet. This morning Hattie and I went out in the woodhouse and sawed some wood for our little stove. this morning Margret, our hired girl, went to Syracuse. Father gave her $6 and a half a dollar for a Christmas present. This afternoon about 5 o'clock Aunt Miriam and Uncle Armstrong came up here.

December 25, Wednesday

Today is Christmas. David and Charlie and I got up before anyone else in the house. And I beat every one in the house in wishing them a merry Christmas. I popped a lot of popcorn and Clara, Charlie and I strung it for the Christmas tree. Uncle Armstrong and his family were coming up here. In the morning we took a sleigh ride down to Granpa's and when we came back it was about noon. Uncle Armstrong's folks were to be here in the morning but their trunk had not come with the presents and Uncle Armstrong and Aunt Miriam went down to the railroad after it but it had not come. Aunt Miriam was going to trim the tree but Mother got so tired of waiting that she trimmed it herself. As soon as she had got it trimmed almost they came. Uncle Armstrong fixed another tree in the place of the other and Aunt Miriam and Uncle Armstrong trimmed it. They came so [late] and we waited so long that it was about half past 3 o'clock when we ate dinner and it was dark when we began to play. We played Goose Sawyer and Blindfold then we were going to have our Christmas presents. There were 3 candles on it. In a little while Eddie nocked at the door for he was santa Claus. Aunt Miriam went to the door and he came in with Granma's Muff on his head for a cap and Father's old Buffalo skin coat on and a pipe in his mouth. Aunt Miriam would take the things off from the tree and handed them to him and he would hand them around to us. I got a donkey with a bridle and saddle and 2 little baskets on each side and he would shake his head up and down. This I got from Mother. A little ship with little sails and a little flag and a little rudder from Eddie and the prettiest pinball I ever saw from Clara and a photograph of Collin Armstrong from himself, a tin whistle from Aunt Miriam, a primer from Charlie and a card from Clara and a box with a spring in that when we open it it will spring up with the face of a man on [it] from Margret, and a slate and lead pencil from Mary Loomis.

Butchering, 1862

January 21st, Tuesday

Today Father is agoing [to] butcher the fat hogs. Eddie and I had to drive the old white cow, the old speckled cow (old Ohio) and a small heiffer (a large calf of mine) down to the stack. When we came back they had 2 hogs scrapping them. I stayed and saw the old "souw" stab bed and when John Connelly was getting over out of the pigpen he stepped on my cut toe and hurt me very bad and made me cry. I went to the house and dressed my toe and got ready for school. Then I went out to the piggery again to see them before I went to school and Father saw I had been crying and asked me what was the matter and I told him and he said I mustn't go to school. I stayed home and took Eddie's and my bladders and blew part of them up.

January 22, Wednesday

This morning I done all my Chores and went to school as usual. It snowed a little today.

January 23, Thursday

This morning I done my Chores early. I was coming up from the barn and a peddler came to our house and Mother [bought] 24 buttons and 1 hankerchief for Charlie and 1 for me. They were colo[r]ed.

January 24th, Friday

This [morning] I had to get my "orthogryphy" lesson. Cornel[i]us Cross had to get his over. Tonight when we were sp[e]lling Emma Cross got whipped because she would not spell.

January 25th, Saturday

This morning Eddie and I done our Chores together. Eddie and I went down to the stack together and Eddie drew me down on our sled. When we came back we fixed our part up in the woodhouse chamber and we are agoing to have a little store there. we drew our boddy wood down from our little woodshed up in our little store to sell.

January 26th, Sunday

This morning I went to meeting. Mr. Fort was here and he preached a Sermon. In the afternoon he went to the "Baptece" Church.

January 27th, Monday

This morning Eddie and I done our chores together. When we was going down to the stack we saw a very pretty snowbank.

January 28th, Tuesday

This morning while I was feeding the cows Eddie filled up the woodbox because we go in partnership.

January 29th, Wednesday

Today it is thawing. And it is quite warm. This noon us boys went up in Mr. Mead's Orchard and road down hill on the snowbanks. There was great dumps and sometimes it would dump us up 2 feet from the ground.

January 30, Thursday

Today Charlie and I brought our sleds. This noon when I was running to hop on my sled I hit my knee on the bottom board and made it lame. It thawed so that we could not go up in Mr. Mead's orchard for the drifts sunk in so.

January 31, Friday

This morning recess Fred Reice and I were [w]restling and Amos Cross come up and pushed us both down and i struck my breast on Fred's knee and knocked my breath out and hurt me very much. It is thawing today and very warm and pleasant.

Boys' work beyond chores, 1862 (see the 1864 entry below describing chores)

February 8th, Saturday

This morning I done my Chores and then us boys had to clean up 11 bushels of wheat and then we had to load up a load of corn. Collin Armstrong come up to our house but we had to work so much that we did not play much. Charlie and I had to clean brine down cellar. The pork is so low now that Father packed his pork and the barrels leaked and let the brine run out. In the afternoon the boys had to yoke up the oxen and draw two loads of wood from the orchard. Then we had to draw some corn and peas over to the other barn. Then we went down to the swamp and we drew up our little wood and Charlie and [?] got some little ash trees for handles to bu[?] and mallets, and then Eddie and I went cross lots over to the stack to feed the cows.

Playing in the snow, 1862

March 1st, Saturday

This morning the drifts were very high and the snow was half a foot deep. As soon as we done our chores we went to making snowhouses. We would take a shovel and dig out from in under high drifts. Charlie did not have any. As soon as I got mine almost done Charlie said he would help me finish it if I would let him live with me. As soon as we got it all dug out I made a large hole in the top at the back end for a Chimney and then put large chunks of snow on the top around the hole. Then we went to the house and got some matches, chips and shavings and made a fire. The smoke all went out the chimney.

March 17, Monday

This morning I done all my chores. The old speckled cow and [my] "heffier' had a couple of bull calves and Father gave them to David to break. The old speckled cow was my cow but I traded her with Eddie for [?] "heffier." Charlie takes care of the youngest one [?] the old speckled cow's calf. He feeds it hay and milk and I tend to the other. we have a stable for each of them.

March 18th, Tuesday

This morning I done all my chores. It has snowed every day for about 2 months. My morning chores are to feed the hens, feed the cows stalks, feed my calf hay and milk. We take turns in filling up the wood box. Charlie fills it up mornings one week and I the next one. When Charlie fills up the wood box morning I do nights. getting the potatoes ditto.

March 19, Wednesday

Last night Uncle Armstrong brought my violin. He saw a little one I made with one string and then promised me one. It is a very nice one and it is about 2 feet long. I can play the scale on it now. This noon I went home for my dinner and last night I was imperfect and I had to stand on the floor 1 hour.

Traveling with his father to a tenant farm, 1862

May 12, Monday

This morning Eddie and I had to take 14 sheep up on the hill. We went down the lot where they was but we could not find only 13. When we was coming home we found her dead. We took the others up on the hill. Peter Row[e] went with us. Today the men are drawing manure out from the barnyard over to the other barn. P.S. Our school began today. Miss Williams is our teacher.

May 13, Tuesday

This morning I went down to Truxton with father. When we were going the wheel to the wagon came off. There was a man "wright" by the side of the road and he helped Father put it on and then he went out to his shop and made an [?]tron to go in the [?]try. He had a bellows to go by water. Charlie's horse kicked so bad that we can not use him and so we had to take Billy and Prince. When we had gone a few miles Billy got frightened and ran away. There was some Beech stakes by the side of the road. Then a colt came running up and frightened him. He ran as fast as he could and Father could not stop him. When Father said "who" [meaning "whoa"] Prince pulled back as hard as he could. I saw a new kind of flower in the woods. We saw some waterfalls in the woods that [splashed] on rocks and they fell as high as the Locust trees. It took all day to get there. When we got there Father and I took a walk up on the new land. Then we went in the house and after we ate supper I sat down in a chair by the stove and got to sleep. Then I went to bed but I could not get to sleep. I had such a cold. In the morning I woke up [and] found myself at Mr. Angle's all alone. Father had got up. I dressed myself and went downstairs and then went out to the barn where father was. After we ate breakfast Mr. Angle and Father went upstairs and brought down some maple sugar. Mr. Angle works the farm by shares. He has 1/2 of what he makes and raises and Father 1/4 and granpa 1/4. When we got a load we started for home. It is 32 [miles?] our house to Truxton. We went a different road from what we did going. We went around the LARGE reservoir. It is 3 miles long and 1 mile wide. We took Dinner at "Deriter" [DeRuyter]. When we came back to Deriter we went down to the oil mill where they make oil-cake. Then we went up to Mr. Clark's Annel house and took dinner again and then we came home.

Regarding the death of David Collin (V), the eldest son, on November 3, 1862

December 17, Wednesday

This morning I done all of my Chores and took some corn in a basket on my way to school to feed to the hens but Father was over there feeding the sheep and he said I "kneed" not feed them because he had. Rocket, Charlie's little bull, had got in between the straw stack and the board fence and could not get out and Father had to get a fork and pull some of the straw out of the stack. Then I went to school and I got there about five minutes before it commenced. At recess I went with Johny Mahon to get a pail of water. This noon Charlie and I went home to get our dinner. Father is quite sick. He was knocking out the old "yorkshears" turks [pigs] and he broke the rope and bit his hand very bad. Stephen went over to Manlius after Dr. Taylor and Fredrick went down to the Village after Dr. Hurd. Dr. Taylor was not at home and so Dr. Smith came over in his place. It has been very cold today, snowing and blowing a little. Eddie is shut up in the libra[ry]. He has had the Diptherior about two months ago and he has not got over it yet. His legs bother him and he can not go out of doors for the Dr. says it is as dangerous as the Diptherior its self. I have got a little yoke steers that were David's. David died about six weeks ago last Monday and he died a very happy death trusting in Jesus. [He died from diphtheria aggravated by exposure after trekking over half a mile to a distant barn to feed the sheep in a heavy storm as part of his evening chores.] Rev. Mr. Erdman preached the funeral sermon. His text was in first Thessalonians, 4th chapter, 14th verse. "For if we believe that Jesus died and rose again even them also which sleep in Jesus will God bring with him." We all miss him very much indeed. About 4 weeks ago little Anna Rowe died with a very bad burn [that] mortified and killed her. She was about three years old. Six days after Peter died the Diptherior and now Johny is dangerously sick with the same sickness and Eva quite sick with it.

A boy's chores when he is two years older, 1864

March 11th, Friday

This morning Emma was up, downstairs when I got up and came down. We bid each other good morning & then I went about my chores. Emma and I are just exactly the same "hight" and her birthday is the 16th of February and mine the 4th of January. Fred went down to the barn with us boys to do our chores. Eddie milks 3 cows and feeds 2 little calves mornings. Charlie and I have to feed the colts, feed the cattle and i have to feed the 3 cows that Eddie milks wheat bran & fill up the wood box and feed the pigs sorted apples and potatoes. Nights: one night I have to feed the cows corn stalks and the next night I have to shell a basket of corn and take it over to the other barn for Father to feed the sheep the next morning, get kindling wood and so forth. Fred and Emma went to school with Eddie and Clara. Eddie said he would get the gun at Aunt Lucy's but he forgot it. This evening we played blindfold and prover[b]s. We had a very nice time playing blindfold. We played that most of the evening. Tonight we played introduce us to the king and queen. We set 2 chairs a little way apart, just far enough apart for another chair, with a shawl spread down to the floor and over the back of the chairs. Then the king and queen sit one on each chair to keep the shawl "strait." Then someone is called in the room and someone is there ready and says: This is my friend the king and queen. Then the king and queen bow and say: Won't you take a seat between us. Then they fall down or rather sit down on the floor because there is nothing but a shawl spread over the open space. Then how we do laugh. Fred and Emma are both very lively and full of fun. They are very nice children and Cousins. Tonight we sugared off and we made lots of candy. We had all we could eat.

The next year, the death of Abraham Lincoln, 1865

March 11, Saturday

 This morning Eddie drove over to Aunt Miriam's [about four miles by road around the hills] for Mother and all of the children but Clara, and then drove back again. We stayed all day and had a very nice time. We went down on the canal a skating with Collin's and Neva's skates till noon. We saw the little lambs and hunted the eggs and jumped on the hay mow and had a splendid time. We went up to the upper barn and hunted the eggs and then rode clear down to the house on the sled. This afternoon we played cards and cracked some butternuts. At chore time Father came after us and Charlie & I rode home with Collin and Silvy and Neva.

April 19, Wednesday

 My school stopped ever so long ago and the work has come on so I have not had time to write in my journal. I have a great lot of news too. The 2nd of march Eddie went up to Cazenovia to school and Sylvester and the girls Sarah and Anna went up too. The term commenced the day after. They like it first rate. Eddie and Sylvester walked down a week ago (nearly 20 miles) Saturday afternoon and Seth took them back about five o'clock in the morning. Before he went up there to school Father got him a shaving apparatus, comb, brush, paper and &c. Eddie rooms [at] Mr. Hays and boards at Mrs. Severences. he studies Latin a and b, and Geometry. he did study Algebra but he had to drop it. I miss him very much. I wrote him soon after [he] went and I received an answer last Saturday. He has written to us all but Charlie, Hattie, Willie & Master [?], Collin he writes very often. Good news. Two weeks ago last Monday

Gen. Grant and his Armies took Richmond and Petersburg both the same day with terrible fighting of nearly a week. The cannons have been firing all day and the bells ring very fast and loud at all the villages and cities around us. There is very great rejoicing. The cannons begun firing at midnight and fired till 12 o'clock the next night. The last day of March, Friday evening, we had a party here and there were about 25 here I guess.... We played whirl the platter, Oats, peas, beans and barley grows, spat, and then came and had supper and had some maple candy and some of them sugared theirs off. They all seemed to enjoy it very much. Terrible news. Last Friday evening President Lincoln was at a theatre and a man came up behind him and shot him with a pistol in the back of the head and got away on horseback. Another man at the same time went to Secretary Seward's house and stabbed him two or three times in the neck and knocked him down and stabbed him 3 or 4 others and got away on horseback. None of Mr. Seward's arteries were cut and perhaps he may get well. Mr. Lincoln was insensible all the time after it and they thought he was dead. But he lived until 22 minutes after 7 o'clock the next morning and then died. I was out in the lot rolling in the barley and Hattie came out and told me the news. Father went out to Syracuse a few days ago and got Charlie & I each a nice little flag and we trimmed them with black and hung them out. in the village almost every house was trimmed with black. The bells were tolling then instead of ringing. April 9th General Lee surrendered his whole army to Grant. The officers and men were paroled and went home. The bells commenced ringing about 10 o'clock in the forenoon and the cannons firing very fast. The first part of the week there was great rejoicing and the last part great mourning. What a week! All the stores were shut last Saturday and in the city too.

October 1865

In October, Roswell's favorite brother, Eddie, aged seventeen, ran away from his school in Cazenovia. Roswell was only thirteen. Part of the diary transcription is missing, but it picks up on October 17:

[It seems he] had been failing some time and hard study and other things we think made him deranged. His things were all in his room but his overcoat, satchel and flute and razor. His trunk was locked with a letter in it to Father. He had [to] break the lock open and then he put the things in it and brought them home and we feel awful of course. Aunt Anna and Uncle Wells and the rest of the Uncles and Aunts came up here and father is a going to have it advertised in the Journal and have some photographs taken from his others.

October 22, Sunday

Last night two of the Dagget children came up here and said that they saw Eddie over [by] Mr. Palmer's swamp about 4 o'clock this morning. The men went over and watched the barn where they thought he would be; they tracked someone that they thought was him into the swamp. About daylight father went to the swamp and he thought the track was Eddie's. William came up after more men and about nine o'clock there was over 100 persons there. Father had offered $100 reward [over $1100 in today's dollars] for him and they marched all through the swamp but could not find him. He was seen out to Syracuse and probably took the cars and went off. there was no meeting in our church. Father went to Syracuse in the afternoon with Mr. Erdman and some others. Mr. Erdman went off to Auburn [about thirty miles west of Fayetteville] with some handbills the next day.

October 23, Monday

Today Father had some handbills printed offering $300 reward [$3,400 today]. We hear lots of stories but we don't know which to believe. Mr. Robinson saw him the next night after he went away and spoke to him. Mr. Justice Wells went to Utica [fifty miles east] and Mr. Wm. Hurd went [to] Oswego [thirty miles north].

December 16, Saturday

This morning Father, Charlie and I went up on the hill and fed the sheep and then brought down 4 of the calves to the other barn. Charlie and I take care of them and I took over some grain for them and Charlie took Clyde over. Clyde is a little Airsheer bull calf that Father bought out near Utica for $100. Then we and Father shelled six bushels of corn and Father took it down to the mill. This afternoon father and Mother went to the village and got some writing books for Hattie, Minnie, Clara, Charlie and I. I made a crossbow for Willie, a Christmas present. An Irishman came up from the village tonight to see father. [The Irish dug the Erie Canal, with great cost to life from malaria, and were generally considered a bare rung above black slaves in the social order, which is why young Roswell identified him as almost a race apart.] The men are using the sleighs today though the snow is only about 3 inches deep. We hear nothing from Eddie.

December 17, Sunday

This morning Father, Mary, Minnie and Charlie and I went to meeting. Charlie and I wore our new suits of clothes. I stopped at Miss Chapman's last Friday and got a part of them. We rode down with Uncle Gardner; we were going to walk. The text was in first Corinthians 4th, 7th. There was only four in the choir. Mrs. Lord is our teacher yet and has been ever since we went to Sabbath School. There is Collin Armstrong, Jessie Wells, Willie Mead, and Charlie and I in our class. We have a new organ for the Sunday School now. Most of them stayed after to sing some new pieces out of the new book. Its name is Happy Voices. We rode home with Uncle Gardner.

December 18, Monday

This morning we rode down to school with Mr. Mead and home part way with Mr. Clark. It is warmer today. We have lots of fun tending to our calves over to the other barn. My calf is halter broke so that she will lead out to water or anywhere else. The men are at work in the woods now days sawing wood to sell. Granpa was here to supper tonight. I have just been whittling on Christmas presents and it is bed time now.

December 19, Tuesday

Last night it rained about all night and it is quite warm. This morning we done all of our chores before breakfast but feeding the calves. I milk Daisy now night and morning now. We walked down to school and Clara came home at recess this afternoon because she did not feel well. Clara has a stove up in the west chamber now that is her room. One of our trees bore 16 bushels of butternuts this year.

December 20, Wednesday

There is lots of good news. Last night about half past 11 Eddie came home [he had been missing for more than two months]. Frank Smith saw him out to Syracuse and brought him home and Mr. [?]ndy. He was coming home and went in the ticket office to get a ticket to go to the railroad and they brought him home. He has been down in Pennsylvania and hired out to a farmer in the coal regions. The woods were 100 miles long and there was lots of wild animals and he bought a rifle and brought it home with him. He had not been seen by anyone that knew him till he got home. He went for his health and is more fleshy and strong than he was when he was here. When we got to school the scholars all knew it. Mr. Erdman, Uncle Wells, Granma, Aunt Miriam, Miss Malty, and some of the school boys came here today. It is quite cold today. Clara was not well enough to go to school today.

Rosy, as he was usually called by the family, was one of the stars in the familial firmament. As he grew up and became more involved in broader family activities, the diaries and letters of others uniformly look forward to his visits. He brightened every party or dinner. He was intelligent, handsome as his father, gay and cheerful. People were grateful for his presence among them. He was not the oldest son but he was perhaps the most favored in skills, wit (in the old sense of that word), behavior, and perception of the world. His father could look upon him with deep pride but, from long tradition, could not leave him the central legacy. That Rosy went on to become a physician of some note and make his own way was typical of his character. He could not nor would not in himself disrupt the family heritage, but close as he was to his father (documents suggest he was the closest in many ways), he saw his own needs in the perspective of the clan tradition.

It is interesting to see how he changed when he went off to school. Suddenly, in his journal, he was no longer recounting sheep tending, milking, or manure spreading, but looking at what seemed to him the larger world—ideas, reason, progress, matters of the heart.

Chief among matters concerning his heart was his double cousin, Cardera. She was the daughter of his uncle from his father's side and of his aunt from his mother's side. The usual family habit of marrying cousins seemed to balk at this level of closeness. Cardie, as she was known, was the other bright star in the familial firmament. There are many diary entries and letters happily referring to "Cardie's arrival," or her visits or her presence at some gathering. She was fair and pretty in a fey way so appealing to the nineteenth century, not gorgeous in the way her aunt Clara was. She had a quality of being, and that quality meshed perfectly with Rosy's. When the two of them were together at some occasion, everyone who recalled the occasion recalled particularly them as the light and spirit of the moment.

There is some record of when Rosy first became aware of Cardie as something more than just another cousin.

From 1866

11/21 Wed.
Today Charlie had the tooth ache and did not go to school. Mr. Edgecome went away today. It has been snowing, raining, and quite cold today. Tonight Eddie went down to coz. Delancy's and brought Coz. Lucy home. Cardie, Hattie, Minnie, Willie and I played some games and introduced Lucy to the sheep fold. Lucy played and sung some college pieces and we are enjoying their visit very much. We were in the library tonight visiting and Lucy took a notion to give us dancing lessons, Eddie, Clara & I had lots of fun.

11/23 Fri.
Today is Charlie's birthday and he is 13 years old. Eddie and I went to school and it was out at 2 1/2 o'clock. I had to speak this afternoon. After school I went down to the shoe shop and had some insoles put in my boots. This evening Charlie and I are invited down

to Collin's and after we got our chores done we rode down & Eddie went with us and went down to the choir meeting. Hattie, Minnie & Cardie, J. Wells, W. Lee, C. Hoyt, Charlie and I were there. We had some nice games and nuts and apples: and a first rate time. Lucy has taught us so that Cardie and I can dance quite well together. The older ones were spending the evening at Uncle Tremain's and when they came back they took the girls home and Charlie and I rode home with Eddie.

1/2 Wed., 1867

Today is the golden W[edding]. Henry went to Syracuse with some frames to get them fixed and I think I have got mine large enough now. Silvy came up to help us and Aunt Maria made herself useful. The company commenced to come a little after 4. There was about 60 here. All the grandchildren [including Cardie] were here and children and a good many other relations. We had the nicest table I ever saw. We had a very pleasant time but for one thing. Carrie Meade came up from Mr. Clark's and said that Seward Clark was dead. He caught cold skating and died from the effects. He was a dear friend of Charlie's and mine and we shall miss him sadly. I received a letter from George Royce today. Grandpa- ma received some very nice fur presents from the children and grandchildren and Mr. Erdman presented a gold ring to them. The history of the family was read and Grandfathers advice and blessing, which was read by Aunt Miriam, was very touching.

1/4 Fri.

Today I am 15 years old. Received a letter from coz. Cardie. [This is his first ever mention of such a thing, rarely mentioning cards or letters at all in his journal.] Rode down to Uncle Wells to tell them that the elder folks would be there. Charlie and I went down to Mr. Clark's and saw Seward. Went to the funeral this P.M. and I drove for Carrie Gardner. Very large procession. Very sad and feel very bad. We boys shelled some corn. F., M., Uncle and Auntie went to Uncle Wells' to dinner. C. Gardner and Amelia Payson called here after the funeral. Seward was 13 years old.

1/28 Mon.

Last night it snowed quite a good deal. We were all late to school. This evening Eddie has been writing to coz. Charlie Collin, Clara to Lucy and I to Cardie. [He was the only cousin to be writing to a cousin of the opposite sex.]

A few years later Rosy is sent off to the Cortland Academy in the village of Homer, about twenty-five miles south of his home, to prepare him for entry later into Williams College. His journal entries from that time show him to have become somewhat philosophical in the way and to the degree that his father became somewhat more philosophical than *his* own father when David Jr. was sent to RPI so many years before. And it is clear Rosy has been doing some reading. The direct and plain-spoken boy has vanished for the moment. We can see him in his rooms in Homer feeling himself far from home, the world-weary chronicler of life.

First entry of the 1871 journal, when Roswell is nineteen

I have, from my earliest boyhood, continued a custom which I commenced, if I remember rightly, at the age of about eight years, by the advice of my parents and encouraged by my own inclinations. I well remember how at this time David and Eddie and Clara all wrote their diaries or home-made journals, and I anxiously waited for the time when I should be old enough and have become a sufficiently good penman to commence such a journal for myself, and I well remember when Mother finished my first little journal, with its covers of wallpaper, how eagerly I stood by and watched every stitch, and slash of the shears, and when at last it was finished and presented in its comely proportions I thought I had never possessed such a treasure, and felt that I was already fast approaching manhood, and felt almost ready to begin a moderate business. So with a few gratis hints and some advice from Father, an encouraging smile from mother, I became the proprietor of a pen and inkstand and with our matronly, cousin and nurse Mary Loomis sitting by for a walking dictionary, I commenced my first journal.

It is a queer almost weird looking specimen, but of all the journals and diaries I have since written, none are so highly valued as this first, simple childish effort, with its primitive penmanship, its fantastic figures, and primary attempts at art in the spare corners.

There seems to be almost a sacred halo hovering over this childish reminiscences of early days, childhood's memories, childhood's affections and loves, childhood's sports and playmates, childhood's joys and sorrows, simplicity and faith, blithe buoyancy and pure artlessness.

My dearest, sweetest, earliest memories, which come to me often, faint and broken, partaking more of dreamy fancy sometimes, than of clear and distinct reality, bursting upon my mind's bewildered and confused vision, like gleams of sunshine struggling through the clouds, shedding around their bright radiance, and suddenly withdrawing, and leaving us lost to grope about in confused fragments of memories, fancies and dream; of these I say, when a faint gleam of light breaks upon my mind, revealing for a moment the sacredness of the early past in all the vividness of which mental conception is capable, at such times my dearest and most sacred memories are connected with my mother.

But I am diverging from my subject.... [And he concludes some 250 words later.] Hoping that my decision will prove a judicious one, that I may be faithful to this practice one of pleasure and utility as may be, and that my journal will prove faithful to the sacred trust and confidence entrusted to it, I will proceed to unfold my records, revelations and such other thoughts as may chance to leave my pen.

There are two further entries of some interest, which are here quoted only in part, for he does go on a bit. The first is a young man's initial social outing with young women and no family or chaperones around. He doesn't seem to notice the comedy his high-flown style sets up. The second is his encounter with problems his cousin Collin Armstrong is experiencing at the same academy in Homer. Together, they create a sense of the changing young man and the changing time in which he is living, so different from that of his grandfather's a mere fifty or so years before.

January 23rd, 1871, Miss Kate Field's Lecture

It was mid-winter. Fairer, clearer, colder weather was never known in this part of the country. The young blood leaped joyously through our veins, and our youthful spirits overflowed with native exuberance. We had been steady and quiet for a long time, had studied faithfully each day, puzzling our brains over the intricate mysteries of the classics, mathematical problems &c., but now we felt that we must have relief, our natures and feelings called for fun! fun! So fun, we must and would have.

This is the time, when "womens suffrage" or "woman's rights" as it is popularly called, is agitated, and filled with their new ideas. Many masculine women are going about the country to deliver their lectures.

One of the most popular of this day is Miss Kate Field and [a] committee of a course of lectures in Cortland, engaged her among other popular lecturers for one evening. Her lecture was to be delivered on the evening in question. We fellows at the Burr mansion had purchased season tickets for the course, but the sleighing was splendid, the evenings bright, and we concluded that on this occasion, we would invite some young ladies to accompany us. So we did, and with results highly satisfactory to us. The next question was how we should go. Some were in favor of going in single cutters and more of getting a large box sleigh and all the party going in it. We had always heard a great deal about the old fashioned way of sleigh-riding, of its preference over every other style, for fun, comfort and economy. Torrence urged this way and others, that having had experience, they knew it was better and had numberless advantages over every other way. "Get a big sleigh," they said, "fill it full nearly, of straw first, then of robes and blankets, and then 'pile in' the more the better." We didn't want any style of formality, but go for a jolly time, and the more the merrier. I confess that I had no experience in this way of doing, but was willing to accommodate the crowd, and thought from what they said they ought to know, and probably it would be more fun.

We knew Mr. Schermerhorn had such a sleigh, and the only one of our knowledge so Armstrong went with me to see that gentleman and negotiate for the sleigh. He readily gave his consent and referred us to his hostler. He agreed to prepare the sleigh for us, and with much better grace after we had presented him with half a dollar.

We found a team from the livery for this, and found ourselves fully equipped.

That evening was clear and bright but most bitterly cold, with the thermometer sixteen degrees below zero. Our party consisted of us five fellows with our ladies, Torrence with Miss Mary Bartlett, Abe Whitehead with Annie Stinson, McKay with Em Leavens, Armstrong with Louise Barber and Collin (*Rosy*) with Alice Riggs.

We went, put up at the Messenger House, attended and were much pleased with the lecture, the subject of which was the much lamented "Chas. Dickens," and got home again safely. If I could justly, I would omit all reference to the ride, in the contemplation of which, I find so little that is pleasing in reflection.

There is a popular expression of slang, "lolligag," and I had never fully known its meaning. I learned it that night.

Anyone with "half an eye" can see that four or five couples of our size to try to crowd into the bottom of any ordinary box sleigh, without seats, where our limbs must be stretched at full length taking double the room we would have done on seats, would be next to impossible. To add to our dilemma, there had to be a seat in front for the driver which shortened the length of the box quite materially. But we had perfected all the arrangements and would not now be balked, so we squeezed in. It may have been an advantage in this respect, that we would almost have frozen any other way we could have gone.

I state merely, plain truth. I can have here no object in pervicating [prevaricating], but I speak strictly and truly fact, when I say that it was from actual necessity rather than from choice that we (I at least) sat, crowded, squeezed so close together, sometimes sitting double, or two thick, that is a lady sitting on a gentleman's lap, sprawled out any way he could find room for his limbs. Oh! how unpoetic! Alas for romance. A fellow squeezed within an inch of his life, with one hundred and forty or fifty solid pounds of flesh and blood, dresses, cloaks, furs, hair pins &c. wearing heavily upon him, staggered by the embarrassment of his position, yet without room to turn, hardly to breathe, is likely to have some new ideas squeezed into his head. He ceases to hold an angel, a fanciful ideal, but tolerates instead a girl of human flesh, bone and muscle, prosy, and unromantic. . . . This then was what was meant by "loligag," and on this occasion it was the rule, rather than the exception. There may have been those present who enjoyed it, but I will only speak for myself. I *most emphatically did not.*

From the entry for March 9–10, concerning closing exercises for the winter term

We went home feeling pretty tired but well satisfied with our success.

I say we went home but then here comes in a part, a very serious part of the evening's drama, that I would could stand unrecorded. But my journal will tell no tales, and it would not be a fair or correct record of the evening as experienced by me, to drop it. After the exercises at the hall I had just escorted Alice Riggs home and as I was to go off in the morning, I stood by the steps saying a few farewell words to her when Collin Armstrong came walking by and spoke some words to me. I asked him where he was going and he said up town and [asked] me if I didn't want to go. I said yes, bade her goodnight and over took him. He acted strangely, and understanding him so well, I was afraid something might be wrong, for he is often given to reckless, desperate spells, so I made up my mind to stay by him. I asked him what he was going up town for at that time of night, he was very much excited and tried to evade my question, but finally stopped and told me frankly that he was going to the hotel to get some whisky. I showed some surprise, and tried all my powers of argument, persuasion and appeal to induce him to go back home with me, but could not move him. I pointed out to him the disgrace of such conduct, reminded him of his pledges, and of going home in the morning to meet his folks. But all to no purpose. He was already inflamed with liquor, of which he had just swallowed all they would give him at the lower hotel, and enraged because they would give him no more, he was going to complete his revenge on himself by plunging madly into a drunken debauch. Something during the evening had displeased him (I don't know what), he had in some way been crossed and thus he was taking a desperate revenge.

I had been very sorry to notice all along through the term at different times, he would give himself up to this debasing habit which, young as he is, has a powerful, a fearful hold on him. Though he would rarely drink anything stronger than ale, and seldom got drunk, though often quite jolly. I am afraid Whitehead has been a [bad] companion for him, for he drinks a great deal of ale and, though a noble-hearted, smart, handsome fellow, is just the one to lead Collin on. But tonight there was something unusual raging in his mind, and he was madly determined to swallow all the "hell-fire" he could get hold of.

When he saw I would really go with him he tried to persuade me to go back. "You don't want anything up here," he said, "it is no place for such fellows as you." But I told him if he must drink, I would go with him. We marched sullenly to the hotel and went in. He stepped into the bar and ordered his liquor. I did not go in to see what or how much, then he came out and we started for home. He said, "Now we will go home. I have got all I want." I walked along by him silently, hardly saying a word, once in a while shortly answering one of his silly questions. He was jabbering and talking silly, more like an idiot than a reasonable man, all the way home and he began to reel before we got there. Whitehead had gone home a few days before so he was in his room alone, but he wanted me to go in so I did. he was very noisy and in a few minutes he began to act wild. I took a book and sat down, pretending to read, but only to watch him and get him to bed. He was now so drunk he could not sit straight in his chair, but tumbled and rolled around while undressing. He kept on growing more and more noisy and wild, pounding the table and door, and throwing his boots around, and trying to undress me, so pitiably silly, and too drunk to stand. He had asked me to stay all night with him, and I now saw that it would be necessary, so I came into our room to get my watch-key and leave some of my clothes, and tell Sid. Collin clung to me and begged me not to leave him, and I could hardly make him believe that I was coming right back. I had hardly come into our room when he came staggering in, and swearing fearfully, threw himself on Sid who lay on the bed asleep, very tired from the excitement and work of the last two days. Being suddenly awakened, and not aware of Armstrong's condition, his temper was quickly aroused by Collin's drunken wallowing on his bed, pounding or hugging him as the case might be, and using the most abusive language. He told him to stop several times and finally threatened violence, when Collin left him and came at me. But Sid's temper was now thoroughly aroused and he came out pale with rage and forcibly put him out of the room and locked the door. This made him perfectly delirious. His oaths and fearful language were terrible and he pounded the door in vain. Presently he went back to his room and called me, and Sid said if he should be any worse and I should need any help with him to let him know. So I went in and found him madly raving in a delirium of drunken rage, like a wild maniac. When I entered the room he came at me as if he would annihilate me, but when he saw who I was, he commenced hurling at Sid the most fearful denunciations, execrations and curses, mingled with oaths and threats. I calmed and soothed him as much as I could with words by humoring his passion, and soon got him to bed for the second time. He was now perfectly crazed by the accursed liquor, and for the first time in my life, I stood in fear of him, for he did not know me, and would sometimes fight me as if I were the fire burning in his stomach. But his blows were wild and easily dodging them, they fell heavily on the wall. But he hurled his boots at me with a fearful vengeance, which were not so easily dodged. His eyes glowed fiercely at me with a strange, unnatural, idiotic leer, which was fearful to see in a bosom friend.

I had never before had experience in such cases, and had never seen anybody so drunk. Three times Mrs. Burr hearing the uproar which he made, rapped on the register pipe from below, but it had no effect on him and I could not keep him quiet.

But soon a reaction took place and I got him to lie quietly in bed. He began to suffer most griping pains in his stomach that made him writhe in agony and plead pitifully for mercy from Heaven, and groan almost constantly. Remorse was now at work, and he seemed to think that his death and judgment were speedy and inevitable. I sat on the bed beside him trying to soothe him and he clung to me with desperate energy as if for life, and begged me not to leave him. Oh! it was pitiable to hear the poor fellow plead and beg for mercy from an offended God, pleading the merits of Christ, to forgive and spare his life yet a few days, to hear him call on his Mother [Miriam] to save him, cursing the fate that brought him into existence. Then he would seem to return to partial consciousness and realize in part his condition, pronouncing the most fearful curses and calling down heaven's direst maledictions on the heads of the rum seller, and then turning suddenly to me with desperate agony of remorse demanded, "Oh why did you let me drink? Why did you not rather shoot me dead? You are to blame for this," he said wildly. He would repeat passages of Scripture and hymns and the clammy foam oozing from his mouth as if to appease an angry God at the last moment. Then he would break down and cry like a little child, groaning, calling on his Mother and invoking mercy. And all the while he clutched my hand firmly. Oh! it was a sad, sad sight and I hope to God I may never witness another such. I could not restrain my tears.

And so a boy begins to see his way into the world of manhood. This troubled evening took place well before the fateful spring drive his father made east down below the homestead, described in the opening chapter. It is one of the few glimpses we have of the underside of the extended family life, one of the few hints that even within this family some things were going on that were less than perfect. Perhaps the news Roswell's father received that later spring morning was not as big a surprise to family members as the documents seem to show.

The care, courage, and sense Roswell displayed dealing with his cousin, fighting to keep his notion of responsibility on top of his fear and anger, were traits that, as he matured, his father came to rely upon and to value. But this necessary reliance presented other problems for the future of the estate and for relationships within the family. Roswell, while perhaps the most able, was not the eldest. What does a family do when the best of them are out of the usual line of inheritance? Primogeniture was not the law, but for the Collins the custom remained that the eldest son still named the parameters of inheritance. To his credit and perhaps to our wonder and incredulity, Roswell never allowed his growing responsibilities to put himself forward or to challenge customs that had bound them all together for so long.

It is not an uncommon perspective to view history as a kind of progression, that we are somehow the inevitable results of this ongoing process toward improvement. From this progression we then assume we are in a "better" place than those who came before us, perhaps even better in ourselves as we view the past with assumed dispassion. It is a view that leads to disappointment.

As the personalities, the reality, of the various characters in this story emerge we come to see we are not so different from them. Certainly not *better*. We see that we exercise as readily as those ordinary individuals who peopled the world and times of the Collins the goal seeking we ascribe to the greed and betrayal between David and Miriam over inheritance. We also seek, as deeply as Roswell, proportion and grace in life. Proportion and grace will elude us as often as it has others before us. We all remain searching creatures alive within a universe of change, chance, and choice at the edge of chaos.

7

Miriam's Questions

> Fathers that wear rags
> Do not make their children blind;
> But fathers that bear bags
> Shall see their children kind.
> Fortune, that arrant whore
> Ne'er turns the key to the poor.
> —Shakespeare, *King Lear,* 2.4.48–53

As we return to the Surrogate Court Hearing of April 4, 1885, the record does not show whether Miriam Armstrong was present. We do know her brother, David, was there, for he was called to testify toward the end of the available transcript. Here her lawyer, Martin Knapp, questions Mr. Stearns, one of the witnesses to the late David Collin's will, asking the kinds of questions Miriam herself would have liked to ask. Hence the interesting and pushy tone of the questioning of a man who was even by his own lights just a small farmer. It is fairly clear that she had made her wishes known to Martin Knapp before the hearing so she could justify her behavior that spring eight years past to herself, to the family, even to the world at large. It is also clear that she and her lawyer felt they could bully this small-time farmer who had been her father's neighbor. They seemed to feel, as good Calvinists might, that he manifestly did not have the skill or wit to get on in the world as her father had. If even one of the witnesses could be caused to raise the least doubt about her father's stability or character, she would be sure to have planted those doubts necessary to support her own claims. But Mr. Stearns, less out of neighborly loyalty than from rugged self-possession, was having none of it.

"Sweet Map" of Manlius and environs, including Collin lands, 1874

Q: Mr Stearns you reside at the Village of Fayetteville, in this County?

A: No, sir, north about a mile.

Q: How long have you lived in that place?

A: I have lived there since 1862; the spring of 1862, I think.

Q: And have you resided where you now do since that time?

A: Yes, sir.

Q: You knew David Collin in his life time?

A: Yes, sir.

Q: How long had you known him prior to his death?

A: Well, I think I first became acquainted with him in 1854 or '55.

Q: And from that time down to the time of his death had you been intimately acquainted with him?

A: Well, yes, as a neighbor I was acquainted with him.

Q: How far did he live from where you lived?

A: Well, something over a mile; we call it a mile.

Q: Did he live in the place where he lived for a good many years, or at the residence of his son?

A: Where he lived,—what they call the Grove Farm.

Q: That was about a mile from you?

A: It was about a mile.

Q: Afterwards he went to live with his son, David Collin, Jr.?

A: Yes, sir.

Q: At a somewhat further distance from your residence?

A: Yes, sir, it is, perhaps, a little over two miles; it may be two and a half.

Q: (Showing witness paper) You identified this as your signature to the paper when this matter was here before?

A: I have identified one; well, I will have to put on my eyes for that; yes, that is mine.

Q: Did you become a subscribing witness to more than one will of the late David Collin?

A: No, sir.

Q: This is the only instrument where you have signed your name as a witness to any document of this description?

A: Yes, sir.

Q: Have you been a subscribing witness to wills of other people at any time?

A: Well, I have since I have been in that town to one; I guess that is all; I think it was.

Q: Do you remember when it was that you signed this paper as a witness?

A: Well, I couldn't date it exactly; it was somewhere in 1876 or '75; somewhere along not far from that.

Q: In 1875 or '76?

A: I should think it was somewhere along there; I couldn't put it down very positive for I didn't keep any diary, and it was a thing I hadn't thought of.

Q: Is the circumstance of witnessing this paper now distinct in your mind?

A: Well, I think it is rather so.

Q: Do you recollect the season of the year when it occurred?

A: Well, I should think it was in the forepart of the season; I couldn't place it very close now.

Q: Do you remember the time of day when it took place?

A: Yes, sir, pretty close; I think I can tell from circumstances.

Q: What time of day do you remember it to have been?

A: Well, after noon some time; that is after dinner, as we call it.

Q: Do you recollect where you had been during the forenoon of that day?

A: I was on my flats,—on my farm about my business; I couldn't tell what I was doing, but I know I was down on my lower lands that forenoon.

Q: Do you know how you came to be called to witness this paper?

A: Nothing further than young Mr. Collin drove down my lane where I was and told me his father was about making his will and requested me to go and witness it, and he told me who the other men were he had talked of for witnesses.

Q: Then the first intimation that you had of it was when Mr. David Collin drove down where you were to work?

A: Yes, sir.

Q: And he told you that his father was going to make his will?

A: About to make his will.

Q: About making his will?

A: Yes, sir.

Q: And he wanted you to witness it?

A: Well, he said the old gentleman wanted me with,—he told me who the other ones was to witness it.

Q: You understood then that you had been sent for to witness the will at the request of the old gentleman, himself?

A: That is the way I understood it; yes, sir.

Q: You understood that he was not only about to make his will but that he had selected the persons whom he desired to have witness it?

A: I took it so.

Q: And was you then informed by Mr. David Collin who the other persons were besides yourself?

A: Well, I would not be positive about that; I think he told me who the other ones were, but I could not be very positive about that.

Q: You say he drove down?

A: He drove down to where I was; I have a lane leading down through my farm, and he could drive to very near where I was at that time.

Q: Well, did you go immediately with him?

A: No, I told him I would be up after dinner; I was with my men down there.

Q: And did he then go away?

A: He left me and went away.

Q: Is that all that took place between you and him at that time?

A: Yes, sir.

Q: After dinner did you go to that place?

A: Yes, sir; I drove up after dinner to Mr. Collin's, the old gentleman.

Q: Where was he then living?—at the Grove Farm?

A: At the Grove Farm.

Q: Did any one accompany you from your house up to his place?

A: No.

Q: Do you recall who you first saw when you arrived there?

A: Well, I saw Mr. Peck and Mr. Clark; they were there.

Q: Do you remember where you first saw them?

A: Well, I think they were in the house; I am quite sure they were.

Q: Do you remember what you did with your horse, or whether you saw anybody before you went into the house?

A: I remember hitching to an oak tree from the house.

Q: And then going into the house?

A: Then going into the house, yes, sir.

Q: When you got inside the house, who did you see?

A: Well, I saw these two men and Mr. Collin set there, and young David Collin, as we call him, was in the house.

Q: And in the same room?

A: In the same room.

Q: Was anyone else there?

A: No, I think not.

Q: What persons comprised the old gentleman's family at that time?

A: Well, he had one son and three or four daughters; let's see, there was . . .

Q: I mean, who constituted the members of his household?

A: Well, I don't know; he had a family in the house; I never knew much of the family.

Q: Were any of his own family living with him at the time?

A: Well, I couldn't say whether there was or not; I could guess at it; I don't think there was, but I still don't know.

Q: Well, his son David didn't live there?

A: No, sir.

Q: How far from there did David live?

A: Oh, a mile or a little over; perhaps a mile and a quarter.

Q: None of his daughters resided there?

A: I think not.

Q: And none of his grand children or his other relatives so far as you know?

A: No, I don't think they did.

Q: It is your recollection that he had a family in the house with him?

A: Yes, he had a family in there.

Q: And do you know what his domestic relations were at that time,—that is with reference to his board and care of his rooms or anything of that sort?

A: No, I don't know anything about that.

Q: Whether he was boarding with this family that lived in his house?

A: Well, I had the impression that he was, but still I don't know anything about that.

Q: Do you recollect enough about it to state the name of the family?

A: I don't believe I could; it was a family I didn't know anything about.

Q: And do you know of how many persons that family consisted?

A: No, I couldn't tell.

Q: Do you know them by sight?

A: Well, yes, I think I knew them; I used to see them occasionally when I passed there; I don't know as I was in the house to see them at all; I don't remember.

Q: You spoke of entering the room,—what room was this?

A: That was what they called their sitting room,—yes, sir.

Q: The house has a front door, I suppose?

A: Yes, sir.

Q: Opening into the hall?

A: Yes, sir; I think there is a small hall there.

Q: With rooms on each side?

A: On both sides.

Q: And on which side was this room that you entered,—well, did you turn to the right as you entered?

A: Turned to the right.

Q: And the room was what was known as the sitting room of the house?

A: I think that is what they called it.

Q: You have been there a great many times before, I suppose?

A: Oh, years before, when I knew the family.

Q: Do you remember how long before it was when you had been to the house?

A: Oh, I couldn't really state; I couldn't tell.

Q: Were you familiar with the location and the arrangement of the different rooms in the house?

A: Not very much; no, sir.

Q: How large a room was this,—the sitting room?

A: Oh, it was quite a good size; I should have to guess at it.

Q: Did you see any other persons while you were there at that time except those you have named?

A: I don't think I did in the house, and I don't know that I did out doors, either.

Q: Was there any other furniture in the room than the ordinary furniture of a sitting room that you recollect?

A: No, but there was a bed in the room; I supposed he occupied that bed.

Q: You judged then, that the room that you entered was used by him as a sleeping room as well as a sitting room?

A: Yes, sir, I would not call that a sitting room at the time, but when I first knew the family that was a sitting room, but at that time I guess he was using it as his private room.

Q: You judged that to be the room where he slept?

A: Yes, sir, I took it so.

Q: Where was the old gentleman when you entered the room?

A: He was sitting in his chair.

Q: About where in the room was that chair?

A: Well, it was not in the centre of the room, but it was within a few feet of his bed; I should think within 4 or 5 feet of his bed; his bed was in the corner and I think it was near the foot of the bed, but I couldn't locate it accurately.

Q: Did he speak to you when you went into the room?

A: Yes, sir, very friendly as he always was.

Q: Do you remember what he first said to you?

A: No, I don't know as I could; the courtesies of the day, I guess.

Q: And you have stated that the other persons were there that signed with you?

A: Yes, sir.

Q: Do you recollect the conversation that followed after you entered the room?

A: Well, I could get at it pretty close; we didn't do very much talking there until we proceeded to business; I was in somewhat of a hurry; I don't know as the other ones were.

Q: Well, what do you recollect as the first thing said after the salutations of the day were exchanged?

A: It is a hard thing to call up; I think we staid there half an hour talking as people would talk without ever telling it again.

Q: Before the business was transacted?

A: Yes, sir.

Q: That conversation you say lasted half an hour or so, you think?

A: About that I should think.

Q: And it was on miscellaneous topics?

A: Yes, sir.

Q: Such as you would naturally discuss meeting these gentlemen?

A: Yes, sir.

Q: Was the son David Collin there all the time?

A: He was there all the time.

Q: Do you recollect where he stood with reference to where his father was?

A: Yes, sir, he stood pretty near; he stood off from us a little,— you might say towards the north-east corner of the room; 6 or 8 or 10 feet, perhaps,—8 feet.

Q: So that he was facing the old gentleman?

A: He was facing us or he stood in a sort of a circle; the old gentleman stood there, (indicating) and Mr. Collin set here facing us all.

Q: Well, when you approached the business which brought you there, do you recollect how it was introduced and who brought it up?

A: Well, I cannot tell you exactly how that was brought up; all seemed to know what was in there what we come for.

Q: But who it was introduced it you don't know?

A: No.

Q: Well, do you recollect anything that was said after the business was actually transacted?

A: No, not particularly; no, sir, I don't know as I could call up.

Q: Had the old gentleman been engaged in the conversation which you speak of?

A: Yes, sir; talked with the rest of us; I think he had more to say about the settlement of the country there and who came in there with him; it strikes me that he called some names of those who came in there about that time.

Q: Your recollection is that he had something to say about the early settlement of that town?

A: Yes, sir, I think he did.

Q: The early settlers there.

A: Yes, sir.

Q: Was there a table in the room?

A: Yes, sir, I think a small table with papers on it.

Q: And do you recollect whereabouts in the room that was?

A: I won't locate it exactly; I think it was near him; I think it was a small table; if I recollect right it had the prints of a place where he had been writing pretty close to him.

Q: Well, during this conversation he hadn't been sitting at the end table?

A: He wasn't at the table; when he was talking the table was close by him.

Q: Did he leave his chair during that time?

A: I think when he signed the will he picked up his chair and drawed it towards the table.

Q: No; during the half hour you have been speaking of?

A: No, I don't know as he did; I know we shook hands and I guess we set.

Q: (showing witness paper) That is the paper that you signed on that occasion?

A: Yes, sir.

Q: Do you remember precisely where you saw it first?

A: It was on this table; the table that he wrote on.

Q: Were there other papers on the table?

A: Well, I kind of think there was, but I couldn't be positive about that; it seems as though there was other papers; it might have been newspapers; it seems to me as though there was others; I rather think some books, but I could not be positive about it.

Q: Do you remember that is a small table or a table and desk, such as a man would use to transact business on?

A: I rather think it was a small table.

Q: Nothing that looked like papers of business,—securities?

A: No, not as I recollect now; I couldn't be very positive about that.

Q: You say you first saw that paper lying on that table?

A: Yes, sir.

Q: Well, when and in what way did you learn that the paper lying there was the paper which you were to sign?

A: By what the old gentleman said to us after the things was introduced; what we was there for.

Q: That is when mention had been made of the occasion what called you there, then do you recollect precisely what he said?

A: Well, yes, in substance he says, "I have made my will and I would like to have you witness it," and worked himself around to the table; that is, moved his chair around where he could get to it and picked it up; drawed it along where,—I had the impression that he wrote it himself from what he said,—and I remember I couldn't help thinking it was a nice looking document for an old gentleman to write,—from the impression that I got from him.

Q: When it was there on the table do you recollect whether it was folded or not?

A: I don't think it was folded; I don't think it was when I first saw it, but still I won't be very positive about that.

Q: Whatever there was in the paper was completed before you got there?

A: Yes, sir, I didn't see any writing there after I got there; only saw him sign his name.

Q: Was there a seal on the paper at that time?

A: I couldn't say that I noticed it at the time; my impression is that I didn't examine the paper much; didn't read a word of it, of course.

Q: Will you be kind enough to state again exactly what he said?

A: Well, I ain't stated yet exactly what he said.

Q: Tell us as nearly as you recollect; giving his words as nearly as you recollect them?

A: I couldn't state the conversation there any more than I could a hundred years since; there was a great deal not pertaining to this at all.

Q: No, but I mean when the business which brought you there was introduced, and you came to this transaction, will you give me as nearly as you recollect the precise words which he used himself?

A: Well, he said this; says he, "I have made a will here"—I think he said he had made other wills, but this is the last—I think that was about all there was about the will,—I think so.

Q: He says, "I have made a will."?

A: Yes, sir.

Q: "I have made further wills."?

A: Yes, sir, he said that he made other wills.

Q: "But this is the last one."?

A: Yes, sir, "This is my last one," he said.

Q: Then what did he do?

A: Signed his name to it and asked us to witness it.

Q: Did he ask you to witness it before he signed it?

A: Well, I think not; I think he signed it.

Q: Well, after he had signed it, give his language as accurately as you can recollect it?

A: Well, as nearly as I can recollect, he asked us to sign it as witnesses to his will.

Q: Who signed it first?

A: Well, I am sure that I did; I would not be very positive about that, still I have seen my signature on there, and it is my impression that I signed it first.

Q: Have you any recollection about it independent of the paper?

A: No, sir, I couldn't tell you anything about it; I have seen it here and I think it shows on the paper, but I couldn't remember anything about it.

Q: And have you any recollection as to which of the other two persons signed first?

A: No, I don't know as I have; I don't think I have.

Q: Well, after all three had signed, what, if anything, was said pertaining to the will, if you recollect anything?

A: Well, my impression is that the son, David, said to his father, "State to these gentlemen whether you have been influennced [sic] by any one in making your will." I think that was the case.

Q: Well, did the old gentleman make any reply to that remark?

A: He said he hadn't; he said,—

Q: Was there any occasion for the son to make that remark?

A: I don't know; I don't know but there might be. I don't know anything about that.

Q: Well, did you observe anything which gave occasion for such a remark to be made?

A: No, sir. A person could surmise what he was a mind to, but he would not know anything.

Q: Well, did you surmise?

A: Well, I don't know whether I did or not.

(Objected to)

(witness continuing) My surmises would not amount to anything.

Q: After the last of the three persons had affixed his signature do you recollect anything being said by anybody before the son made that remark?

A: No, I don't recollect.

Q: Had the son made any remark that you recollect during the time the old gentleman was signing his name and their witnesses were signing theirs?

A: No, sir, not during the time.

Q: Will you please state again, giving the language as accurately as you remember it, what the son said?

A: He said to his father as near as I can recollect, "You state to these gentlemen whether you have been influenced by anybody in making your will." I think that is the substance of it; it might not have been worded just like that.

Q: That is the substance of it and the language as nearly as you can recollect?

A: Yes, sir, as nearly as I can recollect.

Q: Well, didn't that occur to you as a singular remark for a son to make?

A: Well, I don't know. There might have been some reason for it, of course.

Q: Now, how soon after that did you go away?

A: I wasn't there a great while. I might have staid half an hour.

Q: Afterwards?

A: Afterwards, I might.

Q: Did the other witnesses go away when you did or afterwards?

A: I think Mr. Peck who was on my road went away with me on my wagon; I am pretty sure he did.

Q: And how was it with Mr. Clark?

A: Mr. Clark lived the other way from me.

Q: Do you recollect whether he left the house before you did or afterwards?

A: I think we all came out together.

Q: Have you read over this paper?

A: No, sir.

Q: You know what is meant by the attestation clause in a will?

A: The attestation clause?

Q: Yes.

A: I am not a lawyer. May be it is some phrase that I don't understand. I don't claim to be a very highly educated man.

Q: It is a pretty long word to express a simple thing, but it is an endorsement above the signatures of the witnesses to the effect that they all saw it signed, etc.?

A: Yes, sir.

Q: I desire to ask you whether that was read over in your presence before you signed it?

A: I don't think it was. I don't remember as to that.

Q: It is in these words immediately following his signature: "The above instrument consisting of one sheet was at the day thereof, signed, sealed, published and declared by the said David Collin as and for his last will and testament in the presence of us, and at his request and in his presence and in the presence of each other, have subscribed our names as witnesses thereto." Was that read over?

A: No, sir, it was not read.

Q: Do you know that there was any such writing as that on the paper that you signed?

A: I didn't read it.

Q: Were you aware that any words of that import were on the paper that you signed?

A: I don't know as I knew. I didn't read a word of it.

Q: Do you recollect whether there was some writing on the paper between Mr. Collin's signature and the place where you signed?

A: It seemed as though there was, but I would not be positive about it.

Q: You are positive, however, that no writing of that description was read in your presence?

A: No, I don't remember there having [been] anything of the kind read. There might have been. My memory is not very accute [sic] on a thing of that kind; I didn't charge my mind with it. It was a thing I didn't think of again.

Q: Do you recollect what was done with the paper after the last of the three persons had signed it?

A: No, the last I saw of it, it was there by the old gentleman.

Q: Was it folded up in your presence?

A: I would not say. I couldn't say.

Q: Is it your recollection that when you left the room it was still lying on his table?

A: I think it was.

Q: Do you recollect the conversation which ensued after the signing was had?

A: No, sir. It was not much more about the will. I couldn't call it up.

Q: Well, it was on miscellaneous subjects not connected with the business which brought you there?

A: No, I don't think there was anything more about the will.

Q: Do you recall whether the old gentleman took part in the conversation?

A: Yes, he did.

Q: When the three persons who signed as witnesses went away, your recollection is that they went together. Did they leave the son there with the old gentleman?

A: I would not be sure about that. I don't know as he came out when we did and I don't know but he did, couldn't swear positively.

Q: Did the old gentleman give any information of the contents of the will?

A: No, sir.

Q: Was there any conversation while you were there which gave any information as to what disposition he had made of the property by that instrument?

A: I don't know as there was. I don't recollect of anything of the kind being said.

Q: Did he at any time while you were there have anything to say about matters of recent and current happening, or were his remarks mostly confined to his earlier experiences?

A: Well, I recollect about his talking about the improvements of the town and the change in the country and the like of that; that is one thing that he would almost always call up if you talked with him a few minutes when you would meet him. It was one of the things that he talked about there.

Q: He was at that time advanced in years?

A: Yes, sir.

Q: About how old?

A: Well, he must have been quite an old man, perhaps 75 then. I don't know but that he might have been older.

Q: Do you know what his age was at the time of his death?

A: I saw it in the paper, but I couldn't tell you exactly. It was some 90 I think; not far from 90.

Q: And when did his death occur?

A: Last Fall.

Q: In 1884?

A: Yes, sir.

Q: Well then in 1876 he must have been upwards of 80?

A: Well, probably so. That is merely a chance shot.

Q: Had you seen much of him during the few months preceding the signing of this paper?

A: Not very much. I saw him occasionally.

Q: Can you recall when you had seen him before that time?

A: I couldn't; he used to pass down by my house to the farm he had below the Center. That is about a mile below me. I used to see him along through the seasons and that season, but I couldn't tell when.

Q: Had you been in his house within some months before?

A: No, I hadn't.

Q: And had he been in your house?

A: No, sir.

Q: The most you had seen of him was occasionally passing along?

A: Yes, sir, passing along. Sometimes I would meet him on the road, but not very often.

Q: On those occasions you would have conversation with him?

A: He was very apt to stop and talk with me if he knew me, and he generally knew me.

Q: Well, were there times when he didn't seem to know you?

A: Well, I don't know as there were; still, he was a man that would sometimes drive by you and wouldn't notice you; seemed to be studying about his own business.

Q: Well, of course when in full possession of his body and mental powers he knew you very well. He had known you for a good many years?

A: Oh, yes, he had known me.

Q: Did you notice anything in him to indicate that he was absent minded or forgetful?

A: No, sir; I don't know as I did anything in particular.

Q: Well, had anything given you the impression that he was?

A: No, not that I had seen.

Q: Prior to going to your present residence, did you for a time occupy a farm belonging to Mrs. Armstrong, a daughter of the late David Collin?

A: I did.

Q: Where was that located?

A: It was about a mile east of where I now live.

Q: How long had you lived on that farm Mr. Stearns?

A: I run that farm 7 years, I think.

Q: And where did Mrs. Armstrong live during that time?

A: She was in Troy most of the time.

Q: And you removed from that farm to your present home?

A: Yes, sir.

Q: After you left her farm did she occupy it herself?

A: Yes, sir.

Q: Moving there about the time you left?

A: Yes, sir.

Q: And how long did she continue to live there?

A: 2 or 3 years; I don't know but it might have been longer, but 2 or 3 years certain.

Q: Lived there 2 or 3 years with her family?

A: Yes, sir, perhaps longer; I would not say; I don't know but she might 3 or 4.

Q: That must have been along 1863, '64 or '65?

A: She came in there in the spring of 1862; the spring that I left it.

Q: Now, do you recollect about the time that you signed this will,—I mean by that in those years,—the old gentleman coming to you and asking you if his daughter had in fact lived on that farm?

A: He came and asked me some questions that pointed that way. I can tell you what he did ask me.

Q: Well, you may, if you please?

A: He asked me if Armstrong come on there after me; that is her husband. He didn't speak of his daughter.

Q: Well, how did he come to ask you that question?

A: Well, I don't know. He drove around to my door,—you have to drive out of the road a little,—and I went to the door and that seemed to be his errand to ask me that question.

Q: He didn't know himself whether Armstrong had lived there before you?

([O]bjected to)

The Surrogate: That he may answer.

A: Why he asked me that question; there had been several tenants on and I think he had got bewildered about who had come on first. That is the way I took it; that was what was said.

By Mr. Knapp:

Q: Do you recollect about when that was?

A: No, I couldn't place that very close. It was quite a good many years ago. I guess I had been down there 10 or 12 years when that occurred; perhaps longer, I couldn't tell.

Q: When you came out of the room on that day you signed this paper, do you recollect whether he raised from his chair and accompanied you to the door?

A: No, I don't recall. I couldn't say whether he did or did not.

Q: Have you any recollection of his standing or walking about the room at any time while you were there?

A: No, I don't know as he did.

Q: What was his apparent physical condition at that time?

A: Why, he appeared to be well, I think as well as any man of his age.

Q: Was he a man of large stature?

A: Pretty large man, yes, sir.

Q: Fleshy or otherwise?

A: Not a very fleshy man, but a pretty large man,—a large bone man.

Q: Do you recollect how he was dressed?

A: No.

Q: He seemed to you to be a man in a good state of preservation considering his years?

A: I think so, yes, sir.

Q: Now, earlier than that did you know him quite well,—that is to meet him and talk to him quite frequently?

A: Frequently. I used to be at his house quite a good deal while I was running this farm.

Q: While you was on Mrs. Armstrong's farm?

A: Yes, sir, that 7 years that I was there I used to be occasionally at the house.

Q: Was he a man of marked characteristics,—a decided and positive man?

A: Yes, sir, I always considered him to be a decided man.

Q: Ordinarily of pleasant and agreeable disposition?

A: Quite so, to me; as pleasant a man as you would meet anywhere.

Q: He always met you in a very friendly and courteous way?

A: Yes, sir, very.

Q: Was any mention made at any time while you were there that day of his other children?

A: Well, I wouldn't say.

Q: In there by him or anybody else?

A: I couldn't say. I was in quite a hurry; I don't remember of it.

Q: You don't now recollect?

A: No, there might have been something said. I would not like to say there was not anything, because I don't remember.

Q: You knew his other children, who they were and where they lived?

A: Yes, sir.

Q: And were more or less acquainted with them?

A: Yes, sir, as neighbors.

Q: And Mr. Collin had been or was at that time a man reputed to have quite large means, was he not?

A: Yes, sir, we all thought he had.

Q: Considering the business in which he had been engaged and the place where he had lived, he was a man somewhat conspicuous for his property?

A: Yes, sir, he was.

Q: Did you know anything about his having transferred a large amount of his real estate to one or more of his children at the time this will was executed?

A: No, sir, I didn't.

Q: You have since learned that that was the fact?

A: I have heard a good deal of talk about it, but I don't know anything about it.

Q: Do you recollect that there was any mention that day at the house of the transfer of the property?

A: I don't recollect that there was; I don't think it was stated.

Q: Were you acquainted with the situation and condition of the different pieces of realestate which he was reputed to own in Fayetteville, or that vicinity?

A: Yes, sir, I have a sort of general knowledge of the property he owned.

Q: You knew the general location of the different farms that he had owned?

A: Yes, sir.

Q: And had given to his daughters?

A: Yes, sir, around this lake.

Q: Do you recall how long after this information he left the Grove Farm and went to live with his son?

A: Well, I should have to guess at that. He was up there some two or three years, I think he was.

Q: That is he remained at the Grove some two or three years after this?

A: I think he did.

Q: And then went to live with his son David?

A: Yes, sir.

Q: With whom he resided down to the time of his death?

A: Yes, sir.

Q: Have you stated all that you recall that was said by Mr. Collin with reference to his will and its being witnessed by you gentlemen?

A: Yes, sir, I don't recollect anything further.

Q: The substance of it then is, that he said he had made his will; that he had made wills before that, but this was the last one?

A: Yes, sir.

Q: And he did, in some form of language make a request that you gentlemen should sign it?

A: Yes, sir.

Q: Now, was that request before he signed himself or afterwards?

A: I couldn't say, it was all done in a minute, he signed his name and we did ours.

Q: Did any doubt arise in your mind at that time as to his competency to make a will?

A: No, sir, I hadn't seen anything.

Q: Well, judging in simple from what you saw that day and from your knowledge of the man, his mode of living, his conditions and surroundings as well as what you saw at that time, did it in any way occur to you that there could be doubt about his mental capacity?

A: No, I didn't see a thing that made me doubt that he was competent to do anything he chose about any business.

Miriam had waited less than six month after her father's death in November 1884 to take her brother to court. But the community of Fayetteville had known for many years of the disturbances within its most prominent family. It was not in the character of David Collin Jr. to go about the village influencing opinions. We must assume people had formed their own ideas about the unpleasantness. Miriam Armstrong and Martin Knapp made a serious miscalculation in their effort to make a case, for to question the credibility of David Collin Sr. was to question also the credibility of those upon whom he had relied for support in his old age. Each question was seen as a kind of insult to both the individuals and to the community and was met with stone-hard resistance.

8

The Civil War

Tis time to look about,
the powers of the kingdom approach apace.
—Shakespeare, *King Lear,* 4.7.94–96

Drums and bugles ring out,
Violent, cutting the heart. . . .
The bitter cry of thousands of households
Can be heard above the noise of battle.
Everywhere the workers sing wild songs.
The great heroes and generals of old time
Are yellow dust forever now.
Such are the affairs of men

—Tu Fu

It is autumn. The skies are clear. A light breeze blows the leaves with a brilliant rustle—orange, red, gold, amber—while the somber greens of cedar and hemlock make a silent counterpoint. In the distance a hammer is at work, banging siding onto someone's barn or shingles on a roof. Further away a dog barks. Nearby a rooster, having forgotten it is no longer dawn, crows. A few fields away another responds. You can hear these things. You can hear as well geese from high above, vast flocks, thousands in number, honking and plying their way south to the Chesapeake and other soothing, warmer waters as the world makes its turn. Nevertheless, listen. There, voices, no, a voice, booming across the farmyard while women and children kneel on the kitchen floor and farm hands stand silent, hats in hand, in the rutted yards and fields. The thin clouds of October reach high above the human gestures.

No hum of traffic. No white noise. No motors of any kind. Fresh air and breezes out of the northwest. Rolling fields of wheat and corn. Here a man on a rig calls to the team of horses drawing the harvester. There is the sound of horses clopping along the dry dirt road toward the village. Sheep and cattle in different pastures on the hillsides.

The middle of the century, between 1845 and 1875, was largely a prosperous and peaceful period for the central area of New York State. When we look at the prosperity of the midcentury we typically think of it as part of a necessary evolution, as progress. There is a vanity about it, about its rightness, a knowingness, a sense of deserving, that seeps into whatever is done and accomplished. Isaiah Berlin asks in *Concepts and Categories*, "Does knowledge always liberate? ... The freedom is that of self-realisation or self-direction—the realisation by the individual's own activity of the true purposes of his nature ... which is frustrated by his misconception about the world and man's place in it." When we look at individuals from the past we have only what records they leave us by which to know them. We cannot know the sound of a voice, a particular personal gesture unique to them. And we tend to forget they did not live in isolation. As Hermann Hesse notes in *Magister Ludi*, "[T]his man ... possessed a certain world-feeling and had been conscious of the transience of all events and the problematical nature of all that had been created by the human spirit."

I offer here an extended representation of the Civil War because it shows the Collin family in the larger context of the world around them. What the writers, including the two who joined the family somewhat after the events in this narrative, describe, and how they describe it, indicates a pervasive set of values shared among family members and gives us some more insight to the unfolding events within the family. The personal narratives in the face of death extend the experience of confronting death at every turn in life, even after the wilderness has been conquered or "won." The battle of mortality rages on.

In the middle of these three prosperous decades (the mid-1840s thru the 1870s), many days' travel distant from the staid farms of the North, hundreds of thousands of men raged in inconceivable slaughter, a war that was just transposing late medieval techniques and strategies with modern weaponry. The results were devastating to the combatants. The three members of the extended clan who fought in the war kept journals or wrote many letters documenting their experiences. Each served for three or four years and so received a full taste of what was involved in the experience of battle and death. Each was eventually engaged in the final siege of Richmond, although with different war perspectives, in different capacities, and unaware of one another. They were also individuals quite different from one another. The picture they paint cumulatively of the war years is a mix of romance, boredom, luck, fear, and whatever it was that each as an individual brought to the vast slaughter. In *A Turn in the South,* his book about a broad tour he took of the American South some years ago, V. S. Naipaul, acerbic observer of the human condition, recalls that not a day went by when he didn't read or hear of General Sherman, as though his march to the sea were still an actuality to be avenged. To someone living outside the deep internal hatred and bitterness that make up part of the buoyant American character, this was a shock. Could people not let go of or forget after 125 years? The context in which these young men fought is still with us.

The first of these Civil War figures is Captain John Bingham Collin (first cousin to David Collin Sr. through his father's brother Solomon), known in the family memoirs as "Captain Jean." His chronicler is his eventual wife and cousin, Lucy Collin (another first cousin to David Collin Sr. through his father's other brother, Norton). John died on October 8, 1894, in Hillsdale. He achieved the rank of major during the Civil War but was so crushed by the war that his health was ruined and "only the loving care of his wife" preserved his life until 1894.

His wife, Lucy, was a talented artist. She and her invalid husband lived in later years in Rutherford, New Jersey, where she had a studio. They retired to a Hillsdale farm, which John inherited from his parents. Lucy bequeathed the farm after John's death to her beloved sister Cardera, of whom we will learn more later.

Lucy provides the romantic version of the war, envisioned by a young woman, wanting her man to appear and actually be heroic. It was, in fact, not always so. The story she created from his many letters home to her has the quality of a wish, a preconceived myth. It is one perspective, but it tells us much about where we were at certain points during the war. The captain's "Lute" (Lucy) was the love of his life, whom he eventually married (though that is not noted in her story as such) and who kept the record of his service and wrote it up as a sort of novel. His return to the village of Hillsdale as a fresh volunteer in uniform could be right out of Hollywood.

From The Story of Captain Jean and His Lute

> Long years of the most prosperous peace had passed over our happy country, even the bitter struggle for independence was scarcely remembered as a reality, yet treasured as the theme for heroic glorification. The thought of war seemed an impossibility—the very name but a desperate struggle on the historic peace never again to be recalled. When suddenly and almost without premonition on the thirteenth of April, Eighteen-sixty-one the rebellious guns were fired on "Fort Sumter." With the speed of lightning the sound reverberated over the land rousing the spirit of the Nation and thousands of patriotic hearts from that instant rushed to protect their Country's Standard.
>
> Upon one of the loveliest mornings of this never-to-be-forgotten April "Jean" and "Lute" were seated upon the broad verandah of "Meadow Bank" cottage indulging in pleasant conversation. Lute marked an unusual restlessness in the manner of her friend, a warm glow on cheek and brow, yet little dreamed of the spirit that burned within. Suddenly raising his cane to his shoulder and marching up and down the gravel walk, Jean asked—"Don't you think I would make a good soldier?" Truly a noble one, Lute thought as she followed his march across the lawn, where again leaning against the fence shadowed with shrubbery they lingered and chatted until taking a photograph from his pocket Jean hurriedly said, "Lute, I leave you my counterpart, I am going to volunteer," and with one bound sprang over the fence and hastened down the road. Amazed, startled, yet doubting Lute exclaimed, "You are jesting," yet with a beating heart wondering if indeed he were in earnest silently watched him until out of sight.

This was the first expression of the result of thoughts that had taken possession of Jean's mind from the moment the news from "Ft. Sumter" had reached his ear. Nor was it merely an enthusiastic resolve, but an earnestly thoughtful decision thus to commence life when just of age by taking his first step forth from the home of his youth in his Country's service.

Inspired by his noble example two of his friends concluded to accompany him. Thus on the 29th of April 1861 the "Trio" enlisted at Albany as "friends" in a company then forming under Capt. Seymour.

The three were the only ones in town who "volunteered" thus early in the breaking out of the War, and every patriotic heart warmed towards them, loading them with good wishes and advice. Especially did the village Pastor musing on the perilous life they were to lead remember them with exhortations and prayers, while the village Doctor talked of exposure and disease and felt constrained to present his most potent pills.

Nor were there lacking expressions of wonderment that young men in the very hey-day of youth could voluntarily become soldiers and risk their lives amid the horrors of War.

Especially was it thought strange that one circumstanced like Jean, with wealthy parents and apparently the means of gratifying every reasonable desire could leave all for a wandering life of at least two years and a fate unknown. Nor indeed can one paint with pen the wild tumult of feelings that must have filled the young soldier's heart on bidding farewell to loving friends and venturing upon a life, the trials and danger of which were so wholly unknown, for as they were the first to go they had not the opportunity of listening to the experience of others. Yet in that first hale of Patriotic enthusiasm they scarcely thought of hardships and danger, remembering only the glorious cause and the proud honor of having nobly defended their Country in her hour of utmost need.

Jean and his friends were first quartered with their Company in a barrack on Chapel St., Albany, until it was accepted as Co. "A" 14th Reg't, N.Y. State Volunteers, commanded by Col. McQuade.

They were then removed to a new barrack at "Camp Morgan," a mile or more from the city, where commenced the daily "drilling" and "marching," the regular routine of a soldier's life. Sleeping in "bunks," rising at the sound of "Reveille," or the rough shake of the "Orderly" accompanied by the usual guttural "Fall in;" writing pencil sketches home with a strip of board for a writing desk, and listening to religious services on the Sabbath out upon the green with the Chaplain standing upon the brass "Field piece."

After having remained at Albany a few weeks their quiet little town was thrown into quite a state of excitement by the arrival of the "Trio" home on a three day "furlough." Indeed they were almost a curiosity for as yet scarcely any one there had seen a soldier in uniform, and theirs was a very becoming one, a half "Zouave" costume of deep blue, and deep blue overcoats and capes, with garters or leggings lacing up the ankle.

How warmly Jean was welcomed at his home, and looked upon by mother, sisters and loving friends with mingled feelings perhaps of awe, admiration and sadness. On the Sabbath the "Trio" were all at church and the Pastor, Rev. Lorenzo M. Gates, warmly and beautifully addressed each one personally, then waving a silken ensign of our beloved Country proclaimed loudly against the traitors who had rebelled against it and boldly in favor of defending its sacred folds even by the sword, notwithstanding some *wise heads* in his congregation were dubiously shaken at such doctrine from the pulpit, but *they* have long since become *"Copperheads."* [A Copperhead was a Northerner who sympathized with the South or at least was perceived to do so. The real situation was, as always, rather more complicated.]

On the following Monday evening one of the most influential and patriotic men in town, Dr. Dorr, gave a large reception for "Our Volunteers." The parlors were tastefully decorated with the "Stars and Stripes" and there gathered there from miles around a youthful company with whom the young soldiers were accustomed to associate. Many a kind and earnest wish was there expressed for the soldiers' safe return; healths were drank in sparkling lemonade, and maidens graciously accepted attentions from gentlemen in so attractive a "Uniform." But sadness hovered over the parting hour and heartfelt tears were shed by sisters, cousins and true friends of the departing soldiers, who scarcely dared ask when shall we meet again.

On the following morning they returned to their rendezvous in Albany. And to the loving friends they left behind, the little town seemed more quiet, more lonely than ever. Then Jean was again drilling at the barracks. Often of an afternoon people from town drove out to see their "Dress Parade," and the monotonous life was occasionally relieved by visits from home friends, among them his Pastor. Here too came the news of the death of "Ellsworth" rousing a revengeful excitement among the soldiers, leading to the formation of a regiment called the "Ellsworth Avengers." [Elmer Ephraim Ellsworth (1837–61) was a charismatic figure who created a regiment of soldiers from New York City firemen, dressing and training them in the Zouave manner (a romantic perception of precision and ferocity). He was the first officer casualty on the Virginia front, and his death was the occasion for stimulating a warlike spirit in the North.]

From chapter 4, "Captain Jean":

> On the second of October 1861 Jean received his commission as captain of the U.S. Volunteers.
>
> The nineteenth of November Captain Jean returned to his native town to attend the wedding of a cousin the evening of the twentieth, on which occasion he assisted as groomsman with his friend Lute as bridesmaid. He appeared in full uniform as requested and enjoyed the evening exceedingly. The following evening a portion of the wedding guests spent a merry evening at the Captain's home.
>
> The next day Captain Jean escorted his friend Lute accompanied by a sister graduate to make a short visit among friends at Lakeville. He then remained in town a few days more and saw his friend Lute depart for New York to which place her family then removed their residence.

Jean then returned to the barracks. In a short time as these new regiments were required to go to the field and their ranks were not yet filled up Col. Cowles' Regiment was consolidated with the 91st N.Y. under Col. Van Zandt, and in the month of December ordered to Governor's Island.

The regiment came down the Hudson River on the evening boat and arrived at the island on one of the most bitter cold mornings of the winter. They pitched their tents on the shore, the canvas flapping and blowing in the cold piercing wind that came over the restless waves of the Bay. No preparations had been made for their arrival and they had nothing to eat but a slice of "salt junk" spread upon "hard tack." Col. Loomis commanding the island declared that the soldiers of the Mexican War had not suffered as these. Night came, no straw had yet arrived so they lay down upon the cold ground to sleep, but Jean had taken so severe a cold working all day in the cold bleak wind, that when night came he could not speak a loud word, and dare not sleep exposed to the weather, but crossed over in the rowboat to New York and spent the night at the St. Nicholas.

The regiment remained on the island some three weeks, during a great portion of which time Jean was ill with a severe cold and was cared for in the patriotic family of his friend Lute. Here too he had the pleasure of meeting his brother from Syracuse.

From chapter 6, "Key West":

Sunday morning, January 19, 1862 the "Ericson" anchored half a mile off the coast of Key West to the joy of many a soldier, but they were not permitted to land that day as it was the Sabbath. Captain Jean, however, with the Captains of other companies crossed over to the Island in the afternoon to choose the place for their encampment.

Of the Island Jean writes: "It is rather rough to be sure but then I am pleased with the place as it is wild and romantic, still I would not live in such a place if I were not a soldier. There is quite a city on the Island or what the people call a city, composed of about twenty-five hundred inhabitants black and white. There are three churches, stores, etc. like any large northern country village. The houses are very low indeed but some seem very pleasant. The Island is four and a half miles long, by one mile broad. Most of the land is covered with shrubs. Fruit is plenty, some of which grows on the Island such as oranges, lemons, pineapple, Coconuts etc. Still these do not grow abundantly here (but many are imported from Havana). There are several species of cactus, the finest I ever saw, also the Geranium and Oleander so carefully nourished in the north here grow wild. I saw a splendid Oleander tree in full bloom. I have now seen the Coral Reefs of Key West of which I have read.

"The fortifications here are strong. *Fort Taylor* is a fine fort, our camp will be near it. the Steamship *Connecticut* is now lying at the dock. I saw the officers today and inquired after Lieut. Billis' brother. I shall see him tomorrow as he does not leave here until Sunday morning."

The new camp of tents on their *Island House* was called *Camp Brennan* in honor of the General, and here again was pursued the military drilling, target practice, etc. Captain Jean with a number of officers purchased a little boat and thus often amused themselves with fishing excursions, though it is doubtful whether they ever caught any fish. Their first trip of the kind was in a little sailboat, but as none of the officers knew anything of naval affairs they sailed out some four miles from shore and had great difficulty in getting back. Captain Jean thought it desirable not to venture forth again without someone on board slightly acquainted at least with the sea.

February 6th Jean writes to his mother: "I suppose the weather is quite cold now in the north, but you have no idea how warm it is here. The boys run around barefoot part of the time, and I hardly ever think of wearing my coat unless I am going out or on parade. The climate is delightful and I think this is one of the finest places I was ever in. This little Island is worth more to the Government than the whole State of Florida. It is strongly fortified and there are eight regiments here now. I called on one of the citizens on

Tuesday night, Mr. Ferguson, the Harbor Master. I found him to be formerly of Putnam County [N.Y.]. He is acquainted through Dutchess and somewhat in our own Columbia County. He is a fine man and a good Union man. (One loves to meet thus with a man from one's own State). There are a great many *Secish* [secessionists] here (at heart) still they keep quiet for fear their property would be confiscated. I was surprised to find so much style here. There are some fine looking ladies here. We sometimes see them riding on horseback. The citizens often walk out to camp to see the Dress Parade.["]

The twenty-first of February Gen. Brennen arrived on the transport "Philadelphia;" and on the twenty-second, Washington's birthday, the General reviewed his troops on the Island. The three regiments composing his brigade formed at the General's Headquarters in three sides of a square, the general and his staff taking their position on the open side of the Square. "Washington's farewell Address to the Public" [1796, barely seventy years prior] was then read to the men after which commissioned officers of the different regiments were introduced to the General. The brigade then marched through the city in "fine style" and thence to their respective quarters where they were allowed the rest of the day, and the men amused themselves with "foot racing," "sack racing" etc.

February twenty-fifth Capt. Jean received a compliment from Gen. Brennan. The General inspected the arms, accouterments, and dress of the regiments and found those of Company "H," Captain Jean's Company, in the best order. The cleanest gun in the regiment belonged to a private in Company "H." The General immediately selected him for an "Orderly" at his headquarters, the order for which was read on "Dress Parade" that evening. The general also spoke of the excellent order of Captain Jean's Company, a compliment which had been paid him several times by the Surgeon and Colonel. The evening of the Twenty-fifth Capt. Jean was busily writing in his tent when he suddenly found it necessary to pack up his papers for a "blow down," as there had come up a sudden gale of wind that blew a perfect hurricane for several hours, an amusing description of which was published in the "N.Y. Herald." A number of tents were blown over and some even flew out upon the water. A former Lieut. of Company H laughingly declared that Capt. Jean insisted upon having himself and a brother Lieut. hold his tent over him during the gale, but that even then he would not go to sleep, but kept looking out from the corner of his eye to see if they were still "holding on," though for the truth of this story I cannot vouch as it was related with a mischievous twinkle of the eye.

Capt. Jean was often engaged during guard duty about the town as capt. of the Provost Guard. One evening he found one of the men at work in the Government Storehouse intoxicated. On arresting him he resisted and being a much stronger man than Jean seized him by the collar, at which Capt. Jean would have made good use of his sword, had not the patrol guard at that moment come to his assistance, when the drunken man was speedily marched off to the Guard House at the point of a musket.

Great improvements were made upon the Key by the Brigade as they were constantly employed building fortifications, making and repairing roads, clearing off bushes and trees, and some too were at work on the warfs unloading vessels captured from the rebels as they were brought here to receive the decision of the Admiralty Court.

The rebel Steamer "Magnolia" loaded with cotton was captured while attempting to run the blockade, and while lying in harbor here Capt. Jean with Capt. Hulbert and Jackson spent part of the day aboard her. Jean cut a piece of the wood that had been splintered by a shell for a momento. Everything on board still remained just as the rebels had left it, the Captain's sanctum looked desolate, his instruments were untouched and his hourglass of no use to him now unless to mark the hours while in his prison cell. Before taken the Magnolia had on board about fourteen bales of cotton, but three hundred bales had been thrown overboard to lighten the vessel and when seeing all attempts to escape were useless the crew had attempted to blow up the steamer, but only succeeded in bursting one of the boilers.

Soon after the first of March a fleet of twenty-five Mortar and Gun Boats under command of Commander Porter left Key West to take New Orleans, and to Jean it was a magnificent sight to see the vessels as they left the harbor under full sail for their perilous expedition. It made him the more impatient to be himself amid stirring scenes.

The Sixteenth of March Capt. Jean spent a portion of the day on board the "Niagara" our largest Man-of-War. The ships crew was about six hundred men. This was the "Frigate" that a few years previously had conveyed the Japanese Embassy to this country, home, and while on board Jean listened to an interesting account of this expedition to Japan by one of the Marines.

The evening of the sixteenth Jean wrote to a friend [the author], "I have just returned from church and I don't know of a more pleasant way to spend the rest of the evening than to add a few thoughts more of my letter to you. I had a drink of Croton Water this evening on board one of the schooners. Only think of my drinking Croton water here, and then I thought of you and drank your health. I generally attend the Episcopal Church every Sunday evening. It is the most stylish church in the place and the most frequented by the officers. The clergyman and his wife too were formerly from the north and they are very kind and attentive to the soldiers, especially those in the hospital."

About this time Capt. Jean had the pleasure of entertaining at his Military dining table lieut. van Ness Philip of the Gun Boat "Cuyler" and a resident of the same County as the Captain. he was an intelligent pleasant gentleman full of his jokes and genial conversation, and they forgot not to "toast" the "Constitution and Union" in whose service not long after Lieut. Philip fell, a victim of the yellow fever.

The climate of the south began to affect Capt. Jean's health, and during the month of March he was not at all well. His eyes also troubled him very much, partly in consequence of the sandy soil of the Key as the sun shining upon the white sand was reflected as upon snow and was very trying to the eyes. Still he endeavored not to give up, fancying he would become "acclimated" in a little while. On the third of April (1862) he took his Company out to Battalion Drill, and during the drill was taken with a severe pain in the head. The heat was intense and he was soon obliged to return to his tent suffering severely. The surgeon came but could give no relief, and on the fourth of April the ambulance conveyed him to the hospital where he lay very ill for several weeks with a Bilious Fever [from the old concept of "humors," an ailment of the liver resulting in peevishness, anorexia, vertigo, headaches, slight jaundice, and constipation].

The hospital was a large white wooden building on Broadway with a beautiful yard around it, handsomely shaded with Orange, Lemon, Fig, Almond, Cocoa Nut, Tamarind and many other varieties of trees. Some of them were laden with fruit, and the oleanders were bright with a profusion of exquisite blossoms. But the Cocoa Nut tree was the King of the Island towering in tall majesty and rendering so grateful a shade.

One of Jean's men took care of him during his illness and here he passed many a long and lonely hour ofttimes lying awake at dead of night listening to the ticking of his watch or gazing at the lamp dimly burning on the table. One evening Engineer Ames of the Transport Connecticut came in to see him and carried news of his health to his friends in New York. Jean was sitting up then and thought himself getting along finely, but again he had a relapse and sometimes could not but feel discouraged, though with the early days of May there came renewed strength and he again wrote more cheerful missives to his friends.

Port Hudson, the topic of the following excerpt, was in southeast Louisiana some twenty miles north of Baton Rouge. Located on a high bluff on the east bank of the Mississippi, it was heavily fortified by the Confederates in 1862, just before the Vicksburg campaign. The siege in the spring of 1863, led by Admiral Farragut and General Banks of the North, lasted forty-five days and resulted in the surrender of the garrison of some six thousand men in July, after word had come down that Vicksburg had fallen, thus leaving the Mississippi open to control by the North.

From chapter 10, "The Siege of Port Hudson":

> Having arrived at the outer works of Port Hudson on the twenty-fourth of May, on the twenty-fifth the Ninety-first was ordered to drive the enemy from a piece of woods that the pioneers might make a road for artillery. Skirmishing commenced with the enemy in their lurking place, and in the afternoon they [the 91st] made a charge but before they were aware came upon a masked battery that opened upon them with perfect fury. They fell instantly to the ground, thus saving their men, and in making a second charge were successful and before night drove the enemy from the woods to their entrenchments. At night they were relieved and fell to the rear for rest.
>
> The next day orders came that a general engagement would take place on the twenty-seventh. The morning of the twenty-seventh came—all was made ready for the attack at an early moment. The booming of cannon commenced and the command "Forward" was given. The whole line charged at the same time and after some hours of desperate fighting succeeded in carrying the outer works of the enemy by storm. They were obliged to charge through woods, down deep ravines, up hill and over such natural fortifications that it looked astonishing that they could have driven the enemy as they did.
>
> Col. Cowles was one of the gallant soldiers who fell on the twenty-seventh while leading his Regiment, the 128th N.Y., in the assault.
>
> The bombardment of Port Hudson was kept up slowly and continually so that the enemy was constantly under fire. Still Capt. Jean writes on the twelfth of June: "I am so used to the sound of cannon and musketry that I do not mind it and am sitting now under the guns of the Rebel Fort by a table of rough boards covered with a rubber blanket—quite stylish and very convenient for a soldier to write upon, while everything around me represents an army in active service. Still it is an unpleasant position and I shall be relieved when the Port is taken."
>
> The fourteenth of June was again selected for a general assault. They stormed the enemy's works early in the morning and after

hard fighting all day were obliged to retire without success. The 91st led the advance armed with "hand grenades"; they were ordered to charge the works, throw the grenades, and storm the works at the point of the bayonet. With bravery and coolness the men charged the rebel works three distinct times yet seemed to gain nothing; and on being thus repulsed under the continual fire of the enemy they were unable either to advance or retreat, but were obliged to lay on the field under cover until nightfall when the firing ceased. While in this position Capt. Jean was greatly surprised to meet Col. Van Petten of the [?] who had sought shelter by the same old log as himself. The Colonel had formerly been a principal of a school at Fairfield N.Y. that Jean had attended and was glad to meet an old pupil in his country's service.

Of the two hundred and fifty men led to the charge this day seven officers and eighty men were among the killed and wounded. Among the officers killed was Capt. Hulbert, a firm friend that had been almost like a brother to Capt. Jean and deeply did he mourn his loss. Capt. Jean was now the only Captain remaining who left Albany with the regiment.

Later in June a report came that the rebels were about to make trouble in the rear, consequently several regiments were ordered to the rear under General Weitzel to make a reconnoissance, the 91st among the number. They were out four days but saw only a small number of "Gray-backs" who of course skedaddled at their approach.

Although the rebels still held out they were doubtless suffering much from want of food as they were so closely surrounded by the Union troops. In some places their works approached so close that the Union and rebel soldiers could easily talk together, and often with such laughing and amusing conversation that they seemed more like friends than hostile parties. On the twenty-seventh of June deserters reported that General Gardiner had eaten of the first mule, and that he must surrender soon for they could not live without food.

On the last of June General Banks enthusiastically addressed his troops.

With the first days of July came word of the rebels having made a raid upon Bayou Boenf [?] when there was destroyed a large quantity of baggage and Government property among which was private baggage of Capt. Jean, the officers having stored their baggage on the march. Capt. Jean lost a valuable supply of clothing, with collections of curiosities and packages of letters that he greatly regretted.

On the morning of the seventh of July a cousin arrived at Port Hudson from General Grant with the news that Vicksburg had fallen and that the "Stars and Stripes" were floating over that city. Gen. Banks ordered a salute of two hundred guns to be fired, while bands were playing and the loud and prolonged cheers of the soldiers rent the air. The rebels behind their entrenchments must have been startled by the noise and jubilant commotion among the Yankees.

Early on the evening of the eighth Capt. Jean was awakened by the Adjutant coming to his tent with an order not to allow his men to leave camp that day as a "Flag of Truce" was up and Gen. Gardiner intended to surrender the garrison: it seemed almost too good to be true. But it was an indescribable relief after having been under the fire of the Rebel guns at Port Hudson for forty-three days, to know that the long and tiresome siege was at last ended; and that one might again have a feeling of safety for a little time at least. There was a strangeness too in the cessation of hostilities so long kept up in the perfect quiet that now pervaded the scene,—no booming of cannon, no rattling of musketry.

On the morning of the ninth of July with colors flying, the troops marched in the Rebel works to take possession. The rebel regiments were drawn up in line—they flanked and surrounded them, when General Gardiner ordered them to "Ground Arms" and then the general rode up and surrendered his sword. At this time the "Stars and Stripes" were hoisted where but a few moments before had floated the "Stars and Bars" while the bands played the national airs and then a salute of thirty-four guns in the air. It was a grand scene filling the Union soldiers with enthusiasm, and soon officers and men of both armies were shaking hands with each other so that one would have thought that they had always been friends.

The Monocacy is a river flowing from southern Pennsylvania, north of Gettysburg across Maryland near Frederick. In July 1864, a battle took place there against a Confederate division under General Early, whose troops were posing a threat to Washington. The north, under Wallace, lost the encounter, but it delayed the Confederate advance, allowing Grant's army time to arrive to cover Washington.

From chapter 14, "Monocacy Junction":

> At the mouth of the Monocacy River Captain Jean received "orders" from General Tyler commanding that Military Department to proceed to Monocacy Junction, to take command of that Post and assume the duties of Assistant Provost Marshal. He accordingly marched to Monocacy with his command and established two camps of log quarters roofed with tents on the old Monocacy Battlefield. During his stay here he was engaged in superintending the building of a Block House on a prominent hill overlooking and guarding the long railroad bridge that crossed the Monocacy River.
>
> He had also under his command besides a portion of his own regiment a portion of a Pennsylvania Battery and detachments from Maryland Regiments detailed to work on the Block House.
>
> November 6th Captain Jean received a telegram from General Tyler commanding the department to send for Colonel Knight's Regiment, have him turn over one hundred horses and equipment with which he was to mount one hundred of his own men and send them to guard the "River line" in place of the Colonel's men who were going home on furlough to vote. It was something of a task to get his men properly mounted as they were totally ignorant of the cavalry service and unaccustomed to riding, and Captain Jean could not but indulge in merriment at the expense of his laughable display of cavalry, and fancied that the 91st was to be accomplished in all the "arms" of the "Service."

November seventh the 2nd New York Cavalry encamped at Monocacy on the way to the front.

November fourteenth two of Moseby's men were captured a few miles from Monocacy; rumors were afloat that Moseby was concentrating his forces for another "raid" and Captain Jean received a telegram from Gen. Tyler who thought it probable that he would dash for the camp at Monocacy. [John Singleton Moseby was the notorious commander of a loosely organized force of Partisan Rangers in northern Virginia. He moved secretly and swiftly and his men became an effective, much feared, and detested guerrilla instrument for the Confederates. He was enormously popular in his home territory among the people.]

November fifteenth Captain Jean's hundred mounted men returned from the mouth of the Monocacy [at the Potomac]. They seemed to have quite enjoyed their taste of the Cavalry Service. It was a beautiful moonlight evening and Captain Jean was walking out on the hill in front of his quarters when suddenly the sound of a distant bugle reached his ear, and rockets were bursting high in the air. There was querying then among the officers as to whether these were not signals of an ominous nature. This excitement somewhat subsided, Lieut. Runkle of the 3rd Pennsylvania Battery says "Come Captain up to my quarters and we'll have some 'This-e-hash-e' (his mode of expressing his soldier's fare)" and they were soon having a merry hour over the evening's repast.

General Kenley assumed command of the 1st Separate Brigade for a short time during General Tyler's leave of absence to visit his home, and on the eighteenth of November came up from the Headquarters at the "Relay House" to reconnoiter the Post at Monocacy, and remained to dinner with Captain Jean. The night of December first Captain Jean arrested as a spy Lieut. Harding formerly of the United States Navy, while passing through Monocacy on the train going to Baltimore, and soon discovered that he was the husband of the notorious Rebel spy "Belle Boyd" though he tried to palm himself off for an English Lord, but he had no pass or other papers. He [Capt. Jean] found a handkerchief on his person marked

Belle Boyd, also a few pictures of "Belle." He was kept all night by Captain Jean closely guarded and the next morning he sent him to Harper's Ferry; he was afterwards confined at Fort Delaware. [Belle Boyd was only seventeen when the war broke out and worked largely for Stonewall Jackson, getting unsuspected information of Union activities to him. She was twice arrested and released, escaping to England in 1863, where she went on the stage.]

December 5th General Kenley again took dinner with Captain Jean when he (the Capt.) took the opportunity to inquire of the general whether he would remain at Monocacy long enough to allow him to send for his wife. The General thought it would be safe to send for her, whereupon he determined to do so immediately, and on the 8th of December telegraphed for her to take the first train for Baltimore on Saturday morning the 10th [by this time they had moved house to New Jersey, where "Lute" had set up a studio], and he would meet her at the depot when the train arrived. He had obtained a leave of absence and hastening to Baltimore joyfully greeted his wife after a three month's absence. They spent the Sabbath in Baltimore at the "Eutaw House," receiving calls from some of the officers at Fort McHenry, and on Monday morning took the train for Monocacy, arriving there just in time for dinner at the Maryland farm house close by the camp where they were to board.

That afternoon a long train of army wagons with a cavalry escort from Sheridan's army on the march from the Shenandoah Valley to Washington came winding about the hills and forded the Monocacy River by the old battle-ruined bridge just at sunset. They then bivouacked for the night on the slope of the opposite hill. The ground was covered with snow and it was one of the coldest nights of the winter, but without a tent for a shelter, they built glowing camp fires and laid down to rest, while the bright moonlight reflected on the snow, and mingling with the light from numberless camp fires made a picturesque scene one could not but admire though the soldiers were suffering with the cold. One of the officers came up to the house and chatted with the Captain and gladly spent the night on the dining room floor wrapped in the Captain's army blankets.

These weeks spent in "Winter Quarters" with his wife for a constant companion were greatly enjoyed by Captain Jean, while to "Lute" the very change from her city home was so great and strange it seemed like a wild romantic dream. Surrounded with martial scenes and in the presence of him so deeply loved she almost felt as though she were living a chapter in some old historic lore [?]. Every novelty of a life at camp she enjoyed; with pleasure she listened to the measured tread of the "Headquarters Sentinel" marching on the walk below while she sat at the window and gazed out upon the camp to watch her Captain as he went about the Company streets and then to the Block House to note and superintend the progress of the work there. But it was her especial delight to watch his dignified handsome figure when taking command of the troops on Dress parade; or mounted on one of the fine horses belonging to an officer of the Battery with an orderly following in the rear to gallop by her captain's side on "Scouting Expeditions" about the wooded hills and wild ravines that skirt the picturesque windings of the Monocacy.

When the Captain was busy with military duties sometimes she amused herself with sketching and painting views about the old "Battlefield," the "Picket Post" and "Camp" for future mementoes. Often at evening she assisted her Captain in writing military papers, and sometimes the wintry hours were whiled away with Backgammon and Chess interrupted by pleasant conversation or with groups of officers that gathered at the Captain's Headquarters to indulge in stories of hardships and wild adventures or make merry the time with banjo and song. Frequently too there were pleasant social calls from Colonels, Captains, Quartermasters and Lieutenants of other Military Posts sometimes on business or on their way from one post to another, and now and then there were the calls from the Commanding General.

The trains of the Baltimore & Ohio railroad were almost constantly passing the camp sometimes filled to overflowing with the soldiers of moving armies who filled the air with enthusiastic shouts as they passed the camp, or there were the long trains of freight and coal drawn by monstrous "Camel-back" engines and then the arrival of rations was sure to produce a lively scene at the camp.

On Christmas the soldiers tastefully decorated their camp with evergreen designs in arches, stars and wreaths, and Captain Jean escorted Lute to see the decorations of the Company streets, and called upon some of the officers in their log quarters, where she was much amused and interested in some of their ingenious housekeeping contrivances for convenience and comfort.

From chapter 16, "Orders for the Front—Before Petersburg":

One evening the last of February while sitting by their little table partaking of refreshments after a hard fought game of Chess, an orderly tapped at the door bringing the Captain an "order" from General Tyler to hold his command in readiness to move at a moment's notice to join the 5th Corps before Petersburg. In a moment the officers of his command were gathered about the Captain full of excitement at the prospect of their immediate departure for the front; while Lute was filled with sorrow and dismay that she must now leave the husband who would soon be surrounded by the awful dangers of the battlefield. A late order came to "turn over" all their old and injured muskets and equipment that they might be replaced by new before their departure. These were to be sent to Baltimore in charge of an officer and Captain Jean thought best to send his wife on in care of this officer that he might see her safely on the train for New York. Mrs. Lieutenant Spaulding was also to accompany her. Accordingly during the evening of the 24th of February their trunks were packed and the barracks robbed of all those tasty little arrangements that had made the place seem so home-like and pleasant. It was a sorrowful night. In the gray dawn of early morning the 25th of February the train for Baltimore stopped at Camp Parole; a sad group passed the Parade Ground followed by soldiers bearing their trunks and baggage. As the cars were moving off Captain Jean leaped from the platform and the bitter parting was over. Lute accompanied by Mrs. Lieutenant Spaulding reached her [Mrs. Spaulding's] Brooklyn home at midnight in a dismal rain, taking her family quite by surprise and when greeted with the eager inquiry, "Where are your husbands?" they could only answer, "Gone to the Front."

On the afternoon of the 27th Captain Jean marched his command to Annapolis to take the transport for City Point [partway up the James River toward Petersburg and Richmond]. They remained on the wharf all night suffering from hunger and cold, but no transport came, so the next morning they received orders to return to their camp where they remained until the following afternoon March 1st when they again received orders as the transport had arrived. They were soon packed bag and baggage and embarked on board the steamer "Cossack" at about 6 p.m. After a somewhat stormy voyage they reached City Point about 2 o'clock on the afternoon of March 2nd where disembarking in rain and mud they joined the other detachment of the Ninety-first from Fort McHenry and Marshall. The men were quartered in comfortable barracks for the night while most of the officers remained on board the vessel.

The following morning they were to take the cars and proceed some twenty miles beyond to join the besieging army around Petersburg. The arrival of the Ninety-first was warmly welcomed by the army for they came 1800 strong, thus numbering more than the Brigade then in the field. They were assigned their position in the 1st Provisional Brigade, 3rd Division, 5th Corps; General Warren was their Corps Commander; General Crawford commanded the 3rd Division and Colonel Kelley the Brigade; they were Brigaded with Wisconsin troops.

They were stationed on the advance at a point lately gained by the 5th Corps called "Hatcher's Run" on the left flank of the army. Here they arrived in pouring rain with mud knee deep, and nothing but "shelter tents" for protection until in a few days they could build log huts like the rest of the army. Here Captain Jean tented with his "brother-in-arms" Captain Stewart, but the change from comfortable barracks at Camp Parole to shelter tents in such inclement weather was too great for him and he took a violent cold that brought on another severe attack of fever. The Quartermaster kindly offered his quarters in his more comfortable tent which he was glad to accept, but on the 9th the surgeon desired him to go to the hospital but he hoped this would not be necessary.

The first pleasant day after their arrival their Division was reviewed by General Meade. Rebel deserters were constantly coming in along the lines. March 12th the Captain writes, "Ten Confederate Cavalrymen gave themselves up on our lines today. They were mounted and fully armed and equipped, Government pays them for their arms and horses. They all say they are tired of the Confederacy and wish to come back to the Union."

March 14th the 5th Corps was under "Marching Orders" and reviewed by its Commander General Warren; still days passed by without any movement though all preparations were made for an attack, all surplus baggage was sent to the rear, and they were in readiness to move at almost a moment's notice. March 18th Captain Jean visited the 2nd Corps. March 21st he went out in command of the picket line to be absent from the camp some two days. The first night out the rain poured in torrents and it was so dark he could scarcely see his hand before him; the second night was clear and cold. While going the rounds of the pickets he came to a solitary grave near a wood and paused to read the inscription on the old tombstone—"Erected to the memory of Captain Augustus Ellis a merchant of Petersburg who was killed during the War of 1812."

... [On] the 25th of March a severe battle was fought which was the commencement of the closing campaign of the Rebellion. Captain Jean had a pass for the hospital as he was still ill with a lingering fever and the surgeon thought him utterly unable to endure the necessary marching of the opening campaign; but Capt. Jean refused to go to the hospital. He wished to lead his men to the last. The Ninety-first Regiment being 1800 strong was divided into three battalions of which Captain Jean commanded one. These battalions were larger than a majority of Regiments then in the field . . .

In a letter to the *New York Times* (Tuesday March 28th) the army correspondent writing at midnight March 25th says: "The 5th Corps was ordered out as a column of reserve. The First division was assigned to the second Corps. As far as I could learn no part of the Corps was engaged, but they performed efficient service in supporting their respective active corps."

General Crawford (commanding Capt. Jean's Division) started for the Ninth Corps but was halted and brought back to the Sixth Corps. While on their way, they were halted and a rather hurried and very informal review was held before the President, General Grant, General Meade and other generals, besides a number of ladies. This ceremony was a most singular spectacle. Just outside of the shell range, but within hearing of the terrific engagement then in progress, the Division was forced through a showy parade of a review, not knowing the moment they would be called upon to meet the enemy's fire, a flag of truce flying over the works of both armies near the Appomattox pending the burial of dead rebels, a desperate battle in hot and bloody progress on their left near Hatcher's Run, and a grand review before the president near Weldon Railroad. Of this same day's work Capt. Jean writes: "I feel quite confident that I cannot endure through the present campaign in the army of the Potomac. Still I intend to go as far as my power of human endurance will allow me. I don't know when I ever became so tired as on the 25th. We were routed out early in the morning without breakfast, marched four miles at a double-quick when we reached the front where the Ninth Corps were fighting. Here we remained in line of battle until nearly noon when a special train came with the president who received the Corps." . . .

March 29th the column started at 3 o'clock in the morning to strike for the Southside Railroad in order to cut off this last communication between Petersburg and rebeldom and thus necessitate its evacuation. "A large cavalry force under general Sheridan took the Halifax road toward Dinwiddie Courthouse. The Infantry column (comprising the Fifth Corps) crossed Hatcher's Run on the Vaughan Road, but met with no opposition until they reached within a short distance of the Boydtown plank road, where the evening's pickets were found and driven back. The Fifth Corps had a sharp encounter with the enemy on the Quaker Road, but lost in the affair less than three hundred men, and drove the rebels nearly a mile with severe loss to them, and captured a number of prisoners." This was all the important fighting during Wednesday. The enemy, however, enlivened the night by a furious cannonade along the lines in front of the 9th Corps evidently in the hope of finding a weak spot, but they were disappointed. On Thursday (the 30th) the rain began very early, about midnight, and lasted until 4 p.m. rendering the roads impassable for artillery, and necessarily suspending active operations. A lively fire of artillery was kept up by the enemy and picket firing was rapid and continuous but no serious damage was done. In the morning the whole Fifth Corps line advanced across the Boydtown Road with little opposition.

On Friday March 31st there was severe fighting on some parts of the line from morning till night. The Second Division of the Fifth Corps supported by the Third, was thrown out toward the White Oak Road, east of the Boydtown plank road, and ordered to reach and take position there. After crossing a small branch of Govelly Run, and while about forming in line, our troops were fired upon by a heavy force of the enemy who were lying concealed in the woods, and also by the rebel artillery posted in favorable positions. Our men stood their ground for a while, but the enemy appearing to be moving to the left as if to turn their flank, the line was forced back to their first position where they were sallied and soon checked the enemy's advance. About the same time another attack was made on our right flank of the Fifth Corps, but Gen. Miles' division of the Second Corps being posted there made a brilliant charge and doubled up the enemy, driving them back a long distance, leaving hundreds of their dead and wounded on the field. The Fifth Corps about noon again took the advance, and drove the enemy back about a mile and a half, and long before dark had reached the White Oak Road, for which they had started in the morning, and established their line across the same, driving the rebels into their strong works at Hatcher's Run. The loss in the day's work will not be far from 1200. . . .

[A] correspondent writing of the same Friday's battle to the New York Times April 3rd says—"early in the morning the extreme left of the Fifth Corps, General Crawford's division, occupying a position north of the plank road which it had gained on the previous day without much fighting, was attacked by a large force of rebels, comprising all of Anderson's and part of Pickett's division of Longstreet's Corps, who had been sent over from north of the James since this movement on our side commenced, and massed on the enemy's right. The skirmish line of the Third Division was not able to withstand the heavy force opposed to them and fell back rapidly, but in tolerable order on the line of battle. The troops were at the time getting breakfast, and before they could get into line the enemy came upon them and compelled them to retire to the Boydtown road. Here they rallied and formed, and after severe fighting for four hours, drove the enemy back over the same ground, and about two miles further, being on the left of their own line, within about two miles of the Southside railroad, and within a short distance of the enemy's main line of works south of the railroad.

"In the beginning of the attack, Pickett's division of the enemy sent a brigade around our left flank, and into the rear of our line. Our left was held by the First Brigade of the Third Division known as the 'Iron Brigade' (to which Capt. Jean belonged). When it was discovered that the enemy had got to the rear, the brigade faced about, and, swinging its right back to connect with the next brigade in the line, threw its left around against the enemy's right, and succeeded in driving it back from the rear, so as to enable our line to fall back in order. In executing this maneuver, the two opposing forces were brought into such close proximity that several hand to hand fights occurred. In the temporary repulse of the Fifth Corps it lost perhaps one hundred prisoners, and suffered severely in killed and wounded. Subsequently, on entering the ground, it captured about four hundred of the enemy and two of their battle flags. The enemy suffered heavily. Last evening, March 31st, they could not be induced to make another charge in the Fifth Corps, front, although they had fought desperately early in the day."

Here end excerpts from Lucy Collin's account. Now we turn to James Sanford Sears. He married the granddaughter of Henry Collin, brother to our David Collin Sr. We know a little about the early days of Henry and Nancy Collin in Benton, New York, in the western Finger Lakes region, and all they had to cope with to establish a foothold in an unforgiving environment. It is not an inconsiderable statement to say that the environment was unforgiving. We know about disease and physical weaknesses, but we do not often consider how inconsiderate the natural environment is. If you are not prepared for any travesty when you are out in the deep woods, some sort of travesty will find you and happen. If you are trying to make a life in a world that does not care whether you succeed, one that is godless by your own lights, at least (but not necessarily without spirit . . . a subtle difference), the call to will is powerful, and Henry Collin answered the call with all the will available to the increasingly mighty Collin clan.

Henry's granddaughter did not marry Sanford until 1870, by which time he had begun a nursery business in nearby Geneva. Sanford (known as such apparently by the family instead of James) had enlisted in the New York Heavy Artillery in 1863 and was soon promoted from private to quartermaster (in charge of supplies). The brief selections of his diary that we have give a less romantic view of the war than Lucy Collin's: the feeding and supplying of the men on the line who died or at least risked their lives for the "Cause." Without the plodding and routine effort of such soldiers as Sanford Sears, those on the front could not have functioned. We also get a sense of how hard it was to march from one point to another. General So-and-So moved on to position X, while that compelled us to move on to position Y twenty miles away. Most of the soldiers who had to make these maneuvers had to walk them (going on foot with gear, however many miles the commanding officer, often on a horse, commanded them to walk). It does little to ennoble those on the front line without recognizing those who provided the necessary support enabling them to be there. Here are a few pages from James Sanford Sears's journal, during the sieges of Petersburg and Richmond, to give a taste of the behind-the-scenes action. He was twenty-seven at the time.

April 22, 1864

Started from W. Richmond [New York, on Long Island] at noon[.] Got to N.Y. [City], took steamboat for South Amboy— Took [train] car for Washington. In Philadelphia at one a.m. got breakfast and on we went.

Saturday, April 23

Passed through Wilmington, Del. Passed through Baltimore today. Got started for Washington at 8 p.m.

April 24

In Washington at 4 a.m. and all day. Roamed about the city all day. A pleasant day visited the capital etc. etc.

Monday, April 25

A rainy morning. Started for Alexandria early. Got over to Alexandria at night. Fly tents given us. We pitched them and were busy at our baggage all the evening.

Tuesday, April 26

Busy packing and unpacking goods and drawing rations etc. etc.

Wednesday, April 27

Still at Alexandria and busy at the boxes etc. etc. Tried to get to do something at Pay Rolls but did not do much.

Thursday, April 28

Got our boxes packed and started them for Alexandria store rooms. I sent a box home with some of my things in. Received and issued clothing to company. 124 pr. shoes and 124 pr. socks. Left 35 prs. shoes and 28 prs. socks at Alexandria in Store. In camp near Alexandria struck tents at ten 2 [?] lift [?]. We staid until p.m. Going three miles this side of Fairfax at 11:30 p.m.

Saturday, April 30, 1864

Reveille 6 o'clock a.m. Marched at 7 passing through Fairfax. At house on over the old 2nd Bull Run Battleground at Manassas. Encamped 5 miles beyond. Very weary and footsore.

Sunday, May 1

Marched at 7 a.m. and overhauled the regiment at Warrenton Juncture. Hitched trucks, were 2nd at Warrenton Juncture. Worked at Pay Rolls. Had severe storm of wind and rain.

Tuesday

All day at Warrenton Junction. Made out Pay Rolls. Finished at 11 p.m.

Wednesday, May 4

Marched at 6 a.m. for Brandy Station. Arrived 3 p.m. Rested one half hour and turned back. Marched three miles, encamped. Men without rations. An act of some change of base operations.

Thursday, May 5

We marched at 7 a.m. for Germania Ford. Encamped at 10 o'clock p.m. So tired and footsore we could not pitch tents slept on ground under our blanket. At 12 o'clock bugle sounded an advance.

Friday, May 6

Marched until 4 o'clock and [?] our outer pickets. Our battalion went on picket, remained until 10 o'clock rec orders to advance at 6 o'clock [?] and musketry commenced a new front.

Saturday, May 7

The battle lasted about three hours. On our march we passed over the ground the wounded were strewn along both sides of the way and they were busy burying the dead. But the day was over. At [?] o'clock we halted where the battle was raging and the air was filled with shells. I received a slight sun stroke on the march but went on duty.

Sunday, May 8

... our men built breast works near a mile long all sound as yet. John B. Hall scared half to death and ran to the trains.

Monday, May 9

Marched on and halted a few miles southwest of Fredericksburg. The Brigade was drawn up in a line of battle. Pair out on picket.

Tuesday, May 10

Laid still all day. Jonathan came to me as cook in place of Drexlor. A pleasant day all day and cannonading down on the front.

Wednesday, May 11

Moved up nearer to the front. Some cannonading today.

Thursday, May 12

Rainy. Joshua Reynolds killed. Corporal James A. Robinson killed. A. C. Nelson, John Drexlor, W. G. C. Henry, W. Morgan, R. Evans, W. James Emens, Andrew Br[?]eitwait, W. John and I went down to Fredericksburg with the wagons.

Friday, May 13

Thomas Henderhaw Jr. near Fredericksburg with the train. Rainy. Heavy fighting all day yesterday.

Saturday, May 14

John and I went up to the Rig [?] and cooked beef for Co. all night. Curtis helped. No letters from home yet. Near Spotsylvania Court House.

Sunday, May 15

Stayed in our tent all day except when drawing and issuing rations. Got through at 3 p.m. Enjoyed a quiet hour after that. Had a hard shower. No letters from home yet. Rations issued for five days.

Monday, May 16, 1864

Near Spotsylvania Court House. Still and all quiet until 9 a.m. No letters from home. How nice it would be to hear from all the loved ones at home. How I would enjoy some home scenes now. Will I ever enjoy that privilege let alone know it?

Tuesday, May 17

Much as yesterday. A pleasant day. Issued 3 days rations. No letters from loved ones. No loving words from home. No fighting up to 4 p.m. How sweet are the promises of Jesus to me. My trust is in him alone. How strange seems this life to me.

Wednesday, May 18, 1864

9 miles from Fredericksburg, S. West. A pleasant morning. Cannonading brisk for a few hours in the a.m. Shells flew around me. Some of us were killed and wounded. No letters from home. How I would like to hear from all I love. Jesus is near me and precious. May he ever be so and may my soul find peace and joy in trusting him.

Thursday, May 19

A little rain last night. Called at 3 a.m. and started on South for the evening. Up to now in a beautiful country and a most lovely day. Stopped in a lovely spot. Fixed up our cooking place in a pine grove. Cooked beef. Our days rations of beef. A letter from home. All well.

Friday, May 20

In same place as yesterday. A most lovely day. All quiet. drew 2 days rations up to the 23rd. A letter from home and a letter from Julia Childs. It seems so nice to receive letters once more.

Saturday, May 21

A lovely morning. All quiet. How the weeks do roll on and into eternity. I am delighted with the country and the weather. But how sad that war should thus desolate the country. At 1/2 past 5 p.m. started on a march forward. 1000 prisoners taken. Marched all night. Pleasant moonlight and warm.

May 22 and 23

Halted in the morning and got breakfast. A lovely day and most lovely country. well watered. Nice oak timber. Halted for the night at 4 p.m. in a nice wood by [?] water, Passed a nice church, Little bethel, a pump cloudy, had a nice wash and change of clothes. Had a quiet night. Slept well and got up in good season. Cooked breakfast and started on to Richmond. marched until dark—slowly in the a.m. faster in the p.m. A hard fight near Hanover Court House. A very pleasant day. Up all night cooking beef for Co.

Tuesday, May 24

Had time for breakfast. A little fishing at daybreak, sun ceased entirely. Issued rations for two days. Beef 2 days rations. In p.m. received orders to move across the river. I and the cooks carried rations on our backs, forded North Anna river. rained. I slept with wet legs and feet.

May 25, Wednesday

Up in the morning and carried the rations. lay on the bank of the river all a.m. and slept. In the p.m. made coffee for the men. Wrote a letter to father & Mother & sister and brother. Commenced letter to Tabbie. Slept well all night.

May 26, Thursday

Up early in the morning and made coffee for the men. Next got rations. Took all the a.m. and till almost night, 3 days commencing tomorrow. At 6 p.m. received marching orders and in the evening crossed the river and lay on the North bank. Slept well.

May 27, Friday

A pleasant morning. At sun up we got breakfast. Fell in. Changed position a little. Lay in the woods until about noon. Got coffee ready for the men and had to throw it away. Fell in and marched until 10 p.m. Slept in an old cornfield right on the sand. Wrote a letter to Cary and also to Tabbie Morrow. A beautiful day. Passed St. Paul's church.

May 28, Saturday

Up at 1/2 past four. Made coffee and had time to eat breakfast. A very pleasant morning. Started at 1/2 past 8 a.m. Marched very nicely all the a.m. Stopped at noon. In p.m. passed through a fine section of country and fine clover field. At 8 stopped. On watch until 2 a.m. Tired out. Camped in a wheat field.

May 29, Sunday

Bugler blew at 7 o'clock and off we go. Marched 2 miles and stayed all day. Got a ration of beef and poultry. Cooked it and issued it to the men. Cousin Albert came to see me. At Salem church 2 miles from where we crossed the Pamunkey river I went to general Hancock's headquarters and saw Albert more. Another ration of beef. sent letters home and to Cary Reed.

May 30, Monday

At 9 a.m. we're ready to march. Moved at 11 and only 3 or 4 miles in a pine wood. Drew rations ... beef, tack etc. we stayed 2 miles in rear of rgt. were all the p.m. marching 4 miles. The men built breast works during the night. I was not very well. Slept but little. Fighting just at night.

May 31, Tuesday

A pleasant day. In the woods all day. Moved less than 1/4 of a mile. Drew one day's rations for the Co. Beef at night. John made out a monthly report. I was not very well. My bowels troubled me. heavy firing in various directions from us. No letters from home for some time.

June 1, 1864 Wednesday

A most splendid morning. Slept in an oak wood. Birds singing very sweetly. The beauties of nature have summoned me. But man's hand in war spoils it. how sad. drew 2 day's rations. A skirmish in which company C, D, G, and M were hurt some. A few killed and wounded.

June 2

A very lovely morning. All quiet. Slept well. felt well this morning. Got beef. Washed myself and clothes. Enjoyed it much. 1/2 past 9 a.m. Must take a sleep. Orders to march at noon. Moved to the left. At dusk had a sharp fight. Two of our Co. men wounded. Lt. Bentley and Capt. Kaefer killed and Lt. Tallman wounded. Slept wet and cold outdoors.

June 3, Friday

Up at dawn. Got beef and cooked it in a.m. The battle commenced at 7 a.m. Three lines of battle advanced on the enemy. Several batteries opened on the Rebs. Furious fighting all day. All quiet at night. John quite sick.

June 4, Saturday

As yesterday except some cannonading in various directions. Cooked beef. John real sick. Got ready to move in p.m. Moved at 5 o'clock. halted at dark in an open field. Got a letter from Aunt Maria. Wrote an answer. Sent a letter to De.

June 5, Sunday

Rainy morning. Here I am way down near Richmond out in the rain. yet all is sweet and precious in the heart within for jesus is near and dear. How precious, precious, precious. Saw John Wheeler of the 94th NY Nothing to eat. At ten went after rations, got 5 days. All quiet today. Somewhat discouraged about the Co. & officers. Two miles from the Ohio [railroad?]. Moved just at night about two miles. One days ration of beef.

June 6, Monday

Our men entrenched themselves a little east of Gold W[?] and 6 miles from Mechanicsville. Some shelling from the North. A pleasant day. Wrote letters to father and Sister. nothing of consequence done. Rec'd most excellent letter from Esther & also Uncle Beldin.

June 7, Tuesday

A lovely day. Not much done except shelling in the P.M. Down two days rations of sack coffee etc. and beef. Rewrote to father and Uncle Beldin. Hope to get mail more regular now. How I would like to attend prayer meeting in Castleton.

June 8, Wednesday

A most lovely day. As pleasant as can be. Sent a letter this morning to Uncle B. How much I do love him. McAllister, Pat Rinehan, M. Sullivan, R. Komby. E. D. C. Jones, Frank Epley & L. D. Wolever, E. W. Owens detached for Light Artillery. All quiet all day. Pleasant and warm all night.

June 9, Wednesday

A pleasant morning. In the same position as yesterday. Beef killed. 2 days rations. Issued part raw and the remainder cooked. No mail today. Nothing of importance going on. had a nice wash in river water as could be found anywhere. Went for 2 days rations at dusk. Got to my camp at 12 p.m.

June 10, 1864, Friday

Up early and issued two rations. Sick in the a.m. in p.m. got 2 days rations. Got a paper from [?] containing salt, pepper and cherries. A pleasant day. All quiet. 2 days rations in. Got beef.

June 11, Sunday [Saturday]

Went to see cousin Henry. Had a nice visit with him and Cousin Augustus, and Norton Worden was killed last night while sitting near Henry. The rebs threw a few shells over among us. I got a letter from Mrs. Post. No particular news.

June 12, Sunday

All quiet except a few shells dropped in by Johnny Rebs. Got a day's ration of beef & cooked it. Rec'd 23 pairs pants and 62 socks and issued them. sent a requisition for more. Issued the clothing with little trouble and noise. Had order to move at 6 p.m. Started at dark and marched all night. Rested only a short time. Stopped 4 miles from White House Landing and got breakfast.

June 13

Met John Namick, wish good cheer from R. Mitchell of N.Y. City I must write him. Moved toward Harrison Landing. Marched until 12 p.m. Stopped in a corn field. Slept well. Pleasant country to march in.

June 14, Tuesday

Up early. Got our coffee and tack ready and ate. Started at 7 a.m., Marched all day. Rested occasionally. Crossed the Chickahamong and through a beautiful country. Stopped at 5 p.m. for supper. 1/2 mile from James River. Up till 12 p.m. getting beef. The Rgt. laid on a pleasant hill.

June 15, Wednesday

Up very early—crossed the james River on Pontoon bridge. Stopped a mile from the river and stayed. Got rations and rested until after midnight. Started on for Petersburg. I was very well indeed. A lovely section of the country as can be.

June 16, Thursday

Stopped about 1/2 past 8 a.m. for breakfast. Got tired out almost more so than ever in the campaign. No letter from home in a long time. Followed up the river, it was pretty hot day and I nearly exhausted. Got to the front at dark or a little before.

June 17, 1864, Friday

Laid and slept late in the morning. felt used up completely. The Rgt. was posted in the front line of battle. A hot day. lay in the woods all day. Our rgt. made a charge and took the Reb's breastworks just at sundown. Several wounded and several killed in other Co.'s Maj. Hodges killed. Maj. Reynolds prisoner. Spaulding missing.

June 18, Saturday

Drew 4 days' rations. Got a few beans. The boys very much pleased. Got them issued at 10 p.m. Cooked coffee and went to bed. Got a letter from Tabbie, and from Cary. paper from Mother with a nice mess of dried apples also one from Tabbie and the maple sugar gone from it.

June 19, Sunday

A lovely Sunday. Cooked the beans for the Co. Enjoyed them very much. Slept some. Read papers some, wrote home. How would I love to hear from home. Don't think all my letters get home. Enjoyed a very quiet Sabbath. So all through the campaign. No fighting Sunday.

June 20, Monday

A letter from home. (De and Grandma). De did not tell me what ailed him only that he was on his back. I'll try and be thankful I'm not sick here far away from home and friends. Quiet all day. Down one days' rations. Got dried apples, beans, potatoes and whiskey. After dark moved up to the front line of battle.

June 21, Tuesday

Cooked our beans for breakfast and enjoyed them very much. read some, wrote one or two letters. Did little else. Our Rgt. in the front all day and night. Bullets from sharp shooters very plenty. A few men wounded.

June 22, Wednesday

A fine morning. Up and got breakfast. Went up to CO. Got a ration of beef. Cooked it for dinner. Beans for breakfast. Drew and issued clothing to the company. Sharp shooters firing constantly while I was issuing. Dunbar in command of Co.

June 23, Thursday

A fine morning. Our forces made an attack on the extreme left wing. Took some prisoners. Got beef this morning. Busy at clothing accounts all day. Drawing and issuing rations all night—until after sunrise. Got whiskey in the morning. A very warm day. The Rebs made an attack just after dark. Were repulsed.

June 24, Friday

A very warm day. Did but little. A letter from the Independent Office. Did but little all day. Heavy cannonading for a few minutes while eating breakfast. Issued one ration of whiskey to the men. The Reg. changed position a little ahead and to the right. Drew whiskey for the company.

June 25, Saturday

The same as yesterday. Very hot. No letters from home. Nothing of importance transpired. Drew rations just after dark and kept them until morning. Some picket firing in the evening. Wrote a letter to Hannah Stevens.

June 26, Sunday

A very hot day. All quiet along the lines. Enjoyed a quiet hour by myself in the woods. How different our circumstances from the folks at home. How would I enjoy a quiet Sabbath at home with friends and brothers and sisters. In the Sabbath school and in the choir do they miss me still? A little sick. Another day shall dawn.

June 27

Not very well this morning. The question comes up and I am prepared to meet my Savior should he call me home today. Search me, Oh God, and try me and lead me in the way of life. A precious letter from Uncle Beldin Sears. Answered it. A letter from Julia Judd. Wrote to Tabbie. Felt well in [p.m.?]

June 28

A pleasant morning. Drew 2 days rations and issued them. Got dinner and went to City Parrish and got old Muster Rolls and left some things in the box. Got some paper and envelopes. Enjoyed the ride and saw the community. Got back at 9 p.m.

June 29, Wednesday

Worked all day on a muster roll. Got it ready at dark. A pleasant day. Cool. Wrote a letter to sister Nettie and sent it. Capt. [?] shot dead while swearing at some of his men. Hill before Petersburg.

June 30, Thursday

Drew two days rations and issued them. Tack, coffee, sugar, dried apples, pork, beans, sour kraut, etc. Enough to try me pretty thoroughly in dealing out rations. Mustered about noon. Not very well today.

July 1, Friday

Not very well. Issued whiskey to the company. Sanitary commission gave us 31 lemons. A warm day. Sent a letter to Julia Judd, to Millie Tuttle and Mary Wheat. No letters from home. Drew rations 2 days.

July 2, Saturday

Issued rations to the company. Got very hungry and tired before I got through. Had applesauce for breakfast. Made one copy of muster rolls in all day. Quite pleasant the most of the time. Rec'd a letter from D dated June 28. Answered it today. Our Rgt. moved up into the first line of breastworks (July 3) during the night. A fine morning and well. Commenced another copy of pay rolls. Worked at it until 12 past 4 p.m. Got Lea then drew 2 days of rations. One of soft bread for the 4th of July. The [?] came thick as I was issuing the rations.

July 4, Monday
    I finished issuing the rations and then worked at payrolls all day until 3 p.m. Took a nap and [?]. Did little else.

Here end the extracts from Sanford's diaries. The city of Petersburg did not capitulate until April of the following year, after a ten-month siege.

The third family member to participate in the war was Henry Knapp, grandfather of Betsy Knapp, the guardian of the family archives in our era. The following derives from Ruth Stong's genealogy, from interviews with Betsy Knapp, and from Henry Knapp's letters home from the various fronts on which he served.

According to his granddaughter, Henry Knapp was educated in the common schools and Syracuse High School, which he was attending at the outbreak of the Civil War. He entered the military on September 9, 1862, aged nineteen, as a member of Company 1, 3rd N.Y. Volunteer Cavalry, and performed constant and honorable service (as the letters below attest) in eastern North Carolina and Virginia until July 1864, when he received an appointment in the acting assistant adjutant-general's office at the headquarters of General Kautz's Cavalry Division, Army of the James. When he returned home in 1865 he worked in the office of the city surveyor of Syracuse until the spring of 1866, when he returned to the family farm in DeWitt, currently a suburb between Fayetteville and Syracuse, which he operated for three years while teaching in district schools during the winter. In April 1869, he bought an interest the furniture-making firm of J. & D. Decker in Fayetteville. The firm was Decker and Knapp for fourteen years, then in 1883 he bought out the senior partner and conducted the business alone successfully for many years.

Always a Republican, Henry Knapp was president of Fayetteville in 1893, served as trustee of the village and school for several years, and was a prominent member of the Baptist Church. It might be helpful to note that Lincoln's Republican Party later became what we now think of as the Democratic Party. The issue of slavery had split the old Democratic and Whig parties, making new party alignments necessary. Lincoln's

Republican Party was formed only in 1855, through opposition to the Kansas-Nebraska Bill of 1854 (regarding slavery in western territories). While antislavery factions made up the bulk of the party, abolitionist and Free-Soil (a popular movement in central New York) parties also threw their lot in with the new party. Within a single year they became a national organization and in 1856 competed strongly for the presidency, even though they lost to Buchanan. They did well in the congressional elections of 1858. When Lincoln was successful at the polls in 1860, his election was a signal for the secession of the South. The Civil War followed. In June 1878 Henry Knapp was commissioned as captain of the 51st Regiment of the state National Guard. From 1908–1911 he was treasurer of Onondaga County and often led the anniversary parades in the village and city on one of his fine horses.

His letters give another perspective on the war. They tell of his seeing considerable action, yet have little of the romance of Captain Jean's nor the plodding monotony of James Sears's accounts. It is his youthful enthusiasm and down-to-earth sense of reality that get him through. These traits, these roots are part of the heritage he brings back to his own family and later to his sons, one of whom marries into the Collin clan. His were traits the Collins appreciated well above other values, and so the map of earnest Baptists and Presbyterians continued to expand and interconnect. The Collin family's heritage was fertile ground for these roots to find a rich and varied soil.

At the start of these letters, Henry Knapp is in the river town of Washington, North Carolina, up the Pamlico River from the coast, under siege by Confederate troops who are also blockading the lower portions of the river.

> Henry Knapp
> Washington, NC
> October 28, 1862

Dear Parents,

    I may have little leisure and I thought I would improve the time in writing. I arrived in this place last Tuesday one week ago today. It is a very pleasant village. Much more modern style than Newbern [New Bern, North Carolina]. There are a few very beautiful houses here. I suppose you know they had quite a fight here about the time I enlisted. Well I have seen a little of the effects of that fight. There is one house that was once a very pretty house but is now nearly riddled to pieces with grape shot canister and shell from the gunboats. The principle streets here have been blockaded since the fight so as to prevent them, the rebels, from [getting?] so far next time. We have considerable picket duty to perform here. During the week which I have been here I have been on picket three times. We have to go on 3 times in seven days. Picketing goes very well in the daytime but in the night it is rather lonesome. We send out two men on a road and during the day they both stand together but in the night only one so as to give the others a chance to sleep. We go out 1 1/2 or 2 miles. The woods have all been cut down out as far as we go so that it is rather hard for cavalry to catch us but we just got orders to saddle. Probably going out on a scout.

Thursday evening—it is a good place for infantry to lay in ambush. It was as I expected this forenoon when we had orders to saddle up. We sent out a scouting party on two roads. The captain went with one and the 1st Lieut. went with the other. I went with the Lieut. We went out about eight miles. It was most of the way through the woods. We had to ford one stream where the bridge had been destroyed. The water was about 4 or 4 1/2 feet deep. We were going a pretty good jog when we saw the Rebs. We came pretty close to them before they saw us. They were back behind a barn and when they heard us coming they began to pile out to see what was up. They had no arms on. I presume they had little thought we were so near. As soon as they saw us they "skedaddled" back behind the barn, probably to get their arms, but that we did not wait to find out. Our object accomplished we wheeled about and started for home and that but very slow I can assure you. We went back fully satisfied with the scout. I should have said before there were but eight of us, Lieut. included. It was a pretty bold dash for so few. They might easily have caught us by lying in ambush. The gray horses have got a pretty big name around here. That is what brought the company back here. There is an old [?] out in the country that has offered 13 dollars apiece for every gray horse and rider the Rebs would catch dead or alive. They seem to be a perfect dread to all secessiondom.

I was out on picket day before yesterday on the road where those [were] shot and went to the very spot where they were killed. My health continues good and Charlie's also. Three of the boys that came out in our squad are in the hospital one of which is William Thompson. The rest are all well I believe. It is rather sickly around here this fall. Has been quite so. It will probably get more healthy when cold weather comes. We have had one slight frost. The sickness seems to be mostly fever and ague.

The boat came in tonight and no mail for me. I expected something as much as could be. It is nearly time to blow out lights and I expect to go on picket tomorrow so I can not write much more till day after tomorrow. I got two letters a few days ago. One from Helen and one from Levi Lathrop in Syracuse. Thursday morning—I just came in off picket and thought I would finish my letter. It was pretty cold last night. we had another slight frost. When I was out on picket the other day I took a darkie out with me to pick up some walnuts. He got me about 3 pecks which I have laid by for winter use. I get plenty of apples while on picket from people coming into town to sell them. Provisions are pretty high here. Butter 40 ct. a pound and not first rate at that. Irish potatoes twelve shillings per bushel. Cheese 20 cts. Sweet potatoes we can get any quantity of for 50 ct. per bushel.

There are some beautiful flowers here now. On the road that I picketed yesterday there is a large plantation where I got my walnuts (now deserted). I got off my horse and went into the garden there the other day and picked some beautiful roses (red and white) and made a rosette of them, put them in my coat and wore them into town. I thought they were pretty nice. In the garden where I got them there were a lot of nice sea shells on the ground which had once probably decorated some nice room. I should have liked to have sent some home but could not. The library of the house had been torn to pieces, all the books of any account plundered and the rest lay there at least those that had not been torn to pieces.

I have seen several cotton fields since I have been here. The cotton is just about right for the first picking. I wish I could send you a nice stalk of it. It would be quite a curiosity. Corn has been ripe for some time. Thursday afternoon. A boat has arrived this noon bringing some more troops. They had three pieces of artillery and men enough to man them. They said there were two or three regiments more of infantry and three more pieces of artillery coming within a day or two. (Whether they are going to make an advance or bringing them here to winter or not I cannot say. If they come here to winter we shall think ourselves pretty safe.) I believe I have written everything that would be of interest to you. From your affectionate son . . . P.S. If you can keep any run of my letters you can do pretty well, for it is as much as ever that I can.

November 15, 1862

Supposing you would be anxious to hear from me I thought I would improve this opportunity of writing. I think it is about time for me to get a letter from home. Have been looking for one for two weeks.

I told you in my last letter that we were about to start on an expedition. Well we started on Sunday morning Nov. 2nd. After we had left town about 5 or 6 miles our advance guard had a little skirmish with the rebel pickets and got two horses shot in the legs, but no man hurt. We then went on about 12 or 13 miles further within about 3 miles of Williamstown [N.C.]. There our advance guard got a pretty strong volley of musketry. By the way I will say our advance guard consisted of two pieces of marine artillery and about 20 cavalry men. 42 of which was from our company. One of the marines was shot here and one or two horses but not any from our company. The cavalry here fell back and several companies of infantry were ordered ahead. They went on into the woods (for here it is nearly all woods) and for a few minutes there was pretty sharp firing I can assure you. After a while the rebs left and all was quiet. We were then formed into a line again for forward movement and just before starting we got quite a heavy volley of musketry. The bullets whistled around our heads pretty sharp for a while but strange to say no one was hurt much. We were ordered to [?], dismount and tear down the fence and go into a small cleared lot which was on one side of the road. We were formed into a line and some infantry and 5 or 6 pieces of Artillery went ahead. The infantry had some skirmishing and the artillery opened a pretty brisk fire on them mostly with shell, some solid shots. Soon all was quiet again for a few minutes. The Rebs then brought forward a piece of Artillery and threw some 5 or 6 shells over amongst us, but only the last two came very near. They then just got a good range on us. The last one struck I should think about two rods [one rod is 16.5 ft.] from where I was and rolled in under the horses of the company ahead of us. It did not burst. The fuse burnt down to the shell and went out. I believe no one was hurt by their shell. The infantry in their skirmishing lost 3 or 4 killed and several wounded. We finally succeeded in driving them from their entrenchment and encamped in them for the night. We afterwards learned they had about 3 regiments of infantry and one or two pieces of artillery. I should have said before that we had a pretty good strong force. I believe about ten thousand including 34 pieces of artillery.

Well the next morning at daylight we were underway and when within about a mile of the town our company was ordered to charge into the town and see what was there. With drawn pistol we started and did not stop until we reached the further side of the town. When we got there we found the gunboats there with the American flag hoisted. And I tell you we gave the old flag three good rousing cheers. Then we halted to wait for the rest of the column to come up. Our first Lieut. took ten men to go into several of the houses to see what we could find and I was one of the number. We went into a store and I got an old watch, a pair of gloves and several other things of minor importance. I should say however we entered no buildings except those that were deserted.

The rebs retreated through there the night before and most of the citizens left with them. We staid there until afternoon and started on, encamped that night in a cornfield. Started on the next morning and got into Hamilton in the afternoon. Found the gunboats there and the village deserted. We staid there until about 9 o'clock in the evening. The soldiers commenced burning the houses so that the general ordered us on. We went on two or three miles and encamped in the woods. In the morning we started on towards Tarboro went to within about eight miles of the place and encamped again in a cornfield expecting to attack the enemy in the morning near Tarboro where we knew them to have a strong force. It was rumored around in camp that they had 25 thousand men but not much artillery. In the morning we mounted our horses expecting to have a big battle. Our captain told us to try to keep cool and together, as much as possible. We expected to go back about 5 miles and take another road. We started to go back but for some reason or other did not stop until we reached Hamilton. It rained nearly all day. We got a house to stay in for the night and shelter for our horses. In the morning we got up and found it snowing. The first bad weather we have had. We marched the next day to Williamstown, staid there for the night in a house. We expected to stay there the next day. About 10 o'clock the next day word came that if we would be ready in 10 minutes we could go through to Washington. You can make up your mind things flew for a few minutes. We had about a half-hog on the boiling that the boys had killed and a kettle of sweet potatoes, all about half done. They threw it all out upon the ground. Our company and two others and two pieces of artillery came through in about 1/2 an hour. We came to carry a message of some kind for you. [?]. The rest of the forces staid there and I understand they are in Newbern now. I understand the object of the expedition was to draw the forces away from Weldon. So that Gen. Dix wouldn't take that place. If that was the object and he did it, it was a big thing for it cuts off the [rail?] communication with the South. But if he did not take it I can't see what we did of any consequence.

I came back with the conclusion that destruction followed an army. All along the road and especially where we stopped the chickens, geese, turkeys, pigs etc. had to suffer [?] bees At one place near where we stopped to eat dinner there were a dozen or more swarms of bees. The soldiers would knock over a hive and kick it to pieces, stick their hands into the honeycomb anywhere as if there were no bees. In a short time the man's honeybees and all were gone. They stripped that man completely of everything he had that they could make use of. You may be glad you don't live in the vicinity of the [war?]. You cannot be thankful enough.

Our company went out on scout of five or six yesterday and they came very near getting taken.

The following journal entries were sent home as a letter, but the first page is missing. Internal evidence indicates it is probably from 1863 around Washington, North Carolina, where Henry had been stationed prior to traveling north to Portsmouth, Virginia, to prepare for the push to Petersburg and Richmond.

April 5, 1864[?]
It was pretty quiet all day. No firing in town but considerable down the River.

April 6
But very little cannonading in town.

April 7
The rebs commenced again in the morning, and kept it up nearly all day.

8th
The rebs directed their fire mostly on the gunboats but did them very little damage, only hit them 2 or 3 times. Gunboats did not return the fire.

9th
Pretty quiet. Our pickets had a talk with the rebel pickets.

10th

The rebs opened a heavy fire in the morning from their batteries all along on the hills in the north of the town. Kept it up for about an hour and then ceased for most of the day. A schooner ran the [rebel] blockade last night loaded with ammunition.

11th

They opened fire the same as yesterday and lasted about as long. One of their shells went through our Captain's quarters.

12th

Cannonading about as normal. I sent a letter on a schooner that will run the blockade tonight.

13th

The Rebs opened a new battery across the river. Heard heavy cannonading in the direction of it when supposed it to be our forces coming from Newbern.

14th

The steamer *Escort* ran the blockade last night loaded with ammunition and provisions also the 5th Rhode Island Regmt. The rebs opened heavy fire on her but did not hit her, cannonading nearly all day.

15th

Another schooner ran the blockade last night. The *Escort* ran down this morning with Gen. Foster on board. The Rebs opened very heavy fire on her. Hit her about 17 times. One shot went through Gen. Foster's bed from which he had been only about five minutes. The pilot was killed by a sharpshooter. [Foster was one of the important Yankee generals stationed in the South in New Bern, North Carolina, about seventy miles southeast of Washington, North Carolina, also on a river, to block Confederate access to the sea. He was in command of a larger force than the one in Washington and was working to break up the Confederate blockade of Washington for two reasons: first, to cripple the large force of rebels laying siege to Washington; and second to join forces with the Washington Garrison to then head north to Virginia for the engagement at Petersburg and Richmond.]

16th

The Rebs have left their fortification on the outside of the town this morning. Our company went scouting all around the town but saw nothing of the rebs. Some firing between the batteries across the river and the gunboats but the boats drove them out and we sent some infantry to take possession of their breastworks on Rodman's Point and tear them down. They captured a rebel captain and several privates. Found two guns bursted and one in the mud so that the rebs could not get it away. This was the end of the siege. That larger steamer the *Escort* running the blockade in open daylight I understand was the reason of their leaving. They supposed they had the river effect really blockaded and intended to starve us out. Our casualties w[ere] 7 killed and some 20 or 30 wounded. They had the town surrounded with about 15 thousand men. We had only 15 or 16 hundred. They had orders to charge on our breastworks and take the town but could not get their men to do it and the men showed their good sense in not doing it. It seems as if God was with us. In every movement one might see his guiding hand. I don't believe nor I did not believe any of the time that although at times it looked very dark, that He would permit them to come in here and take all of these praying black men and women back into bondage.

April 21, Tuesday

Last Sunday General Foster got here from Newbern overland with troops. Everything is quiet now. we expect to be relieved tomorrow from picket duty and go to Newbern. I saw Charlie Webster yesterday. [One of the interesting things about the Civil War was its personal nature, in that one could meet friends and relations by chance even though so many were scattered all over the region of conflict.] He is in Co. A and came in the expedition with General Foster from Newbern. [They were going to New Bern after Washington was freed because the river at New Bern was not blockaded as the lower Pamlico River still was.] The 15 or 16 hundred men of which I spoke as being the garrison of this place were white men. We had besides them between 2 and 3 hundred negroes armed by them. The rebs can't say much about arming the negroes because Gen. Spinola who started from Newbern to reinforce us [but was driven back] captured a negro orderly Sergt. between here and Newbern.

I will try and draw you another map of the place showing you the position of the batteries and fortifications, both rebel and federal. Last Sunday we had a meeting, the first one we have had in about 3 weeks. It seemed real good to have all things quiet again.

My love to all.

Yours as ever,
Henry J. Knapp

Washington N.C.
May 17, 1863

Dear Parents,

A boat came today and I thought I would write a few words just to let you know that we are all well.

I have drawn you a map [see illus. 11] of the batteries and fortifications around Washington by which you can have some idea of our position. The batteries below I had no room to draw. They were in "Hills Point" about 112 miles down the river [the Pamlico River, which leads into Pamlico Sound and Cape Hatteras on the Outer Banks] and were only used to blockade the river. The forts "Hamilton," "Jackwick," and Marine Fort were built after the siege commenced. there are two other forts now in process of building. One on the island in the river and the other on our drill ground. Don't know the name of the one on the island but the one on the drill ground is to be called "Ft. Spinola" after the Gen. who has command of this post. The Jackwick is not occupied now and I presume Ft. Hamilton will be left when Ft. Spinola is finished.

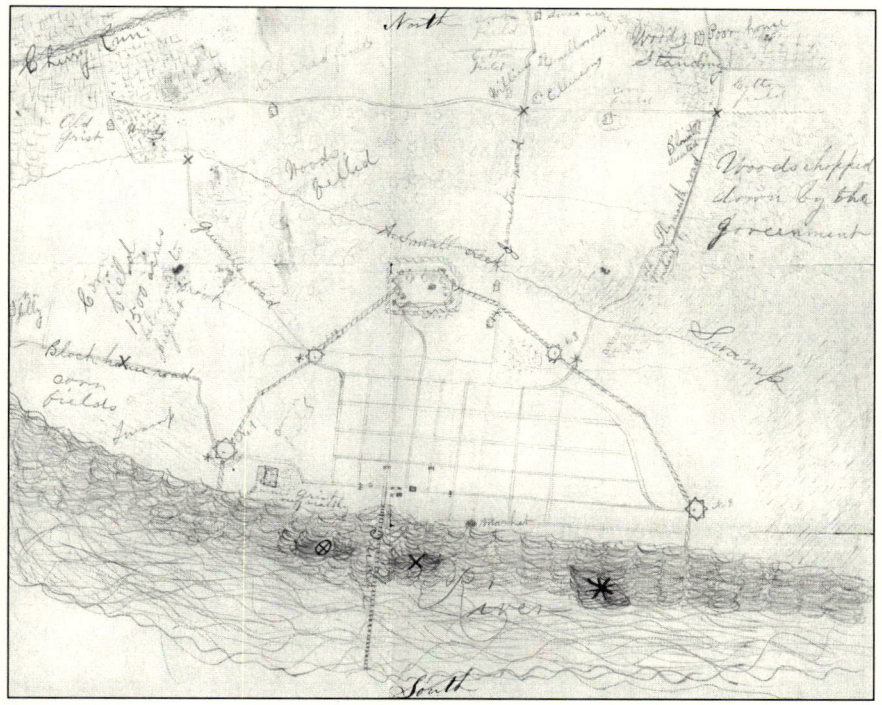

Map and drawing of the siege of Washington, N.C., made in the field by Henry Knapp, 1863

I sent you 40 dollars [$700] in my last letter. I have felt quite anxious to hear from it. Hope you will get it all safe.

We are having splendid weather but pretty warm. Peas have been in blossom abut 2 weeks. We shall have some green peas probably before long. I have had several dishes of strawberries. Got over two quarts in my cupboard now. Wish I could send you some. It would be a great treat for you.

I got a Richmond paper of the 13th yesterday and saw one of the 14th when I was on picket and I intend to send it home. The rebs think they have done a big thing but they lost one of their best generals "Gen. Jackson." I am very anxious to hear our side of the story now. The latest papers we have got is the 8th. The new troops that have come here seem to be dying off pretty fast. They average about 2 a day. They are all drafted Pa. troops but our cavalry the North Carolinians and one regiment of Pa. I believe that was all. My love to all the friends and remember me as ever ...

P.S. Gens. Foster and Potter came up here this forenoon to inspect the fortifications at this place. That paper of the 13th that I was going to send is lost and therefore cannot send it.

Camp near Point of Rocks, Va.
June 20, 1864

Dear parents,

I presume you are anxiously looking for another letter, by this time I should have written before but we have been off in front of Petersburg for the first four or five days and have seen some pretty sharp fighting. But we are back in our old camp now, although are under marching orders and momentarily expecting to move. The first day out (last Wednesday) our company had the advance. We met with but very little resistance except occasional picket skirmishing until we got within about a mile of their outer works where we found a battery of artillery supported by some infantry. We engaged them here until some infantry came up (mostly negro troops) and then our division of Cav. started to flank them before we got around to their rear. However the negroes charged on the battery and took two guns, so of course they are all dispersed before we got up. Our cav. Div. then went around on the south of Petersburg to engage them while the infantry attracted them in front. We got in sight of their breastworks about two o'clock and the fight commenced and lasted until about night. We fought dismounted. We charged up near their breastworks once but were repulsed and under an awful fire of grape and canister and musketry. Our Vol. (Mix) acting Brigadier was mortally wounded and left on the field. We have heard by prisoners that he has since died. It is a wonder how as many escaped unhurt for it was the most terrible fire I was ever under. Had it not been for the protection of a few trees they would have cut us up terribly. About night we retired back to the 18th Army Corps on the east arch of the city. During the night the

18th Corps assisted by part of the 2nd and the Negroes worked the outer line of breastworks and forts. Them Negroes fight like tigers. As soon as we got the outer line of works we turned them on the rebs. The next day we were reinforced by the 5th and 9th Corps. and they have kept charging and taking works as they go until we had possession of their last line of works when we (our fear) left and I presume our troops are in the city now. The [?] Corps have all crossed back to Bermuda [a town on the coast] now. So the force we have South of the James consists of the 2nd, 5th, 6th and 9th Corps across the Appomattox and the 10th and 18th between the Appomattox and James. There is a heap of men come to get them all together. There is a rumor that our Cav. Div. and the 18th Corps are going into South Carolina but I hardly believe it. There is some heavy fighting going on somewhere now for I can hear the roar of cannon in the direction of Richmond or rather to the Northeast of Richmond. I am quite anxious to hear the correct statement of affairs near Petersburg. Am in hopes we captured a good many firearms there. Old Gov. Wise was captured the first night.

The 122nd is in the 6th Corps and staid near our camp one night but I did not get a chance to see them. Some of the boys went over there, however. Steve Goodfellow is there and Jim Hudson takes care of the Col's. horse.

The boys are all well from our part of the community. I forgot to acknowledge the receipt of your letter of the 12th.

Please write often and give all particulars. My love to all the friends. Hoping to hear from you again soon I remain as ever . . .

       Headquarters,
       Kautz Cavalry Division
       September 10, 1864

You will have to excuse me for not writing before. The fact is I have rather been waiting for a letter from home before I wrote and besides time has slipped away so fast that I have hardly been able to keep track of it. This summer has passed very quick indeed to me. It seems but a very little time since we started from Portsmouth last spring. I have now a little less than a year to stay. I only hope that it will pass away as fast as the past six months.

I have heard that Mr. Blanchard and [?] have enlisted. Good for them. But unless they have got a heap of patriotism they will think it rather bad speculation before their time is up, that is if they have to go into active service, particularly infantry. You need not tell anyone I said so for I don't wish to discourage them.

What is the prospect for the coming election at home? But I don't know as I need ask for our part of the State is generally on the right side. I hardly know what to think of Gen. McClellan. I have previous to this pitied him a little and thought that he had not had his just dues from the Government. [McClellan appeared to be a brilliant young general who was at one time put in charge of all the forces, but his age and inexperience caused him to react with too much caution, resulting is disastrous campaigns. While Lincoln removed him from his command, Democrats chose him as a presidential candidate. Lincoln won handsomely.] But when he accepts the nomination for President on such a platform as that of the Chicago Convention I shall sustain him no longer and indeed I had lost much confidence in him of late anyway from the company he has been keeping. When he becomes the accepted leader of such men as Valandingham, Wood, Harris, Long and all the others whose only thought is to end the war in such a manner that the Rebels may gather the fruits of victory, then I think it is time for every well wisher of this country to spurn him as a venomous reptile. "The Gentlemen may cry peace! Peace! but there is no peace." There is but one method of restoring the Union and that is by conquering back its rebellious parts. And that we are doing day by day, and doing well. For what can be more inspiring, more full of hope and promise than the general military situation of today? Farragut at Mobile, Sherman in Georgia, Grant at Petersburg each in his own turn answering the liberty loving people of the North to rejoice over their victories. But I do not propose to make a stump speech. All quiet in this quarter just now. Yesterday they were at it nearly all day. Pretty lively. What was accomplished I don't know.

I understand by Johnny Kellogg that James Baily has been heard from as a prisoner at Charleston. Hope it is so. I wish that you'd ask Mr. Bailey the next time you see him if he got the box of James's things that I sent to him some time ago. Johnny is quite well now. Is orderly for Lieut. Col. Jacobs of our Regmt.

The boys are well a far as I know. I sent some time ago for a recipe for my catarrh medicine. It is in one of Helen's letters received some time November (I think). I should also like to know if you have received all the Phrenological Journals for this year. If not, what numbers are missing? I should like to preserve them.

Remember me to all who take the trouble to inquire after me. Kiss little Ella for me and hoping to hear from you soon, I remain as ever . . .

Friday morning Sept. 16

The Rebs attacked our picket line last night. Haven't heard the exact results yet. They captured some however. We could hear them charge very plainly here at H-qtrs. We may get more of it for they haven't left us yet. The Rgmts. are formed in line to receive them. Considerable excitement. . . . Henry.

Headquarters,
Kautz Cavalry Division
October 18, 1864

Dear Father,

I received your letter of the 12th last evening. Much obliged for sending me those ballots. I went up to the Regiment this morning to get the printed Power of Attorney and Envelope. Found that they had all the necessary blanks but no ballots and no one has attended to it. The regiment is so broken up and on duty so much that they have paid little attention to it. I should like to have you send me one thousand (1,000) ballots as soon as possible if you can get them and unless I have more to do than I have at present I will attend to getting the votes. Please send by mail.

There is nothing new that I know of. The Div. is on the north side of the James doing duty and I am left back at Jones Landing in charge of the office. I have nothing to do but eat and sleep except occasionally when they have reports to make out. They send them on to have copied.

I got my express box all right. I am glad you sent the papers for they help to pass away time. The maple sugar is "par excellence." Boots came just in time.

We are having beautiful weather, only the nights are rather too cool for comfort. Especially for those who have to lay out all night.

I went off after chestnuts yesterday. Got some nice chestnuts as you ever saw.

The boys from our part of the country [?] all night as far as I know of. Kellogg is the only one out to the front now. Thompson and Babcock are at the dis-mounted camp. Thompson has not been very well lately.

I shall send my vote in a few days. Be careful when you open it not to break the inner envelope, and thereby spoil the vote.

No more at present. Hoping to hear from you soon, I am as ever . . .

(ps) I was down to City Point the other day & saw Howard Smith but did not know him. He passed not more than three feet from me. I thought it was him and was going to speak to him, started once to overtake him but thought it certainly [it could] not be him. If I had known that he was in the army I should have certainly have stopped him but did not know that he was a soldier until I got back.

Head Quarters,
Kautz Cavalry Division
November 27, 1864

Dear Parents,

Tis sabbath evening and all quiet for the want of something to do I conclude to write letters.

Am well and enjoying myself finely, only living most too high. The people at the North have been very kind in sending us our Thanksgiving dinner. We've been living on chicken and turkey for the last three or four days. Some of the finest turkeys you ever saw.

We had one for dinner today that weighed fourteen and one half pounds dressed and cooked. Besides the fowl we have had jellies, apples, doughnuts, biscuits, fruitcake and most everything. Many of the articles were accompanied with letters wishing the recipients to acknowledge the receipt of the little goodies, and it has occasioned no little good feeling among the soldiers I can assure you. Yesterday I visited the famous Dutch Lake Canal and went down to the bottom of it. I should think it would take two weeks yet to finish it. Half of it is finished now, and the other half pretty well along. I should think it was between three and four hundred feet long and about fifty feet wide and about sixty or sixty five feet deep. I went down and used the picks a little while so as to have it to say that I helped dig Dutch Gap. The soil has all been formed by the action of water. I got a piece of wood from the bottom partially petrified which has probably lain there for thousands of years. It has a mineral deposits on one side about a quarter of an inch thick resembling iron. The end next to the Rebs is not disturbed, but cut down straight and shows different strata very plain. The mass of it is mostly a blue or slate colored clay. There is a thin layer of sand or gravel every foot or two. The clay, when wet, is quite easily worked. They break it out in chunks with a pick and it has every appearance of plaster in the stone, before I went down I certainly thought it was all rock. When it becomes dry it is quite hard, about like the soft stone I used to get. I brought a piece back with me that has the impression of a leaf on it very plain. I intend to continue my research some day when I can get away, if the Rebs don't throw their shell in there too fast. They were very good yesterday, did not throw one while I was there. While I was there Genls. Grant, Meade, Butler and Warren rode up to take a view of it.

My love to all and ever remember me as
Your Aff. Son,
H. J. Knapp

Who can know how heavily letters from the front weighed when they got home? We can assume that they meant something and that the cost of the war was only a little ameliorated by the increase in need for fuel and grain and stock, which remained a considerable advantage to established farmers such as the Collin family who used the canal systems and the rail systems to their fullest extent.

It is clear from these letters home from the front, not to mention the graphic papers available, such as *Harpers,* that folks in remote Central New York knew what was going on in the war and were indeed profiting from it. The relatively newly developed rails made travel and communication easy and quick, by former wilderness standards. Everyone seemed to adapt quickly and without hesitation to the changes of so-called progress.

But at the same time, something else was going on, something that no one recognized nor most certainly acknowledged: war leads to nihilism, alienation, and desecration of life. In a book review entitled "On War," Chris Hedges wrote,

> The vanquished know war. They see through the empty jingoism of those who use the abstract words of glory, honor, and patriotism to mask the cries of the wounded, the senseless killing, war profiteering, and chest-pounding grief. They know the lies the victors often do not acknowledge, the lies covered up in stately war memorials and mythic war narratives, filled with stories of courage and comradeship. They know the lies that permeate the thick, self-important memoirs by amoral statesmen who make wars but do not know war. The vanquished know the essence of war—death.

So. Three men who did not die in the war in which they all served, who were loosely connected by family ties, never met. One was so broken by the health problems contracted in the war that he is remembered by the family only as the invalid husband of his talented, artistic wife. Another became a modestly successful businessman and churchgoer who disappeared to join the majority of his anonymous silent peers. The last prospered in small ways in his small community, enriching his family heritage, but he, too, is largely forgotten. They returned from the war to a landscape untouched by battle, to communities brushed only occasionally by the immediacy of death from warfare, to a land prospering from the struggle in which they all took part.

The trajectory of John Collin's life (our Captain Jean) was weighted by the myth, the freighted capacity for storytelling, before he ever began to live his life. He was not ennobled by his character nor his actions but rather by the dreams his loving wife wished upon him.

Sanford Sears, on the evidence of his diaries, faced his life as one without choices. He lived a life he might not have chosen to live, was a man he might rather not have been, and found no myths to suit him but, instead, found a kind of acquiescent plodding reality that gave him no power to will things otherwise.

Henry Knapp seems to have lived his life without burden or pretense. The tendrils of loneliness that so often caught those trapped in overlapping myths did not touch him. He remained himself. He learned from what the world set before him. When he entered the Collin family through marriage he had no reason nor context for self-justification. It was a characteristic he bequeathed to his granddaughter, who felt she needed to tell everyone's story but her own.

9

Business as Usual

> Crack Nature's moulds, all germains spill at once,
> That make ingrateful man!
> —Shakespeare, *King Lear,* 3.2.8–9

Meanwhile, the wilderness was pushed further and further back and, at least on the surface, the pastoral ideal was being realized by those willing to work the land. The wisest among them, which included David Collin Sr. always looked for the main chance. The Collins did not really have some romantic ideal of rural prosperity. Whatever enhanced or worked to further the reality of prosperity was viable and just. The landscape of the upstate region of New York is littered with the abandoned mills, waterways, roads, and other detritus of enterprise attempted and discarded after brief periods of success. Much was invested—time, hard cash, and available technology—but modernization, change, and raw invention moved at such an unmanageable pace that many attempts at taking part in the surge of the new failed before they had barely begun.

By the mid-1820s the investments made in the Erie Canal began to see a sharp increase in value. As David Ellis put it in his *History of New York State,* "Few undertakings have so completely fulfilled the highest claims and fondest hopes of its sponsors as did the Erie Canal. The slashing of freighting costs (by more than 90 percent from Buffalo to Albany) released a torrent of produce dammed up by the prohibitive costs of hauling freight overland."

Despite the death rate among the Irish diggers (from malaria and typhoid, things we do not usually connect with the north country, and, as well, the racial disregard for human decency that held the Irish as the lowest of the low), the canal paid its way very quickly, to the extent that lateral or feeder canals could also be built and defray the general costs to maintain the larger system. The Collin family invested in a long lateral canal from the village of Fayetteville that linked it to a wide-water place along the Erie in hopes of drawing trade or commerce into the village and bringing goods from the village to the canal. It helped, but it was not enough. As Ellis points out, "Canal business gave employment to thousands. The captains usually owned their own boats and picked up cargo wherever they could find it.... Boatmen were rough and profane, liking nothing better than a chance to fight for the first place in going through a lock. Hundreds of saloons and brothels lined the banks of the Erie Canal, sometimes labeled the 'Big Ditch of Iniquity.'"

Ellis continues:

> Travelers using the packets complained of tedious delays and overcrowded quarters. The ordinary berth was only five and one-half by two feet, and three berths lined each wall of the tiny cabins. During the 1830s packets charged five cents a mile, including food, and managed to cover about one hundred miles a day. The packets lost most of their passenger business after 1842 when the railroads provided through service between Albany and Buffalo. At first freight originated largely within the borders of New York. Gradually the amount of freight originating in the western states increased, and by 1847 it equaled that of New York. Four years later it was more than double the New York figure. After 1850 the backbone of canal traffic consisted of grain and lumber from the lake states, for Erie Canal boatmen were unable to prevent pork, beef, cheese, butter, wool, and hides from slipping to the railroads during the 1850s.... Farmers and businessmen in the "sequestered counties" of New York demanded that the legislature grant as much aid to them as it had to the counties along the routes of the Erie and Champlain canals. Citizens in the Chenango Valley agitated for a canal linking the Erie canal at Utica with the Susquehanna River at Binghamton, and in 1833 the legislature approved Governor Marcy's recommendation

and authorized the ninety-seven-mile-long waterway. The coal brought up from Pennsylvania enabled capitalists, by 1846, to use steam power in the new textile mills of Utica. Important as this coal trade became, the Chenango Canal never paid its operating costs.

The Collin family needed their link, the little tributary canal to the main canal, to ease the cost of sending wool and grain east and south to the markets in the Hudson Valley and further south in the growing urban environment of New York City. It worked well for them for a time, but they were not sentimental and readily shifted to the rails when those proved more cost-effective. They saw also the value of water power as a draw to industry and hoped to provide Fayetteville with a chance to challenge Syracuse as a growing center of new manufacturing and perhaps eventually to lay the groundwork for electrical power. Thus they became major shareholders in the Ledyard Dyke, another water system separate from the canal, drawn from south of the village. Betsy Knapp wrote about it in the following way, giving the family-authorized version of the story as a natural and historical development, a necessary part of the greater scheme of things, showing them involved in more than the merely parochial. She also, clearly, tramped the damp length of the canal herself to familiarize herself with its details. The dike is a good example of the ruins of a fine idea that seemed viable at the time—one good enough to entice the careful Collin family to back it. But, as we can see from Betsy Knapp's investigation, the technology, while complex, was not forward-looking. Market needs quickly outstripped the ability of the dike to provide power to feed those needs. I believe it is important to see in detail at least one instance of the physical scale and economic scope of what became thousands of such lost, ruined constructions around the state. What we find left is a well-thought-out but uninventive weed-filled relic of hope amidst rapid change:

> Historically, the site of power resources was one of the major factors in determining the location of manufacturing. For centuries human and animal muscle was the major source of power for industry, until the mechanization brought about by the Industrial Revolution brought demands for power in much greater amounts. Until the development of the steam engine in the mid-nineteenth

century, power was primarily obtained directly from running water and mechanized industries were forced to locate along streams that could be harnessed for water power. This pattern is still quite evident in Southern New England, the original area of concentration for manufacturing in the United States, where most of the older industry is strung along the small, swift-flowing streams.

The development and growth of industry was usually the key to success for the small towns and villages of the early nineteenth century. Seven components are necessary for the successful operation of manufacturing: raw materials, power, fuel, markets, labor, transportation, and capital. With readily available supplies of timber, limestone, and agricultural products combined with the recent completion of the nearby Erie Canal, Fayetteville lacked only one of these ingredients—a source of power. Ledyard Dyke is an approximately two and two-thirds mile long hydraulic canal built between 1845 and 1849 for the purpose of providing water power for industrial development within the village of Fayetteville. The dyke [sic] is typical of the conveyances and hydraulic control structures which were once common when water was the primary source of power for industry.

Due to the limited head available, external undershot water wheels were used to supply power for the several mills originally located along the dyke [meaning the power of the stream is applied at the bottom of the wheel, instead of flowing over the top from a dam or millpond, and the force of the flow only is used, turning the wheel in the opposite direction of the flow of the stream]. In later years more efficient hydraulic turbines were employed to supply both direct mechanical and hydro-electric power for several industries. Among these were the Precision Die Casting Company on the location of Syracuse Plastics and the McIntyre Brothers Paper Company. The turbine at the McIntyre Brothers' mill remains intact [as of the 1980s, when this account was written], although no longer in use.

The idea of the canal was first conceived in 1836. There is about 100 feet of natural fall from within the village down to the level of Limestone Creek which flows north along the west end of

Fayetteville. Limestone Creek is a moderately sized stream which drains an area of about 86 square miles above the village with an average flow of about 144 cubic feet per second. It was thought that [if] this water could be diverted from some point upstream to the village, the 100 feet of natural fall obtained in returning the water to the creek would provide a usable source of water power. A site for the diversion was chosen and an earth and timber dam constructed across Limestone Creek about three miles upstream of the village and just west of the village of Manlius.

Ledyard Dyke has been in more or less continuous use since its completion in 1849.... The channel remains essentially intact with only minor alterations to the original design. With the exception of a holding reservoir (now called Beard Pond, which provides [today] the focus for a municipal park with walkways and band concerts in summer and skating in winter), Ledyard Dyke has been largely neglected and, in many places is almost entirely overgrown with trees and underbrush. Large amounts of debris have collected in the channel at many points, constricting the flow. Most of the hydraulic control structures also remain intact, but in deteriorating condition. All machinery has been removed except for a couple of control gates which are inoperative. One diversion structure is still in operation above the McIntyre mill, diverting water into a 30-inch conduit for the mill's use. It is in fair condition.

The Ledyard Dyke begins at a point north of what is now called Troop K Road.... The diversion dam has been modified over the years so that it is now an earth and stone structure capped with concrete. The spillway crest is ten feet high. The south end of the dam was breached by a storm in 1976 and has yet to be repaired [at the time this was written], but the head above the dam is maintained and the dyke continues to function. Several modifications to the dyke have been made in the vicinity of the dam due to washouts and flow into the dyke is now controlled by a 48-inch inverted siphon.

The channel is hand-dug and varies in width from twenty to less than eight feet with the depth ranging between two and four feet. The bottom is generally clay. The cross section alternates between rectangular and trapezoidal, and the channel lining varies from earth to stone and concrete. Most of the control structures are at least capped with concrete but appear to have originally been constructed of cut limestone, which was readily available in the area. Several of the structures have clearly been modified over the course of time, with one structure sometimes being superimposed over another.

The channel of Ledyard Dyke runs northwest from the diversion dam, crossing [what is now] State Route 92 at a point east of Hunt Lane. It then arcs due north, crossing Hunt Lane and Franklin Street before entering the "dough-nut" shaped holding reservoir in Beard Memorial Park. The reservoir, or Wellwood Pond [now Beard Pond] as it is called, has a surface area of about one acre and serves as a focus for the park. It was constructed . . . to stabilize flow in the dyke. . . .

Most of the 100 feet of fall occurs within the last one-third of a mile before the water re-enters Limestone Creek. It was along this stretch that all the mills were located. Ledyard Dyke continues to run west between Orchard and Clinton streets, passing through four small falls ranging in height from two to five feet just upstream of Walnut Street. Another cut limestone arch bridge in fair condition and two small weirs are located along the dyke before it turns north of Washington Street. The dyke crosses Clinton, paralleling Beach Street for about 150 feet before turning west for the final descent into Limestone Creek. About 60 feet west of Beach Street a ten foot high dam with controlled spillway (circa 1940) serves to divert part of the flow into the supply conduit serving McIntyre Brothers Mill. The dyke then descends through a series of four falls ranging in height from 4 to about 9 feet before flowing beneath the McIntyre Mill. At some point beneath the Mill the diverted flow is returned to the main stream which then flows into a 48-inch concrete culvert running underneath Mill Street. The dyke then completes its course by dropping about 7 feet out of the culvert back into a channel which returns the water to Limestone Creek.

As a whole the Ledyard Dyke hydraulic canal constitutes a fairly well preserved and operational example of the hydraulic technology employed in harnessing the controlling water for the purpose of producing mechanical power for manufacturing. Such technology was once a common and vital part of American industry, but few examples remain today.

The war (not to mention the profits excited by the war through supplying sheep, beef, and grain, etc.) and the rather quick demise of the investment value of the canal after the huge success of the railroads, made for some interesting shifts in community investments. According to the Manlius town historian, Barbara Rivette, "David Collin Sr. was one of the original investors in the Ledyard Dyke power canal and, with first choice of mill rights, chose the waterfalls in the center of Fayetteville. This location, bounded by Clinton, Walnut, Lincoln (earlier Canal), and Chapel (earlier Water) Streets was the location for his lumberyard. Later, the family's factory for church and household furniture, which became known as 'the bedstead factory,' was built there and eventually the village's first electrical generating plant used the waterpower. David Collin's stature as a business investor led him to be a founder of the National Bank of Fayetteville and a founding director of the Farmer's Bank."

Barry Lopez writes in *Resistance,* "In the theologies of redemption (Islam, Judaism, Christianity) the presumption is that though humanity has started off badly and is burdened with sin, it can achieve a state of perfection through diligence and self-improvement.... In the theologies of creation (such as Native American)—the world is beautiful and we are part of it—that is all. Our work is not to improve, it is to participate." The diligence and self-improvement not only prevent us from participating in the world, but that faith traps us in our own separation from the world, because self-improvement and our faith in it suggest the self is something apart. For the Collins this faith in self-improvement seemed irreversible. As irreversible as Miriam never again returning to the family homestead, her one-time home; as irreversibly embodied in her brother David's straight back as he rode off, whipping the buggy away that bitter afternoon.

Her father invested in local banks long before she was old enough even to know what banks meant. Indeed, the whole idea of a local bank depended upon local support and a heavy hand on the return of loans or other investments. David Collin's investments experienced substantial degrees of activity, not all of them ultimately positive, but as a noble figure of the settled community he was expected to produce support. That he did, usually wisely, indeed almost always wisely. But there were a few rather large local investments that did not pay off as well as this careful man had anticipated.

The idea that a local large landholder should be engaged in some banking activity went back two or three generations in the Collin family. Both David's father and his great uncle, Captain John Collin, acted as bankers to neighboring farmers and businessmen, lending cash and then carrying their "customers" until the crop was in. By the time David Collin Sr. could afford to be a lender, rural life and New York State banking laws had become too complex for private wealth to be used this way. Before 1850 capital resources grew very slowly, but they began doubling within the next decade. Initially, as deposits in banks increased, it was not understood by either bankers or state officials that those deposits, as well as any notes issued, had to be covered by a reserve. There was a panic in 1857 when many banks could not redeem their notes. The National Banking Act of 1863 required a minimum reserve, holding stockholders liable, and used a bond-deposit concept to protect notes. It wasn't until the twentieth century that lawmakers took steps to protect both depositors and banknote holders, a serious need, as shown in the demise of two banks within a few years of one another in Fayetteville, in both of which David Collin was heavily invested.

In the face of the raw wilderness, farming was one of the few viable and sustainable growth businesses. David Collin proved himself highly skilled in that endeavor. Around 1870 he became a founding director of the Farmer's Bank, seeing the interrelationship between growing population, farming, industry, and cash flow. He wanted to be right there for the decision making and the profits.

David Sr. died in 1884. Three years later the Farmer's Bank crashed with considerable ramifications across the village. In November 1887, David Jr. wrote to his beloved son Roswell about family and village matters. Toward the end he mentions a Mr. Severance getting out of jail. Mr. Severance was the chief clerk at the Farmer's Bank. David writes:

Dear Ro,

I have just read your letter to Charles which Ed and Mary brought up with ours from Min to Sarah, telling of the good times she and Hattie are having and that Hattie is attending a kindergarten school [as a teacher] from 9 to 12 and enjoying it very much with a small class of little girls from 4 to 7 years of age from the first families.... Frank writes of being very busy working very late and one night all night so as to have everything balanced up by the first of Nov., which is now to be the close of the year with the firm, but he is in good health.... It is very pleasant to hear from the children and read of the good times they are having, but not so easy from the quiet standpoint of home to make up a letter that would interest them and also with the daily routine of home life and care which requires about all the time and strength and yet from last winter's experience there is nothing like a letter from home and friends. I received the suit you sent me soon after I got your letter. It seems very nice and as the weather has not been very cold I have not put them on but I shall this week. We had about three inches of snow the last of the week and it is now about gone and raining some tonight, and hope it will continue for a while as it is very dry and wheat has but a feeble growth for winter and we have very little fall feed and streams are very low and many cisterns empty.... Will has been at his place in Sullivan [seven to ten miles to the east] most of the time lately in building a house. He has the cellar dug and wall built and some of the lumber on hand and hopes to have it enclosed before winter sets in, which with his clearing land and cropping takes a good deal of his time. I expect to sell him the [Oak] Grove place and if he can get a loan by mortgaging it and pay me for it so that I can take up some of my obligations. Mr. Severance was released on bail last Saturday. The bail bonds were $12,000 [$240,000]. Some ten of his friends went bail. I went in for $1000 [$20,000] till time of trial. It seemed best as he could not prepare to defend himself when he was confined, and it will not prejudice the bank's interest and at any time I feel unsafe about it I can take up the bond and he will have to get someone else.... We are all in usual health and hope to hear from you as often as you can write.

Affectionately yours,
David Collin

Shareholders have to take up responsibility for the liabilities and losses for a bank. It was not just neighborly altruism that motivated so many friends to stand bail for Mr. Severance. According to the Manlius town historian, Mr. Severance's biggest crime was that he could not say no, and he overextended the bank's reserve to the point where the bank couldn't make good on its own notes. The *Fayetteville Recorder* reported it this way, first on June 2, 1887:

> At the afternoon session of the court the matter of the Farmer's Bank against Eli Bangs and others, was referred to Attorney M. A. Knapp [no relation to Henry Knapp, but he was Miriam's counsel]. The defendant's attorneys say that the action is a friendly one, brought in the interests of the creditors for the purpose of closing the affairs of the bank. They of course deny certain statements made in the complaint and will put in an answer. Myron Bangs is the president of the bank and Frank Severance cashier and treasurer. The bank is closed and Fayetteville is a little excited. The assigned cause for the weak financial condition of the Farmer's bank is that Fayetteville is not a large enough place to support two banking institutions, the National Bank securing the bulk of the business.

Then on July 21, 1887: "Orders have been obtained from Justice M. H. Merwin providing for the selling of the Farmer's Bank's real estate by the receiver, directing the Superintendent of the Banking Department, Willis S. Paine, to deliver to the receiver the United States Bonds, amounting to $1000, now, in his hands, and authorizing the employment of an expert accountant to examine into the financial condition of the bank and report. The assets of the bank will be converted into money and a settlement made."

And finally, on the next day, July 22: "In the matter of the dissolution of the Farmer's Bank at Fayetteville, orders have been made by Justice Merwin of Utica providing for the sale of real estate to the value from $10,000 to $15,000 [$290,000] and for the delivery to the receiver, W. S. Andrews, of the $1,000 in United States Bonds held by the Superintendent of the Banking Department. The bank's books will be examined by Lawrence W. Myers, the expert accountant."

Seven years later that "other" bank, the National Bank of Fayetteville, also folded. The causes in that case were less parochial and personal than with the Farmer's Bank, stemming in part from the statewide Panic of 1893, which was a recurring problem throughout the state's economic development during periods of explosive industrial growth. The reasons closer to home had more to do with certain significant employers being unable to cash in on bills due them through the bank. There was a run on the bank in the fall of 1894, which it was of course unable to meet. The story is important because it involves the Collin family furniture factory, owned at the time by David Collin Jr.'s son Edward, the one who ran away from home in his youth and caused such consternation. The *Fayetteville Recorder* reported the story over the period, starting on October 5, 1894:

> The Fayetteville National Bank is closed pending examination by National Bank Examiner Van Vranken, and at the present writing it is impossible to say when the examination will be complete.... The directors were dissatisfied with the manner in which certain accommodations were being carried on and a meeting was accordingly held Saturday evening to consider the question. At this meeting Cashier R. W. Eaton, tendered his resignation and Platt H. Smith was appointed to fill his place.
>
> On Monday morning the bank opened for business with Mr. Smith as Cashier.... Rumors of the change had already been spread abroad and a number of depositors became frightened. A run was begun on the bank which was brought to a crisis when Eli T. Bangs presented a check for $2,800 [$55,000], which the bank did not have ready money to cash....
>
> No one questions Mr. Eaton's integrity. He has been connected with the bank in different capacities for about 27 years and has been cashier for 15 years, and everyone who knows him knows also that his word is as good as his bond....

Meanwhile the depositors will be inconvenienced by having their ready funds tied up, but no fear need be apprehended, but that they will receive every dollar of their deposits as it is one of the points of the National Banking System that depositors are protected....

The closing of the Fayetteville National Bank on Monday was followed by the general assignment of Collin, Sisson & Pratt, furniture manufacturers [the bedstead factory].... Owing to the hard times Collin, Sisson & Pratt have been obliged recently to do much of their business on paper. When a consignment of goods was made to any house it has been customary for the firm to deposit drafts on such house, in the bank, and when checks were received the drafts were canceled. But of late the collections have been so slow, that at the time of the assignment it is estimated that about $3,500 [$68,000] in drafts still remained uncancelled at the National Bank. Had not the bank officials ordered the bank closed, this amount would have been met, when the collections were easier.... This firm has been doing a good business and was in a most prosperous condition until about two years ago, since which time the firm has been losing money.... [T]here are orders now ahead to keep the firm busy for a month at least. After that there is no certainty as to what the firm will do.... The firm is composed of Edward Collin, George Sisson and John D. Pratt and manufacture a high grade of furniture. About 50 men are employed the year round [no small number in a village that size] and the news of the assignment was a hard blow to the business interests of Fayetteville.

On October 11 the paper continued:

The National Bank of Fayetteville still remains in the hands of the Examiner Van Vranken. Payment of discounted paper is demanded, and we understand that as soon as a sufficient amount is collected to pay depositors in full, orders will be issued by the Comptroller of Currency to open the bank....

The firm of E.& C. L. Collin has dissolved partnership, Charles L. Collin [Edward's younger brother] purchasing the interest of Edward Collin. In this purchase Charles L. Collin assumes all obligation, and also all right, title and interest in the firm, together with all the accounts, claims and demands, due and owing said firm. Mr. Charles L. Collin will in the future have the entire management of this concern, which consists of saw-mill, lumber and wood yard, planing and shingle mill. There is no change in the business situation at the furniture factory. The firm is kept busy daily filling its large orders. Mr. Sisson informed a "Recorder" reporter that if the present crisis had been averted, the firm would have had a class of orders during the coming season that would have necessitated enlarging their forces considerably.

In November the *Recorder* reported on an October 25, 1894, meeting: "A meeting of the shareholders of the National Bank of Fayetteville will be held at the Banking House in Fayetteville, N.Y. on the 26th day of November, 1894, to vote on the question of going into liquidation and closing said bank." By the beginning of December it was gone for good.

In February 1881, when things were prosperous and full of hope, the *Fayetteville Recorder* published an article about the family firm that gives a sense of its scope, its importance to the community, and what was at stake and suggests the economic power of a vertically integrated business (the latter being possible because so much of the materials and processes involved derived through family connections, from raw materials to major shareholders). The Collin family supplied the wood from their own lumberyard, power from the dike in which they were major investors, and capital from the bank they helped found. These various stories about life and business in Fayetteville through the old age of David Collin Sr. and his son's maturity, from just after the Civil War to the beginning of the 1890s, suggest how complicated and layered life in the village, with its increasingly frequent connections to the larger world, had become for all the original settlers. Large families and intricate marriage relationships, business successes and failures, and the changing scale of the community created a society very different from the one in which pioneer families shared their Sabbath celebrations in one another's front parlors before any churches were built. It is not unreasonable to suggest that the Collin clan had come to be regarded as something like local nobility, respected to be sure, often loved by many, and through the sheer visibility of their power and prominence subject to a perhaps unfair scrutiny by those who loved them less well. This was the world in which Miriam staked her claim for dignity.

By the 1890s all of this began to change rapidly. The *Recorder* piece of February 17, 1881, however, gives a fine picture of a nineteenth-century American manufacturing operation within a mere generation of pushing back the wilderness:

The Bedstead Factory

> The factory of Mssr. Collin, Arnold and Sisson is spoken of as "The Bedstead Factory," but the title seems a little inappropriate, as the manufacturing carried on there is not confined to bedsteads alone, but embraces many other kinds of household furniture for the general trade, such as extension and other tables, lounges and, in fact, any article of furniture that may be ordered. The firm have filled some heavy orders for church furniture, and the beauty of the work has given the greatest satisfaction.
>
> Messrs. Collin, Arnold and Sisson last fall found it necessary to enlarge their establishment to enable them to employ a larger force of employees to keep up with their increasing business. An addition was attached to the building then in use which added 26 x 40 feet on two floors for new and improved machinery and bench room for workmen. A store house was also erected on the premises and at the time of our visit the latter named building only contained about three hundred bedsteads, or the product of one week's manufacturing—that number being about the weekly average of that kind of furniture—which show that the products of the factory meet with ready sales.
>
> The boiler used in the factory is utilized to its utmost capacity. In addition to driving the machinery it furnishes steam for heating the entire establishment. A few months since steam heating pipes were put in the building, proving not only a great saving in the way of fuel, and adding comfort to the employees by an uniform heat, but reducing the danger from fire, which is always a consideration in establishments of this kind. The boiler also supplies the

heat for the dry kiln, which is situated near the factory. The kiln has a capacity for seasoning about 10,000 feet of lumber every two weeks. The boiler now in use has done service for many years, and the proprietors are about to replace it with a new one made for them by A. C. Powell & Co. of Syracuse, and which is now ready for delivery. It will be in position in about two weeks.

The factory uses about 600,000 feet of lumber during the year, principally black walnut, ash, maple and basswood. The bedsteads manufactured embrace every style, from the most expensive to the very cheapest. Machinery is used in every instance where it can be made to supply the place of hand labor. Lathes, gig, cut off and wabble saws, smoothing and sandpaper machines perform in a few hours what would require weeks of hand labor by the same force of employees. At the present time Messrs. Collin, Arnold & Sisson have twenty-two employees, and the payroll amounts to about $170 a week [$3,100].

Another article of manufacture in the factory, and by no means an unimportant one, is fly fishing rods. These are made exclusively by Mr. Sisson, who is acquiring a national reputation in the manufacture of them. They are made from split bamboo, and some idea may be formed of the nice workmanship required on them when we state that an eleven foot rod, fully trimmed, will only weigh seven and a half ounces. Wherever these rods have been introduced orders come for more. Sportsmen greatly admire them, and orders are received from Kansas and other remote States, and the local demand for them is quite large.

While Syracuse and neighboring cities and villages take a large part of the products of the factory, still the proprietors have large orders from remote places. During the past year they shipped nine full [railway] car loads of bedsteads to New York City. To manufacture over fifteen thousand bedsteads during a year, together with other kinds of furniture, by a force of employees no greater than we have named, requires not only varied but perfect machinery, and the factory possess all the facilities for rapid manufacturing. That the work produced gives perfect satisfaction may be inferred from the ready sale obtained for all the furniture the factory can turn out. This establishment is but one among the varied manufacturing interests which serve to increase the prosperity of our village, by furnishing employment to a number of men who reside here and assist in the support of other branches of trade.

When Edward sold the business to his brother it was not to escape creditors, nor was it some machination to keep the enterprise in the family. It was the last of a string of crushing events, any one of which might have stopped a lesser man. Tall (for the time) at five feet eleven inches, fair, with the rugged good looks of Collin men, he had a peculiar walk deriving from a partial paralysis following a bout of diphtheria. Certainly, as the oldest surviving son, he felt a heritage of pressure to perform, which must have contributed to his prodigal escape from home as a youth. But he settled down, marrying his first cousin, Mary, and eventually taking over his grandfather's sawmill on the Ledyard Dyke, using the then new Gridley Automatic Circular Saw, which allowed him to cut logs into planks for veneer. In 1870 the mill burned to the ground, and Edward had no insurance. Nevertheless, in true Collin fashion, he rebuilt the mill, became senior partner, purchased a lumber firm making those bedsteads, and expanded it into manufacturing all lines of furniture. Seventeen years later it all burned to the ground again. Once more he rebuilt it, and just as things began to look promising, his bank failed.

As it happened, the business Charles bought from Edward eventually ended up in the hands of another pair of brothers. Leopold Stickley and J. George Stickley broke with their hugely successful older brother, Gustav, founder of the Craftsman empire (whose products are highly collectible today), to strike out on their own. In 1902, the company they bought from L. L. Chapman had been the Collin bedstead business. Originally their work was a blatant imitation of their brother Gustav's mission style, but when his empire collapsed around 1915, they switched to a very high standard of early American reproductions. The company is still in Fayetteville and Manlius today, although now, since yet another fire destroyed the factory on the original site by the dike, they have a new location and are reproducing those mission and Craftsman designs they once left behind, to international acclaim for the quality of the work. Looking at the vast warehouse on the edge of the village of Manlius one might feel that David Collin would have approved.

There was, however and despite all this economic history, an incident in the summer of 1871 that on the one hand shows the evil of suggestive rumors and on the other perhaps suggested to Miriam some grounds by which she could later challenge her father's will. On August 22, 1871, the pastor of the Presbyterian Church in the village, Rev. D. W. Bigelow, wrote a letter to David Collin Jr., cosigned by many, but not all, of the elders of the church. The letter is clearly in response to one David had written to the pastor earlier, the tone of which, it seems, was not very forgiving. What had happened? Who were the missing elders, and why were they missing as cosigners? It must be remembered that David Sr. was a founding elder of that church and had contributed substantially to its building and future prosperity. First the letter from Pastor Bigelow et al. (it is a masterpiece of convoluted apology and self-justification):

> Fayetteville
> Pastor's Study
> Aug. 22, 1871

Mr. David Collin, Jr.,
Our esteemed brother in Christ and our coworker in His cause:

> We know that you feel hurt at the action taken by session with relation to your father, and we do hereby express to you our sorrow that we should have given you pain.

> We can and do assure you that whether the course we took in this matter was just and wise, or not, *our motives were pure*. We then felt and now feel not only a true desire to preserve the purity of the Church and its good name, but also a most tender regard for the reputation and happiness of your father and yourself.

> Of all this we do assure you as we are men who fear to make this deliberate manner, or in any way a fare representation, and as we would still keep a good conscience before Him who knows our hearts.

> If it seems unusual that men should thus declare their motives pure when to suppose otherwise would be to make them in truth

most guilty, it is because we wish *to emphasize the fact,* believing that if you are convinced that we acted in kindness, you will not feel cold in heart even if you still think that we blundered. And now in explanation of our action, allow us to call your attention to these facts.

1st, An Elder's meeting should have been called in any case, at that time. Four months, an unusual time, had elapsed since session had met for ordinary business. The pastor without any knowledge of this matter purposed to appoint a meeting a week earlier than he did, and would have done so but for the many claims upon his time following his vacation. That meeting was not, therefore, unreasonable.

2. At the time the appointment was made nothing had been learned to show the falsity of rumors afterwards to be mentioned.

3. When the session met there was no reason to suppose all would not be present, and at no stage of the meeting would we have been surprised to have had you come in and listen to all that was said.

4. In view of rumors that involved the reputation of your father's character and the purity of the Church—rumors that had for months been circulated, and as we believe had gained more & more credence in the community, we felt that it was not only proper but our duty to speak of the [matter?] together and to consult about what could be done.

5. Although almost fully persuaded at that time (by statements made by the Pastor who had *that day* had an interview with Mr. S. J. Wells) that there was no foundation for the rumors alluded to, it was now proposed and the measure met with the approval of everyone present that two of our oldest members should talk with the brother whose reputation was at stake; and this was done in the full belief that such consultation with him was frank and scriptural, and that it would result in fully clearing up the case and putting a certain and quick stop to all false reports.

6. It was not official action any further than this, that it was the Elders whose duty it is to watch over the Church, who thus

consulted and thus requested two of their number to go quietly and see the brother.

7. By this action the matter was made no more public than before, for this was impossible.

8. The interview was in every way kind and fraternal and resulted in just what was hoped for and confidently expected: the fears of many have been wholly allayed; the mouths of gainsayers have been stopped, and the reputation of one whom we have held dear, and now doubly so, was at once cleared from all suspicion!

If still, our dear brother, you believe that our action was injudicious, we deeply regret that we had not found a plan that would be better and that would meet with your approval; and if we did indeed blunder we ask your charity and forgiveness in Christ our common Lord; looking for and expecting this we remain, as your sincere friends in Christ,

     Rev. D. W. Bigelow, Pastor
     Philip Flint
     Henry Hoag
     Justin Nedly [?]
     R. L. Hatch
     Jas. J. Hand

Curiously, there are no records of this meeting of the elders in the church archives, which are held at the Presbyterian Historical Society in Philadelphia, though there are records (minutes and correspondence) for the meetings preceding and following it. The "brother" whose reputation was at stake was David Collin Sr. S. J. Wells, who was interviewed by the pastor, was also an elder, though he was not at the meeting, and was Mr. Collin's son-in-law, not to mention a wealthy businessman in his own right. There is no other correspondence in the church records to fill out some of the gaps in information but it would seem, from internal evidence in that letter and from a letter written a year later by Mr. Collin's grandson, Roswell (probably to his cousin Cardera), that David Jr. had written to the pastor an angry letter suggesting that he and his father, both elders and trustees of the church, had been deliberately excluded from a secret and impromptu meeting of the elders that was called with the intention of saving the church from a potentially compromising situation and perhaps to drum the senior David Collin out of the church, the very one he had helped establish. Judging from Ro's letter, Samuel Wells was absent from the elder's meeting *not* because he was supporting his father-in-law, but because his wife, Anna, was working with Miriam to discredit their father. The rumors apparently alluded to David Sr.'s ailing wife (also called Anna), who had been in poor health and died two years later, and to an unmarried middle-aged housekeeper who lived with Anna and David at the Oak Grove farm. Mr. Collin was frisky, but mind you, also seventy-seven at the time of these rumors. Clearly he was exonerated, but David Jr. felt the meeting and secret interview served only to fan the fires of rumor further. One dearly wishes at least David Jr.'s letter to the pastor was extant. Maybe the paper itself was consumed by the heat of his anger.

At any rate, not many of the family affairs were private by the 1870s. When things began to simmer around the 1876 will of David Collin it was generally known that there was "some contention" within the family, as indeed is brought out in the Surrogate Court hearing a decade or so later. David Collin Sr. wrote three wills during his lifetime, or at least only three are on record in the Syracuse courthouse; he kept outliving his heirs and having to revise his bequests. Of those three, the major will was that of 1869 in which, it may be recalled, he insisted that his daughter Miriam pay off her husband's enormous debts by May of that year or else sell off, at her father's death, what she had already been given (each daughter had already been given a farm, among other things) to cover them before she got anything else. Surely that was a hard blow to Miriam. But seven years later, after his wife, Anna's, death, he wrote another will (the third and last on record), the one later contested in the Surrogate Court. It is not long. It is entirely in the words of this tough old octogenarian who, despite his poor frontier education, had no trouble with the necessary legalese. It gives an eloquent sense of his character, his mood, and that he is quite aware of what has been going on around him, not unlike Lear on the heath asking, "Is there any cause in nature that makes these hard hearts?" (*King Lear*, 3.6.81–82). I quote from the original contested will here in full, written out in his own hand:

In the name of god, Amen. I David Collin of the Town of Manlius in the county of Onondaga and State of New York, of the age of eighty-two years, and being in good health and of sound mind and memory and bearing in mind the frailty and uncertainty of human life and being desirous while I have the strength and capacity of adjusting my worldly affairs and directing the disposition of the estate which it has pleased God to bless my labors; do make, publish and declare this my last will and testament in manner following, that is to say: First, I commend my immortal being to Him who gave it, and my body to the earth to be buried by my executors hereinafter named with little expense or ostentation.

Secon[d]. I direct my said executors to pay all my just debts and funeral expenses out of my personal estate as soon after my decease as can be conveniently done.

Third. I give and bequeath to the children of my daughter Caroline now deceased wife of Sylvester C. Gardner now deceased who shall be living at my decease the sum of fifty dollars [$800] to be divided between them equally share and share alike. Also I give and bequeath to my daughter Lucy, wife of Porter Tremain now deceased the sum of fifty dollars; also I give and bequeath to the children of my daughter Harriet now deceased, wife of Nathan Seward now deceased who shall be living at my decease the sum of fifty dollars to be divided between them share and share alike; also I give and bequeath to my daughter Miriam wife of Ethan Armstrong the sum of fifty dollars; also I give and bequeath to my daughter Anna wife of Samuel Wells the sum of fifty dollars which said several legacies or sums of money I direct and order to be paid by my executors to the said respective legatees within one year after my decease and in case any of my said daughters now living should die before my decease then I order and direct that the legacy of said daughters be paid to their heirs to be divided between them equally share and share alike.

I desire to declare that this item of my will is maid [sic] after long deliberation and reflection and that my determination as I have expressed it therein is deliberate and intentional and that I came to such determination in part because heretofore I have given to each of my said daughters a good farm and land besides, such gifts amounting in all to over eighteen hundred acres of land and I have paid for or on account of my sons in law, husbands of my said daughters and my grandchildren, children of my said daughters about the sum of thirty thousand dollars [$480,000] including interest to this time and in part for other reasons which after such deliberations and reflections seem to me good and sufficient.

Fourth: I give, devise and bequeath to my son David Collin all the rest, residue and remainder of my estate both real and personal, together with all the hereditaments and appertinances [sic] belonging or in any wise appertaining to said real estate to have and to hold the same to the said David Collin his heirs and assigns for ever, this item of my will is intended to include all my real estate of every name and nature whatsoever and wherever situated which I may have at the time of my decease and all the remainder of my personal estate, goods and chattels of every nature and kind whatsoever after deducting that part thereof herein before disposed of by the former items of this will.

Lastly: I hereby appoint my son David Collin of said Town of Manlius farmer and my grandson Edward Collin of the same, lumber merchant, executors of this my last will and testament; hereby revoking all former wills by me made. In witness whereof I have hereunto set my hand and seal this Thirteenth day of May, 1876.

[The document is subscribed with the names of Wm. G. Stearns, Marquis L. Peck, and Ambrose Clark.]

Miriam, her sister Anna (who I believe did not receive a farm—or certainly did not live on it if she did and was anyway quite comfortable as evidenced by the mansion she and her husband built next to Beard Pond), as well as the Tremain and Gardner children, felt the fifty-dollar bequest was an insult, rather like tipping someone a quarter today.

There is a letter from Roswell, from September 1877, probably to Cardera, that explains a little of what was going on behind the scenes that led to so much public speculation. Ro had by then graduated from Williams

College and was studying to enter the Columbia University Medical College. He was showing his mettle to his father and grandfather in terms they could understand and was therefore being brought into central family issues even though he was quite a bit younger than Edward, the seeming heir of the family legacy after David Jr. died. The letter, in part, follows:

> Last Saturday afternoon, Sept. 15th, Charlie [his younger brother] and I went down to "the Grove" to call upon Grandfather and shortly after, Father and Ed came. We found Grandfather down under the barn taking care of the pigs, and finding a place to sit down we engaged in conversation. Grandfather did most of the talking and the substance of his remarks was as follows, as nearly as I can remember. He began by saying that as we boys were there, it would be as well that he should tell us about the division line between Mrs. Armstrong's farm [he usually referred to her as Aunt Miriam in his journals as a younger boy—he was now twenty-five—and presumably this is how his Grandfather was referring to her, and he makes no mention of his uncle at this point] and Father's 50 acre lot, about which there is now some difficulty. He said that when he gave Mrs. Armstrong her land, it was understood that the old fence between the 50 acre lot and her south line—running from Smith's South-West corner, West—was to be the boundary and division line, without any variation. He directed Mr. Tremain to run the line and make out a deed *on this basis*. Mr. Tremain told Grandfather that he had done so, and it was with this understanding that Grandfather signed the deed. Recently, to the great astonishment of himself, Mrs. Armstrong has claimed that this old line fence was *not* the boundary between her land and Father's 50 acre lot, but utterly ignoring this line, she has set the fence several rods further upon Father's lot—ie. starting from the same corner, she has run a line at a considerable variation from the old line. The deed in her possession seems to call for this new line. She has removed the old fence and the stake and stones in the woods which marked the corner. All this Grandfather bitterly denounced as wrong, ungrateful and fraudulent. It

was evident that either by trickery or by error, her deed was not as he had directed it to be made out.

Mrs. Armstrong refuses to yield her new line or anything called for by the deed in her possession. This Grandfather denounced as a wicked attempt to take advantage of an error. Grandfather said he used to think and speak of giving Mrs. Armstrong the 14 acre wood lot, but never had done by deed or word—that he allowed her to use it as a grazing lot for stock on condition of her supporting the fence between it and the rest of the woods. That in consideration of heavy debts which Mr. Armstrong owed Grandfather, he had allowed him to cut Basswood logs from this lot to sell and turn the proceeds toward payment of those debts, that Mr. Armstrong so abused this privilege that Grandfather withdrew it. In answer to a question from Father why he had disposed of his property as he had and who had told him to do so, he said no one had told him and that he had used his own judgment in the matter and disposed of his property "as he thought best"—that he had a perfect right to do this as he had come honestly by his property, had been generous to all his children and like any other man, he had a right to dispose of his property as he thought best.

In answer to a question from Charlie whether Father had tried to influence him in his favor or had ever asked him for any property, Grandfather stoutly denied both. Father asked if any of his children had asked him for property, and he said he believed none but Miriam and Anna. That they had done so repeatedly—especially Miriam—that Mr. Armstrong had borrowed large sums of money from him from time to time—a small part of which he had ever paid back—that this had now been running for some years, and that there was still due him over twenty thousand dollars including interest [$330,000]. That when in consequence he had been obliged to raise large sums of money, he would have been greatly embarrassed but for Grandfather's aid. That he had taken all these things into consideration in disposing of his property, and that when he could not get his due from Mr. Armstrong, he had counted that indebtedness in with what he saw fit to give that family. He also said that in a similar way, the Tremain family had received large sums of money, principally Charlie Tremain, that through loose management and expensive living, they had allowed this to slip through their fingers and this he also reckoned in to them when he disposed of his property. The amount of the Tremain indebtedness Grandfather stated to be about eleven thousand dollars [$190,000].

In answer to the question whether Father had ever prejudiced him against the Seward girls, Grandfather said never, but he had always spoken kindly of them and in their favor. That he (Grandfather) had done well enough by them, that they had shown very little interest in him and used to hardly ever come to see him. He said he had never been lacking in affection for his children, that he had given to each a farm and done much for them, but now in his old age [he was now eighty-three] most of them shamefully ill-treated him. We then went into the house and Grandfather read and explained to us some papers he had been writing, in which were statements with reference to the division line and disposition of property of which we had been speaking. After finishing he said, "Now I wrote that myself and it is all true every word of it. I would take my oath to it in court."

Father asked him with regard to the woman (Mrs. Worden) who was keeping house for him, what their relations were? Grandfather said he hired her to do his housekeeping and cooking, that she had always done well for him and before Grandmother died, she had taken good care of her—better than anyone else he had had and that Grandmother got along well with her. Father asked if he paid her wages and he said yes, he paid her every month two dollars per week [$33]. Father asked if that was all—if there were or had been any other relations between them and Grandfather said there had been no other relations—that everything was "straightforward and upright" between them. He said he knew that some talked about the way he lived there, but that he had repeatedly asked that one of his children or grandchildren might come to live with him. That he had offered to hire what help he needed and make things as pleasant as he could if they would only come and keep house for him, but none of them had been disposed to come. That he could not live absolutely alone and do his own cooking and washing—that he was too old to marry again, and so under the circumstances he had done the best he could. He said he did not think he should live very long when Grandmother died, but the Lord (had) seen fit to spare him.

Grandfather again spoke bitterly of the outrageous way in which he had been talked to and treated by some of his children and denounced it as outrageous and wicked. Said they would be rewarded—that the Lord would never prosper such wicked treatment of a parent. He said they tried to make him out a law vagabond, base in character and incompetent to do business. That if all they said of him were true, there might be some little excuse for the course they had taken—but none of it was true—he knew perfectly well what was about as much as ever and had always tried to do right. But in their wickedness and ingratitude they forgot all he had done for them and treated him as he would never believed they could. He said Mr. Pierson had used such abusive language to him—that he was a mean man and he believed he had had a bad influence upon Mrs. Pierson [his granddaughter Caroline, daughter of Caroline who had married a Gardner, whose farm was just a little east of the homestead and where the fateful meeting took place] who used to be a very nice girl, but now treated him very badly. He said there were always those who would much rather speak evil of one and undermine his reputation than to say anything good of one.

A few days later Father, Ed and I called upon Grandfather, and Father asked him more explicitly with regard to two or three points, upon which my aunts have proposed to prove Grandfather's incompetency. They have said he lived with his house-keeper, Mrs. Worden, as if she were his wife and that there had been criminal relations between them. Father asked him if this were true, and Grandfather gave an indignant and vehement denial. Mrs. Worden chanced to be in an adjoining room and heard this conversation, and said repeatedly that it was all false—that she never had been the means of injuring Grandfather's character in any way. She threatened and so did Grandfather, to bring a suit against the defamers. Grandfather also said that when these sums of money were loaned to the Armstrongs and Tremains, it was understood and stated that if these debts were not paid, they would be deducted from the properties which he should finally see fit to give to those families.

Miriam was desperate for a bright place in her family and her community, a sense she was also among the Chosen. It called for desperate measures. But like the rumors of her father misbehaving with the housekeeper, which it appears she fostered, the source of the desperate measures could not be kept secret long. And that May morning, a year later, she saw her father, her once-beloved brother, and the legacy for which she had so patiently waited, being drawn inexorably away by a smart, well-bred horse under the pale new leaves of elm and maple.

10

The Romance

> Men must endure
> Their going hence; even as their coming hither;
> Ripeness is all ...
> —Shakespeare, *King Lear,* 5.2.8–10

On an autumn afternoon a young man sits at his desk by a window and looks at the long shadows of the bare trees that stretch across the fine, leaf-strewn lawns. The sun is red and slipping below the gray mountain ridge in the west. It had been dull all day, gray, cold. He and other young men had walked quickly between buildings in coats and mufflers as the wind picked up out of the north, stirring the leaves with large invisible hands.

But this flash of amber light heartens him. The rich smells of the season return in memory with a palpable immediacy. He takes in all at once the suddenly brilliant red leaves, the barberry in the hedges between the few houses he can see from his room, the scent of windfall apples hidden under the leaves that when stepped upon released their cidery scent.

He takes a piece of paper, dips his pen in the much used and abused well, and begins in his neat flowing hand, "My Dear Cardera ... "

It is now 1874. The quiet but very handsome, bright young man, unaware of his fine appearance or his good mind, is Roswell Park Collin. He is writing from Williams College (chartered in 1785) high in the old mountains in northwestern Massachusetts, a few miles from the New York and Vermont borders, and within a long day's ride of family members, some of his many cousins in New York's Columbia County. He is writing to his beloved cousin

Roswell Park Collin, son of David Collin IV

Cardera, a double cousin as the books would have it, whose frequent letters have made his time away from home, some 150 mile to the west, bearable.

Cardera is small, blond, bright-eyed with a ready smile, pretty rather than beautiful. But she has, also, a fine mind, an equal to that of the young man, a sharp perception of human nature, the entire mix of which brightens any room she enters and fills all who know her with affection. He is twenty-two. She is sixteen.

Roswell, or Ro, was the first of David Collin's children (this is David Jr. we are talking about here) to go to a four-year college of some reputation.

He was what we'd now call a premed student and the first to set his sights well beyond Fayetteville. He carried with him, as was just beginning to be made clear to him, the burden of being one of the leaders of his generation within the extended family (certainly he was as popular and beloved as Cardera from Hillsdale to the Finger Lakes). His father was also beginning to see him as someone he could trust with issues of family business and affairs and frequently wrote to him concerning such matters.

Ro turns his eyes from the window to the paper before him:

> Nov. 19, 1874
>
> ... You were quite right in supposing I had not forgotten my promise, but I was none the less delighted to hear from you. You were also right in thinking I might have other invitations for Thanksgiving, but wrong in thinking they might be more tempting than the "quiet Thanksgiving with my uncle, aunt and cousins." I was afraid I should not be able to go anywhere, as the faculty were undecided whether to give us a vacation, or rather, a recess, now or not; but their decision was such that I think I can accept with safety and certainly with *pleasure,* your very kind invitation.

In this letter, written on that November afternoon, we meet a man quite different from the frightened youth who nursed his Armstrong cousin through many bouts of heavy drinking or who wrote with such self-conscious eloquence about life. Here he is just beginning to get to know Cardera as a young woman in her own right and not merely as another female cousin in an army of cousins. Cardera's name, by the way, came from a place in North Wales, Cader Idris, which her mother had read about and liked, in the way Celtic tales began to have their romantic hold on the Victorian imagination after the publication of the spurious "Poem of Ossian" by James MacPherson earlier in the century. From Roswell's letter dated January 24, 1875:

> Now I will tell you a little about my vacation. When I reached home I was disappointed not to find Em there and they had written that none of the Benton folks [the homestead in the northern Finger Lakes region] could come. But Tuesday of Holiday week,

Uncle Henry and Aunt Maria came unexpectedly and we enjoyed a very pleasant visit from them. Cousins Henry and Cora Baldwin came from Pitcher the same day I believe. New Years Day Glover, Henry Baldwin, Charlie and I started out about eleven o'clock and made fifty *very pleasant* calls. We did not get home until about nine in the evening and it was one of the gayest and "pleasantest" days I have spent for some time. Don't you wish you had been near enough to receive us too? I do. What would you have offered us to drink? Coffee I suppose. We had nothing offered us stronger than coffee and lemonade, though some wine was presented last year. We of course did not indulge. Clara, Hattie and Cora Baldwin received a number of callers. The older folks went to the Gardner's to meet the Uncles and Aunts and passed a very pleasant day.

Saturday Uncle Henry and Aunt Maria went home and Em and Will came. George had to stay to keep house. Of course we were delighted to see them and made the most of the time, for Em only stayed over Sunday and started for her Western home Monday. How strange it seems to have her going off there, don't it? I told her you were anxious to hear from her and she said she would soon write you. I presume you have received a letter from her already. Will stayed until Thursday morning, though he had intended to go the day before, on his way back to college. Most of the gaieties of the season had passed by then, but we had some good times and enjoyed his visit very much.

We have a very fine young pastor in our church at home and I enjoyed attending his prayer meetings, which were very interesting. Ed and Mary are as cozy and happy as they can be. I always enjoy going there very much. Charlie and I stayed with them one night and had such a good visit and pleasant evening. Ed gave me the Bric-a-Brac series elegantly bound for a Christmas present and Hattie gave me a very pretty volume of "Poems of Home Life."

Charlie was away on lumber business for Ed across Oneida Lake a good deal of the time while I was home and is there now. I have had two good letters from him since I came back, more than he had written me in a whole term before. Charlie is not much of a hand to write letters, but an "awful good boy" I think. Nearly a week of the time I was home Clara was gone to Coventry to attend the wedding of an old school friend and she reported a splendid time. Charlie and I attended one social party while I was home, quite select, though it was held [at] the hall and club rooms and there was quite a good deal of dancing. I have been trying to teach some of the fellows here that little dance you taught me—Esmerelda—I believe you call it—but I don't succeed very well. Wish I could try it again with you and Stelle. Hattie left for Saratoga about a week before I came away, and Ed and Mary were hoping to go to New York sometime during last week or the week before. Perhaps you have seen something of them. I certainly have not heard, for Charlie's letters were not sent from home but from Oswego County, and I have not received my usual home letter.

The level of family engagement in togetherness is remarkable, considering the difficulty of travel despite the trains. The draw of the homestead was powerful. From a letter of April 12, 1875:

My Dear Cousin Cardie,

It is a rainy morning and I don't know what to do with myself. I first thought I would write some letters and then I thought I was too restless to keep quiet so long. After reading a chapter or two from Arthur B[?] Castle, I came out here where Charlie was ciphering before the fireplace on the bearings and measurements of a recent survey, and concluded to attempt a letter. It will keep me busy and if I do not finish it no harm is done you know. Perhaps you have heard that I have been a cripple for nearly four weeks. It will be two weeks tomorrow since I came home and all this time I have been shut up here in the house, instead of going to Homer [a village some thirty miles southwest of Fayetteville where he went to secondary school] for a merry time and visiting about home, as I had anticipated. Of course it is a disappointment to me but still it gives me a good deal of time for reading and I divide my time about equally between my books, guitar and the piano. Then every day when it is pleasant Charlie takes me out to ride and as he is breaking a colt of his own, we have some splendid long drives. Saturday morning we started out right after breakfast and did not return until dinner time. But most of the time I spend quietly in the house. Now Cardie, if you were only here what a good visit we could have, with nothing to do but visit and read aloud etc. And then you ought to see the lovely little wild flowers that the boys brought from the woods yesterday. They are too sweet for anything. There are several bouquets of them about the house. Now if they would only go and keep fresh in a letter you should have one, for I imagine you don't see many of them in the city [meaning at her sister's in Rutherford, New Jersey]. But I think the most fun is to gather the dear little things fresh in the woods; would it not be nice! I shall be able to walk in a week or two without crutches I hope. You see I sprained my ankle very badly and broke ligaments so it is a long time getting well. Our term opens again next Thursday, but I shall not go back until I can walk all right. How do you like being out of school again and do you read much? Have you read "John Halifax, Gentleman"? I have just finished it and am delighted.

Clara has been down to Ed's and Mary's most of the time since I have been home and is very busy sewing. I expect to go down there tomorrow for a few days. They are real well and just as happy as can be. I just missed seeing Hattie as she returned to Saratoga the very same day I came home. Frank Glover was out here a week ago and spent Sunday with me. Last Thursday evening I went to the village to attend the graduating exercises of Minnie's class. They passed off very nicely. The girls were dressed in white and Minnie's essay was considered the best of the evening. That is the first time I have tried to go anywhere except to ride.

I heard some time ago that you and uncle Norton were going to take a trip to Florida. Is it so? How is Estelle now? Charlie says, "give his love to Cardie and regards to Estelle and yours at the same time." So here you have it from us both. Charlie told me to send word to Estelle that he wanted one of her pictures which she promised him. He has some but they are so poor he will send them away, but expects to have better ones very soon and then will send one.

Aren't you coming out to Fayetteville this summer? Father was speaking of it the other day. We are all agreed that the pure air and free exercise of the country would be the best thing in the world for you. I need not say we would be delighted to have you come, and would try to make your visit pleasant, you know it is so. But enough for the present. I am so quiet there is little to write. We are all usually well, though Grandpa is sick with a hard cold. Minnie will answer your letter soon. Love from all to all; and Mother adds that she hopes to see some of you here this summer.

    Your aff. cousin,
    R. P. Collin

After his treasured time at Williams, where he made a friend for life, his roommate, Charles May, Roswell left the rural world of Fayetteville and Williamstown for New York City. There he entered the College of Physicians and Surgeons at Columbia University, receiving his M.D. in 1879. In 1878, however, he had to take a leave of absence from the city to go home and care for his older brother, Edward. His brother had contracted what Roswell called a *vilious fever,* a form of typhoid that affected the small intestine, was often fatal, and at least was a wasting disease from which it took considerable time to recover. By this time the family was looking to Ro as a knowledgeable and experienced man. He himself never questioned his responsibilities, despite the increasing tensions surrounding his grandfather and the old homestead. Edward was happily married to Mary and doing well with the bedstead factory. His life had not all been smooth, but for a while it looked as though things were going well for him. Then he took ill, and it was clear to everyone that this illness was serious. Edward survived but was badly broken by the experience. Roswell writes to his beloved Cardie to explain things in February of that year:

> You will be surprised to receive a letter from me at home and I will explain. Saturday night came a letter from Mother saying Ed was quite ill, though I had no reason to suppose his condition dangerous at all. I received the letter just before dinner—and just after dinner came a telegram from Charlie "Come home tomorrow." Of course this laconic message together with the letter alarmed

me and at the same time left me in great suspense. I left New York on the first train which was at eleven o'clock, but Sunday is not an auspicious day on the Central and I had a slow and tedious journey—reaching Manlius about 8:30 p.m. One of the men met me there and brought me directly to Ed's, and here I have been ever since playing the role of doctor nurse. Ed is very sick with a vilious fever, but if we can avert typhoid complications I think he will sail through all right. There were two reasons for sending for me. One was that Saturday he was so very ill that they all—including the doctor—considered his condition alarming. The other reason was that they needed me to help take care of him. Mary is not strong enough, so Charlie and I share the care of him between us, and he requires constant care. I cannot tell you how long I may be home—it will depend on Ed's condition. If he is no worse, he will probably be enough better by the last of the week so I can return. I have been fearing it would be my bad fortune to miss the senior dinner, by absence—tho. I have no more reason for supposing it will come this week than any other. Please tell Stelle so she will know what to do, in case the dinner should be appointed for this week. All last week I was busy at the hospital and should have been this week also but for the circumstances. This has been a beautiful day and the sleighing here is perfect. You may think this scrawl is written at an unseasonable hour, but doctors are privileged you know—and the time passes slowly when there is little to do but struggle with the somniferous god. One thing is certain, this pen of Mary's is a complete failure—even if it is gold and sports a pearl handle. I take the liberty—which I know is assured, of sending love from everybody to everybody.

Your aff. cousin
R. P. Collin (written 3 a.m.)

Over the next few years, while Roswell was setting up his practice in New York City and living in a boarding house with other students and young physicians, Ro's love for Cardie began to deepen. He was approaching thirty and she was into her twenties, a very marriageable age. In writing to her, he is full of family news, reactions to his trips to Hillsdale. These letters keep affectionate comments formal, in good Presbyterian/Victorian custom, but there is a growing empathetic energy in the tone of them. Cardera was often in New York City or summering at the Hillsdale farm, called Collinwood, that she inherited from her sister. The first letter excerpted here is not, however, to Cardera, but to his mother, Clara, who was to die within a month of its writing. The letter, dated February 23, 1881, is written from New York City—we can almost feel the pace and responsibilities of generations shifting:

> Yesterday was a perfectly beautiful day here, but today the rain and sleet is falling and it is altogether disagreeable—as I suppose we are to expect it to be at this season. It would be a good day to be in the country, if we could be in the house out of the mud and wet—and as that would probably be the way I would take it, I wish very much I were home with you all. I received Minnie's letter this morning, and feel very much elated over the new dignity to which I have arisen in the past few days. Every now and then Mr. C. May has proudly exulted over me with the announcement that "he is another uncle." [There were two "Charlies." One was his brother, and this other, Mr. C. May, was his best friend and roommate from Williams, who, like Roswell, was in love with Cardie.] Only about a week ago, he was crowing the same thing for the fourth time—but now he can't "uncle" me anymore. We shook hands over it and declared quits this morning. I feel an almost irresistible desire to see my niece and though the young ladies of that age, when I have been accustomed to meet socially or professionally, have not been interesting specimens of humanity, this one, I am sure, is a remarkable exception. I know she possesses extraordinary charms and attractions. I feel that she does "in my bones," as they say. Think of a Collin with black hair. What a contrast in the family bouquet of blondes. I must certainly see this young lady before so very long and get her Grandmother's opinion of her, and in the meantime I congratulate everybody interested—and especially Chas. and Sarah. Perhaps now Charlie [his brother] does not approve of such familiar address and will hereafter be spoken of as "Mr. Collin, of the Collin family"—or

the father of Miss Harriet Beebee Collin [this Harriet Collin was Betsy Knapp's mother] etc. etc. If so I feel inclined to humor him, and acknowledge his claim to special consideration.

This does not seem to be much of a letter, but somehow I can't keep my niece out of my head and heart—I hardly know which.... Mr. May enjoyed a holiday yesterday and we spent most of the day together.... He is always so jolly and cheerful and witty that he always keeps me laughing. He is a splendid antidote for blues.

I am glad you feel able to ride out so often as it must be very pleasant for you as well as beneficial. Minnie writes me that you are not feeling quite as well, for a few days, but I hope it is only a temporary depression. How much you must have enjoyed Aunt Hattie's visit. I should like very much to see her too. I am glad to know Cousin Hatty seems so happily settled. I judge from a letter I received from George, that he thinks Will is about the luckiest and happiest man living....

You know I think of you a very great deal Mother, and shall be very glad when I can see you again. It would be a great pleasure to be at home with you now, but since my duty seems to be here, I try to content myself with it, take what comes thankfully, trust for what does not yet come, and leave as we all must, everything else to the Good Father. And I pray that He be your comfort and strength, in these weary and trying days of illness, and I bless you always for the dear good Mother that you are—and always have been. With great love, as always, for you and all.

Your loving son
R. P. Collin

Some time later he is living at 133 West 34th Street, and in the fall of 1885 he writes to Cardera, who is visiting Fayetteville:

This week I am going to send my home letter to you—both to show you my appreciation of your note and because as a member of the family you are entitled to a letter. I was glad when the letter came, for I had been looking for it every day for more than a week, and was beginning to feel rather badly treated. It was all very interesting when it came and I was very glad to hear what good times you were having. The weather has been simply perfect and I cannot help thinking all the time how lovely it is in the country and wishing I could be home with you all.... Have you read aloud any more and is Aunt Eliza still industrious over the rugs?...

Yesterday afternoon I spent most enjoyably at the Staten Island Cricket Grounds playing tennis.... I have this morning been offered the opportunity to travel for a year—around the world in fact, with a wealthy family, with a pecuniary consideration about equal to my practice. Probably you will think as I do, that it is a very tempting offer, and before you hear from me again, I may have decided to go. I shall have no opportunity to consult the family in the matter, as I have only a day or two in which to make my decision, and if I should decide to go, may not be able to see them for a year. Please pass this letter around....

I suppose you know without my telling you that I appreciate your efforts to keep me supplied with weekly letters from home—as well as that it is always a pleasure to hear from you. It begins already to seem a long time since I was home and saw you all and if only we possessed some magic for eliminating distance and expense, I am very sure I would manage to spend a Sunday and perhaps also a Saturday and a Monday at home.... How is Minnie's cold and what are you doing all these days? Is Aunt Eliza still at work on the rugs?

A month later he is indeed home in Fayetteville, but Cardera is now gone, her fall visit over. From a letter of November 1885 to Cardera:

It seems much longer ago than yesterday morning since I said "good bye" to you at the depot, and were it not that the lack of news to write seems to prove the fact, I would hardly believe it. I really have no news to tell you, but I knew you would be anxious to hear from Miriam [his sister, not his aunt] soon, as the first few days after separating always seem the longest. So while I am waiting for Father to come from the Shakespeare Club, I will scribble a brief epistle to you. I tell you, Carderica, we miss you dreadfully, and Miriam especially. She was nearly heartbroken after you went, but feels better today. The Doctor came to see her yesterday and told her she must stay in her room for a while as the cold air of the halls was very bad for her. It will be pretty hard for her to be shut up so close, but I guess it is the best thing, for she seems quite a little better today. The Dr. came again today and brought some salt for her to take and has changed her medicine. If she knew I was writing to you I know she would send her love.

Your "Aunt Eliza" commenced her fourth rug today.

Gus has invited me down there to spend Thanksgiving evening. Don't you wish you were invited too? When you answer this I shall not be offended if you write Miriam's name on the envelope as she needs all the company she can have just now. Wishing you all a very pleasant Thanksgiving, I am,

Your cousin,
"Billie Taylor"

Two weeks later he is writing to her again from the city. The "Minnie" he refers to is, I believe, the family name for his sister Miriam, who in the end lived to be over eighty, well into the twentieth century. From a letter of December 6, 1885:

After my return from Fayetteville Wednesday I wrote you a short note asking you to call and see me if possible. In reply I find upon my desk, your address in Lu's hand, at No. Andover, which I suppose means you are there. I wanted to talk with you about Minnie, and what I had to say I could much better talk than write. To be brief, I am very anxious to have Minnie go South as soon as possible and when I left home, the prospect was that she would do so. As I told you the day I saw you, I would rather have you go with her than anyone else—and so would she—and Aunt Eliza is willing you should go—and if necessary she is willing to go too. Now what I want to know is if you would be willing and could arrange to go South with her pretty soon. I know it is asking a great deal and I do hate to interfere with any pleasant plans you may have, but, Cardie, the necessity is great. I feel that it is a matter of life and death with Minnie, and the sooner she can go the better. I wish she were already there and would be glad if she could start within a week, in fact the first day she is well enough to travel, and I urged them at home to begin her preparations at once. How long do you expect to be away, and how soon may I hear from you? Please drop me a line as soon as possible. I must confess to you that I forgot to take the lamp shade you got for Minnie. You must forgive me and I will send it to her. With much love and hoping to hear from you soon.

     Your aff. cousin
     R. P. Collin

Less than a week later he responds to two letters from Cardera. She spent time between her home in Hillsdale, traveling to see relations, and another home near New York City in Rutherford. From Dec. 10, 1885:

Your two letters were received and greatly relieved my mind. You don't know what a comfort you are. I cannot send you definite word yet for I have heard no definite word from home, though I know from a note received from Minnie she is talking of starting next week. You know how much time you want at Rutherford before you start, and I want to see you before you start. As soon as I hear anything definite about the plans I will write you again and probably Min will write you too. It seems most likely that she will go to Lake Como—though I think Thomasville Ga a rather better place. Yes, I knew about Kittrel and mentioned it to you. It is a nice place but rather too cold and too far north for Minnie at this season. With thanks for your letters and much love,

     Your aff. cousin,
     Ro—

Roswell becomes busier as his practice builds up. His tone becomes almost a breathless shorthand. He thinks constantly of home, but he is driven by his work, though perhaps motivated to be driven there by other factors. From June 1886 he writes Cardera a series of brief but intense notes:

[June 16]

Thanks for your note received this morning. I am going to try to get home Friday, but may not until Saturday and hope I shall find Aunt Eliza and you when I get there. I had expected to attend the Benton reunion but since that is given up, I shall probably have more time at home. Your note was the first report of Father for several days. Give him and all the rest my love, and with a generous portion to yourself.

Your aff. cousin,
Ro

In July he wrote her from Quogue, on Long Island. There are times when she seems as illusive as a dream or a mist:

> I felt *very sorry* to miss you and Aunt Eliza when I reached home—all the more when I heard how near I came to seeing you. Had it been possible I would have gone to Rutherford after my return, but after the week at Williams—and *such* a delightful one—and my packing up and a good many things in town to attend to and a flying trip to Long Branch, I was already more than a week late here and did not dare to stay away any longer. . . . I found Minnie *very* well and Father doing nicely. He walked around and took most of his meals at the table with the rest of us. I hope he will continue to gain strength. You and Aunt Eliza were sadly missed by us all and I shall never forget what you have both been to us this last winter.

An excerpt from a November 15 letter, written now from 50 East 31st Street in New York:

> I was very glad to receive your letter and definite information about Aunt Eliza'a condition. I am glad to hear that her condition is no worse and hope she is improving all the time and that she will soon feel like her old self again. . . . It is no doubt a great relief to her to have you with her, and you must not forget to take good care of yourself, as well as of her, for you know it would be a great deal worse to have two invalids than one.

The wedding passed off nicely and was very pretty. [His younger brother, Will, was married to Louise H. Cameron in November.] There were *many* expressions of regret at the absence of Aunt Eliza and yourself and your vase was very much admired and appreciated. The day after the wedding we were all down to Ed's to dinner and had a splendid time—and Edith and I returned that night. I enjoyed having her with me very much and the day we went up we had the company of Mrs. John O. Evans, who had just returned from abroad. You see I am in my new quarters and very comfortable and pretty they are.... I have not heard a word from home since I came back, but I expect a letter by each mail.

And in December 1886 he writes from New York:

Charlie [his friend, not his brother] felt obliged to return home last night, in spite of all my efforts to keep him another day, and he was *very* sorry, as I was—that he could not stay and go to you today.... I hardly need to tell you that amidst all my work and the preoccupation which it brings, I still have had you constantly on my mind, and my heart has been filled with the same sadness which is yours [Cardie's mother had just died]. How well and dearly I know what it all is! I do feel for you all more than I can express.

Charles May, the "Charlie" of the above letter, studied law after he graduated from Williams with Ro. He lived in New York City as well and often saw his old college roommate. He was a partner in the firm of Baldwin and May and did quite well for himself. He met Cardera through Roswell and fell deeply in love with her. A cheerful and optimistic young man, he courted her despite the unwritten pact (at least in available documents) between Roswell and Cardera not to marry while they were both alive. He was a dear and loyal friend to both. The three were often together, and Charlie frequently saw her on his own both in the New York area and at her place in Hillsdale. The following letters from Charles May to Cardera tell us a little about the friendship and indicate his earnestness in pushing his suit forward. Cardera loved him, too, but he was not her first love. In October 1888 Charlie wrote:

My dear Miss Cardie:

I am vanquished I admit and have lost my call besides, a matter I have been grieving over, ever since I received your letter this morning. Wednesday, Thursday and Friday at Lee I looked for the missive which did not come. Friday night I went to Pittsfield leaving directions to forward my mail (plural you see) and during my stay there I amused my friends' curiosity as well as wonder as they had never known me to be so anxious about my letters before. Monday I gave it up and went to Northampton instead of Hillsdale a little bit vexed, I admit, but of course without reason. I spent a very pleasant day at Smith College, however, with my niece and yesterday returned to the City. My brother forwarded the letter here and now I have nothing but regret to express that I did not get it sooner and thanks for your kindness in sending it. I appreciate fully your reason for not writing sooner, although you magnify the effect that a disordered house would make on a bachelor. My college experience in a room which I took care of myself has prepared me thoroughly for any kind of disorder. I care not how great it is, and in spite of my club experience and the reputation for love of luxury, which I am sorry to see, it is garnering me. I never feel quite as natural as when everything is in confusion and I can put my feet on the mantel piece and tip back in my chair with the consciousness that I am right in the style of everything about me. And the open fire! Ah me what have I missed!

Please give my kindest regards to Mr. & Mrs. John Bingham Collin. It was very thoughtful of you to distinguish them so scientifically from John F. Collin, for I wager that I would have gone to the latter's house and if I had I am afraid I would have astonished him, if he is a good man, with an ejaculation.

If you should do me the honor ever to communicate with me again by letter while I am in town (a bit of good luck which I can hardly expect now that I have exhausted my bribe) will you please address it to me at my office, No. 32 Nassau St., as I am more certain of getting it promptly there than if you send it to the club. Thank you very much for your [?] & permit me in view of my disappointment to subscribe myself your meandering,

Charles May

The next whimsical letter is in many ways a metaphor for his courtship of Cardera. He is always welcome, thought of with affection, but she is just not there for him.

>32 Nassau St.
>N.Y. City
>July 27th 1889

My dear Miss Cardera:

On the 19th day of July in the year One thousand eight hundred and eighty-nine, a traveler might have been wending his way from the depot in a small town near the foot of Mt. Washington, known by the euphonic name of Hillsdale, toward a pleasantly situated farm house about two miles from the village. He was evidently a stranger in the neighborhood, for shortly after he left the depot he stopped a native whom he met and enquired the way to Mr. John Collin's house, but though a stranger he evidently knew enough to distinguish the John Collin whose residence he was seeking from all other possible John Collinses who might be living there, since he was careful to say not John F. or John S. but plain simple John, for which reason the directions given him were plain and lucid. "Turn to the right when you reach the first street, go along it till you reach the church, then turn to the left and follow the winding road till you come to the bridge over the brook, then turn to the left and keep on for about a mile, when you will come to the house which is on the left hand side of the road." With such guiding it was not strange that the traveler found his way very easily and along the road he trudged past the church, past the old burying ground, past the beautiful cemetery, over the clear bubbling brook, by the lovely grove up the hill and on and on by the farms till at last after another enquiry to make sure of the house, he arrived at his destination. But *where where* were the people? He knocked at the front door, he knocked at the side door, he shouted so that he feared the neighbors would be alarmed, but it was all in vain. Evidently there was no one at home. There were signs of recent occupation, a chair under the tree, a window open on the [?] floor, a chair under the tree in the orchard, and more than all a dog, belligerent at first, great at barking and showing teeth, but afterwards when he saw that it was no ordinary tramp that was coming, full of friendly welcome and of tail wagging apology for his mistake, but the signs and the dog were all. For two long hours under the tree on the hill above the house did the traveler sit with one eye on the front yard and the other roving around in quest of people. Far up on the mountain he could see moving figures in the field. He conjectured that one of them might be John, but the fact was he didn't come to see John, and if he should travel up the mountain and find it was not John, he might feel bad, and if he found that it was John he might feel bad too, for he would then have just time enough to say "How do [ye] do, please tell Miss Cardera I called." and then to walk down the mountain again and back to the depot to take the afternoon train to New York. This disappointed traveler therefore concluded that he had better wait until twelve o'clock when if anyone was coming to the house at all, he, she or it would be apt to come, but if no one did come by the house then it was likely that he might have to wait there until late in the afternoon, in which case there would have been nothing but a skeleton under the tree on the hill, for hunger already had begun to fall upon his wasted frame. Moreover dark clouds were gathering and a deluge threatening. He did not wish to be put to the task of deciding which was pleasanter, starving or drowning. Therefore this disappointed traveler, shortly after twelve o'clock, gathered himself together and wandered his way back to the town, by the lovely grove, over the clear brook, past the beautiful cemetery, over the winding road to an Inn, even so he held gratefully in his remembrance, since there he had a dinner which banished from his mind for the time being all dread of starvation. Then in the pouring rain he was driven to the depot and took his departure for the City. Would you know the name of this luckless traveler? It was,

Your humble servant,
C. May

Charlie had proposed to Cardera several times in his long courtship, and each time he was affectionately turned away. But he was persistent.

As Roswell worked through his thirties and his practice matured, so did his love for Cardera. His expressions of affection become more overt. In one place he refers obliquely to a conversation they seem to have had regarding marriage and the heartbreaking decision they made not to marry. It is the closest reference that I have found, in the documentation available, to this choice of theirs. He is deeply engaged in his work, worried about his aging father, and trying, though with only moderate success, to stay in touch with his increasingly widespread extended family. Indeed, he is experiencing the onset of the complex responsibilities and intense busyness of midlife. A part of his practice, for the summers, is now in Quogue, located near the Hamptons on eastern Long Island's southern shore. The area is not quite the enclave of the very rich that it has since become, being made up largely of potato farms and fishing villages, but some families with old money lived there, and his early roots matched theirs. In this first excerpted letter to Cardera, from June 1889, he is actually writing from Fayetteville and his brother William's house (the Oak Grove Farm that had been his grandfather's and that his father had passed along to Will):

> Here I am at Will's house, writing you from my very early "stamping ground" where as a child I have spent so many pleasant days with Grandmother Collin, in excursions from the cellar to the mysterious attic. It is very interesting to be here again, and they have repaired and improved the old house so that it is really very comfortable, while retaining most of its old features. We have just finished a very toothsome dinner, and now, my dear cousin, a few words with you while I enjoy my post-perandial cigar and my thoughts of you together (as to time, of course). I wonder if I am not to see you? I only reached home this morning and learn from Minnie that you are to leave Hillsdale next Friday. I wanted to see you in Hillsdale, but if you are not there, how can I? Yet next to seeing you there, is seeing you in New York [where she spent most of her adult life] or in fact anywhere. I hope you are to be in the City long enough to see me when I return—which will be either by the Saturday or the Sunday night train. I am going to try desperately to get away by the Saturday night train, so as to spend part of Sunday at Park's house [another cousin]—for among all my

other shortcomings (and you know my dear how innumerable they are), I confess with sadness and mortification that it is considerably longer since I have seen any of his choice little family, than since I have seen you—and both failings I profoundly regret. I know perfectly well how you will elevate your eyebrows, and the possibly skeptical—certainly agnostic smile that will dally with your mobile features—but my dear cousin, of whatever other sins you convict me (alas! that they are so many) do not I beg of you, impeach my genuine affection for my kindred—especially for those who are nice, like yourselves and Park's family. I left the city Monday evening and saw Em yesterday as she was on her way home. I am sorry to say I do not find the family very well. Minnie is miserable with a bad cold. Louise ditto, Clara home and rather tired out, and the baby with a severe cold. But Niles Collin Hand is a magnificent boy of whom I am very proud and Clara is much better here than in Kansas City—better in fact than I expected to see her. The others are all pretty well. Carrie and Miss Annie Kelly are at Edward's house but I have not yet had a chance to see them. Won't you please drop me a line addressed to my office so that it will be there Saturday, telling me where and when I can see you? I hope you are well and strong again, and that your potato-sprouting bucolics not only inspired your mind with brilliancy, even more than usual, for your decennial address [she was president of the Mayflower Society], but also invested your nerves and sinews with strength perennial. I have a great deal to tell you—too much to write, and must wait till we can speak face to face. Wishing that may not be long, I am, My Dear Miss President with great respect, yours to command,

       Roswell P. Collin

In late September he writes to her from Quogue:

This is the day I had expected to leave Quogue but it will be impossible now for me to leave before Monday. Then I will have a very ill patient to carry to town. This you see disposes of the question of next Sunday at Hillsdale. C. May writes me that he has sent you word of his inability to join us there, and Minnie I know could not leave home at this time—as Niles and Clara are both home now and waiting for me to join them. My dear, it was very good of you to arrange such a delightful little plan for our pleasure and I wish it might have been carried out. What a good time we could have had all together. I still hope I may stop at Hillsdale for a day or two on my return to New York, which will probably be not before the 10th of October. I want very much to see you all and the old homestead. I am hoping for a good rest and great pleasure in my few days of vacation. This has been the hardest summer I ever spent here—in one way. I was rather tired after a hard winter when I came down here and I have been more busy here all summer than ever before—in fact overworked.... The result is that my friends have been neglected. For the first time since I left home as a boy, my weekly letters home have failed—and I could only write about once in two or three weeks. All this I regret, but could not help.... Much love to you—also to John and Lu, Aunt Hattie and Martin.

In October, a week or so later, he writes again:

As you have either judged from my last letter, or heard from Miriam [his sister], or both—I am at home again. Left Quogue Monday P.M. last week with a very ill patient, who could go no further than New York that day, but whom I attended to her home in Newburgh the next day. There I spent the night and came as far as Syracuse by the limited express next day. It was too late for the train to F. and too cold to drive out, in summer attire, so I spent the night there (the Leland Hotel at Franklin and Fayette Streets, across from the N.Y.C. Railroad depot, per the letterhead) and went home Thursday morning. It is good to be home as I hardly need tell you. I have never enjoyed or felt the need of the homecoming more than now—for I have had a summer in Quogue—but no vacation. All are pretty well except Clara [who had just come home from Kansas to have the baby Niles]—and she has improved greatly this summer, but still has very little endurance. The boy is simply superb—and so is his father—whom it is a great pleasure to see, after six years. The weather has been wretched since I came, but every day we are expecting sunshine. I came out this P.M. to do some errands for Min and myself, and this evening we are all going to Ed's to tea. Saturday evening we all spent very pleasantly, except Father—who does not go out evenings—at Dr. Evans'. Yesterday we had the usual family Sunday re-union at the homestead. Miriam is splendid as usual and we are both wishing you could be here now. She has received your letter announcing Edie's approaching marriage. It is hard to realize it, is it not? I hope she will be very happy. She is a fine girl and deserves to be. How are you "Liebchun" and when can I see you? How are John and Lucy? C. May told me of his visit to Hillsdale. I saw him a few minutes Monday night. It is train-time now and I must go. With love to the cousins and a great deal to your good self.

Your aff. cousin
Roswell P. Collin

Roswell had become one of the best throat specialists in the city, but he developed, through the brutality of urban medical practice, through his thoughtful nature, and through his doomed love for Cardera, an increasingly lonely yet profound vision of life. It has the ring of experience that carries his family's troubled legacy and the frustrating helplessness of a discipline that was only beginning to break out of the almost medieval, pre-Pasteur world of incurable diseases. Typhoid and smallpox were the terror of crowded cities (and New York was swarming with new immigrants living in appalling conditions), where epidemics could attain plague proportions. It would still be another twenty-five years before the Typhoid Mary incident led to learning how to prevent the spread of the dread wasting disease. Yet Roswell had been inculcated with a deep sense of duty, a love of man and nature—realizing there is no real separation—and a passion to give of himself. Some of that need he learned at home, as he watched the dissolution of his family and the ideals by which they had lived. Much of it came from a need to give himself and his life meaning when the person who gave him the most meaning could not be part of his intimate heart. He loved his work—lost his *self* in his work (and his relationship with Cardera gave him permission to do so), brought him to a nothingness beyond faith, but it was not emptiness. Eido Shimano has written, "When we ... completely accept our fate, then we can take a different attitude. When we take a different attitude, a positive attitude, then, no matter what the situation, we have a great influence on other people. This *giving influence* to other people is the meaning of life."

Ro writes to his friend Charlie May in July 1891, while he is in Quogue, just before returning early to his winter practice in the city to help in the battle against one of the many epidemic outbreaks of typhoid fever. He begins the letter, however, referring to an episode in which he almost drowned at the beach, then moves quickly to a case he handled, a black child with typhoid. Obviously, from what Ro says, Charlie has heard something of these things, most likely from Cardera. The no longer quite so young doctor's tone and language have changed dramatically:

> The beach episode was an accident—pure and simple, without one element of imprudence. We were unusually cautious, as the life-lines were not out. The same conditions now, as the lines *are* out, would be free from danger, as the sea-pull would simply sweep us to the cross line, where we could all cling and rest, and come in on the ropes, if we could do no better. As to the [other] dangerous case which exhausted me, I have not the slightest regret, except that I could not save the little black stalwart bit of humanity. I would not only do the same thing again, but would do it all or more, and with genuine *pleasure*. In fact I could not possibly do otherwise, when once a life is committed to my hands, I am impelled by a force as irresistible as the fatal magnetism which draws one to the brink of a giddy precipice or height. It may be fatal—one may topple over the edge—but be powerless to prevent it all the same. Old soldiers prefer to meet death on the field. So would I, in the service, when my call comes.... My life is not so precious to me that I would become a coward to save it.... Desperate cases make me desperate.... Still more it is what I *like* to do. It gives me pleasure—and I have none too much. My greatest interest and pleasure in life is in my work. It may exhaust me—but it brings me no pain or bitterness or sorrow—or fear. It did once—but never since. Of all diseases in the world, I had the greatest dread and horror of smallpox. When it became my duty, as well as opportunity, to take charge of the smallpox hospital, I was almost paralyzed with fear, and had a fearful battle to fight my cowardice.... Pride and conscience won the day, and I entered the wards prepared to do my

duty, at whatever cost. Since that time, disease has had no terror for me—and this case was worse than smallpox. It might have cost me my life, but I do not think I would have minded very much if it had. Experience has taught me well, the lesson which probably most people of my age learn—"Blessed be nothing." The early hopes and ambitions for personal happiness are most seductive—but they are frauds and sure to fail. One may plan his own plans, exercise without limit the privileges of "free agency" and attain his ends, all of which were motivated by a craving—natural enough, but most likely selfish—for satisfaction and happiness. But when all is done, some subtle influence has spirited away the object of it all, and only [vani]ty or mockery are left. There *is no happiness.* One is crushed. It is better to be crushed early, as you and I have been, than to be educated by Fortune to an elevation of high certainty, and then let drop like a charred rocket stick. I believe this is the great lesson of life—and that the sooner one learns it the better. It seems like the end of all things but it isn't. It seems to bereave June of all its roses, the sunlight of its glory, music of its harmony, and life of everything it seemed and promised. It is a very large, nasty, old school dose and cannot be swallowed all at once. But it is finally injected, assimilated and as a result, self or selfishness is largely eliminated. The bottom seems knocked out of everything—and one expects nothing. Well, the truth is, that is just the time one begins to live. The Ego had to be pulverized, and when practically extinct, the weak remnants first revive to a consciousness that if "nothing" is not blessed, it is at least tolerable. By way of relief, ego begins to take interest in others, since there is not enough left of itself to interest anything or anybody. It is not so bad—in fact rather agreeable. "What fools we mortals be"—to take all that time and suffering to learn what we were taught in the beginning. I find all my plans for my personal pleasure disappointing. When I forget myself and turn to others helpfully, I find that by some curious necromancy, I attain the greatest satisfaction.

Unlike his aunt Miriam, who looked outside herself for affirmation, vindication, and hope for a place among the elite, Roswell was turned by his work in on himself. It has been said that to search for and to study the truth, as Roswell came to do, is to search for and to study the self. To search for and to study the self is, in the end, to forget the self. To forget the self is to be affirmed by all things. Perhaps here, if we are willing to step back a couple of years, we can let Cardera tell her side of the story as it runs up to the time of this letter by Roswell and a little beyond. Her voice is a necessary missing piece of the music, and until now we have heard only from those who knew it by heart. First a letter to Charles May:

(from Hillsdale)
August 2nd, '89

Dear Mr. May,

On the morning of the nineteenth of July 1889 the family of a certain country gentleman arose very early, for the evening before two thirds of the family had persuaded the other third to leave his farming for one day and make with them a long-deferred trip to Albany to purchase a long-desired carriage, which was to add to the comfort of the family and of any guest who might be tarrying with them. The morning was perfect and having arranged for the mid-day meal of the men in the rife-lot on the side hills or "on the mountain," as it has been called, the party set out in high spirits and with anticipation of an enjoyable day. The train connection from their little village did not allow of sufficient time in Albany for their purpose, so this trio had before them a fifteen mile or so drive to Chatham. The road, after a little way, became unfamiliar and extremely rugged, full of the most unexpected ups and downs—picturesque, of course, but retarding. There were moreover so many turns to right and left that it was a puzzle to know if they were on *a* road to Chatham, and the country gentleman had often to stop at a farm house to inquire the way, and as often, or so it seemed—he found the house apparently unoccupied, which led him to exclaim, "Well, I never *did* see such a deserted region!" whereupon one of the party members [said], a little deprecatingly, "But you must remember that if anyone called at *our* house to make inquiry today, he might think the same of *our* region." They were in time for their train, however, and moving on rapidly to Albany, they made there their purchases according to their wishes, and returned to Chatham. As they resumed their places in their topless buggy for the homeward drive, a gentle rain was falling, which they were pleased to call a shower. A little later they spoke of it as "a perfect drencher," and the one waterproof in the possession of the party was handed out and made to cover the backs of the three people, and the one umbrella was held in as protective a manner as possible against the furious blasts of wind and rain by two and sometimes three people. Night was coming on and the anxious wish of these benighted travelers was to get over the mountains and past certain remembered steep places before it should be quite dark. They hastened on, the wind forgetting not to blow nor the rain to fall. But darkest night overtook them and at times not even [?] before them could be seen. They gave themselves up to providence [?] and on they moved by wishes! enveloped in blackness, except as a blast of lightning revealed the road. And yet this party of three despite the fact that they were dripping, declared they were enjoying the drive. It was not cold, they did not after a time have even the trouble of holding an umbrella which no longer protected, and then there was an element of danger that added excitement to the night's experience. But this weird enjoyment came to an end as they drove into their own domain and were welcomed by William, one of the men from "the mountain" "No [?], no one's been here, I suppose?" one of the family found breath to say, and as she ran into the house. "No, ma'am, guess not, haven't seen nobody." And she was half amused herself at the question, as though anyone *would* come, anyone more interesting than a buyer of wool or a seller of mowing machines.

 One afternoon, some two days later, she sallied forth, as was her custom, for the day's mail. As the letters were [to] her, she ... needed only to read a line or two to guess the rest of the story, and "Oh," she cried in utter dismay, "He was here and gone! Isn't it dreadful!?" And the more she thought about it the more dreadful it seemed. "But why?" she wondered, "why did not he let me know he was coming? ... [?] ... He couldn't have cared very much about seeing us, else he would have made care of our being home. Oh, I see how it was. He happened to be passing through our village on his train, so he thought he would stop and walk out to the farm. If the family was home, well and good—if not, it did not matter very much, he would have had a pleasant walk."

But to *her* it seemed dreadful that he should [come all that] way and find no one to greet him; dreadful that there should be no one to offer a cup of water even, or a morsel of bread to a half-starved man; dreadful that she should be robbed in one fell hour of even the anticipation of a possible call. For she felt that after such an experience he would never never come again to such an inhospitable house, and she could not blame him, she would not if she were in his place. At first she felt that she would never dare even to suggest his coming again—she seemed to see his smile and hear his thoughts—"Oh no, one visit is quite enough for me." "But I'll never be satisfied," for so her thoughts ran on, "till he does come again and let us redeem ourselves from apparent inhospitality. I'll never be satisfied till I meet him at the depot and bring him home in the carriage that was, alas! to be the cause of something beside comfort to the family! Could he be persuaded to spend a Sunday with us? Not some indefinite Sunday but one near at hand, the eleventh of August, say, or the one following?" Such was her thought and [?] such is the wish of the country gentleman and his whole family.

x x x x x x

Would you know the name of this country gentleman and of the [?] "he" of my story? Would you, Mr. May? Tell me that you know "he" will come again and I will tell you—what you will.

Awaiting most surely the summons to meet him at the station on Saturday August tenth (please don't let "him" fail), "she" and I are sincerely yours,

Cardera Collin.

By 1891, when Cardera was thirty-three, Roswell resigned himself to a life alone. He knew that precious time was passing for his still-young, beloved cousin, and he was of such a nature that he could not bind someone else to the life he felt he had to choose. Unable to love anyone else as he

Cardera Collin, first cousin and first-cousin-once-removed of Roswell Park Collin

loved her, he chose to be alone, but he set his dearest friends free. At some point that summer it appears that he made it clear to Charles and Cardera that the earlier pact between himself and Cardie could not continue and that she and Charlie were both free to make other choices. The cost to him was profound. We learn of his being ill in the early fall, having returned to the city. Cardera's brief diary entries tell the rest of the story for the ensuing couple of months of 1891, while she also was in the New York area, probably over in Rutherford, New Jersey:

Saturday, Nov. 7
    A lively afternoon, & [?] and I drove to the [?]—called on Aunt N. & Mrs. Chinels [?]. Found a dear letter at the office from Charlie. During our absence Mrs. LeRoy Hunt & Mrs. McAlpine called.

Monday, Nov. 9

Very rainy all day. Sent James for the mail at night. He brought a letter from Charlie. I went up to my room to read it and half laughed and half cried over it. A letter also from Sara begging me to come to town next week.

Tuesday, Nov. 10

Worked very hard at house cleaning etc. all day. James went to the village at night and sent a single word to Charlie.

Wednesday, Nov. 11

Wrote a note to Charlie telling him to come on Saturday as we had planned. I went to the village in the rain to mail it. House-cleaning all the afternoon. Read introduction to second volume of Life of Josephine, & then wrote to Charlie. Dr. Cornell here.

Friday, Nov. 13

Went to the village in the a.m. to see Dr. Cornell on business. Two letters from C. One from the "legal friend," one a note telling me he was coming on the afternoon train. Wrote a letter to Ro this evening, also a note to Sara.

Saturday, Nov. 14

In the dear old library by the great open fire I was betrothed this night to Charles May.

Thursday, Dec. 10

Left for N.Y. on 8:39 train. Forgot trunk and had to telegraph back. Rather a good joke on myself. Went to see [?]. Went to Mrs. Woodward's [her husband, Dr. Woodward, was a friend of Ro's and was caring for Roswell in his home]. Ro had had a relapse, could not see him. Charlie spent the evening with me.

Friday, Dec. 11

Went to Park's office & told him of my engagement. He was delighted. Went to the Union League after lunch with Sara then for a lovely drive in the Park with her. Charlie with me in the evening.

Monday, Dec. 14

Shopping. Went to a lovely concert with Sara in the afternoon at Munro Hall. Charlie's birthday & the anniversary of a month of our engagement. He brought me my ring in the evening, an exquisite solitaire. We spent the evening at Park's.

Friday, Dec. 18

A note from Charlie this morning that Roswell is worse. I went right on to Mrs. Woodward's. Had a sweet talk with Mrs. Woodward. Waited to see Charlie Collin [Ro's younger brother]. Dr. Swift came in and said there was nothing discouraging about Roswell. I went to Sara & we called on Virginia Bailey. Sara & I spent the night with her.

Up to this time no one had spoken the dread words that Roswell had contracted typhoid fever, most likely when he worked with the young child out on Long Island, as mentioned in his letter to Charles May. Neither had the young couple set a date for their wedding as they waited and worried through Roswell's illness. In her way Cardera was holding back on her new commitment as her Ro fought to hold on to his life.

Monday, Dec. 21

While at breakfast a telegram received from Charles May that Roswell was very low. The doctor gave no hope. I prepared to go to the City immediately. A second telegram told me that my beloved cousin Roswell had died at nine o'clock. I arrived in Syracuse at night, was met & was with Minnie a little later.

Tuesday, Dec. 22

A dark, rainy day. Charles Collin arrived this morning with his precious burden. That was hardest. But when we looked on Roswell's face, it was not so hard. That face so beautiful, so whole. Oh, Lord, why? Why?

Cardera Collin and Charles May were married on May 26, 1892. Cardera Collin May died in April 1936.

11

Wherefore One Hundred Years of Silence

> Let it be so; thy truth, then, be thy dower:
> For, by the sacred radiance of the sun,
> The mysteries of Hecate, and the night;
> By all the operation of the orbs
> From whom we do exist, and cease to be;
> Here I disclaim all my paternal care,
> Propinquity and property of blood,
> And as a stranger to my heart and me
> Hold thee, from this, for ever.
> —Shakespeare, *King Lear,* 1.1.110–22

At two o'clock on the afternoon of April 5, 1885, David Collin Jr. is called before the Surrogate Court. He is now sixty-three, a man of substance and no longer referred to as Mr. David but as Mr. Collin. As he answers the questions he is stiff, reluctant. Martin Knapp, Miriam's attorney, has to pull every fact from him as they go over his father's wills and the details of his estate. At first it seems he is just angry at being there. Gradually we guess that he must be hiding something, some fact about the estate that would explain why Miriam Armstrong went to such lengths to overturn the will of 1874. In the end we discover that he was indeed hiding something, but that his reluctance had little to do with the family finances or how well he made out from the arrangements. It was something else altogether.

DAVID COLLIN,
Recalled and cross examination resumed.
By Mr. Knapp.

Q: Mr. Collin, did you know of a will executed by your father at Mr. Tremain's house in 1871?

A: No, sir.

Q: Did you ever understand that a will was executed by him about that time?

A: I didn't know anything about it.

Q: I didn't ask you what you know. I asked you if you understood that he executed a will about that time?

A: I have no recollection of it.

Q: Mr. Tremain married one of your sisters?

A: Yes, sir.

Q: He is not now living?

A: No, sir.

Q: When did he die?

A: I should think perhaps 10 or 12 years ago; I don't recollect.

Q: He was living then, in 1871?

A: I think so; yes, sir.

Q: Were you present at his house at one time when there was some talk about your father's making a will?

A: I don't recollect of it.

Q: Were you there at one time with your father when the disposition, which he should make of his property by will, was the subject of conversation?

A: I have no recollection of it, sir.

Q: Were you present at any time when instructions were given by your father for the preparation of a will?

A: No, sir; no recollection of it.

Q: And did you know of your father executing a codicil to the will in 1872?

A: No, sir.

Q: And you never heard that he had executed a codicil to the will in 1872?

A: I don't know anything about it.

Q: Now, don't let us have any misunderstanding about it. The question is a fair one and you don't answer it fairly. You say you never heard that he had executed a codicil to the will in 1872?

A: I don't recollect anything about it.

Q: Do you mean by that, that you don't recollecting hearing about it?

A: I don't know anything about it.

Q: Do you mean by that, that you don't recollect hearing about it?

A: I have no recollection about it.

Q: Have you any recollection of hearing of it?

A: I have answered all that I know in regard to it.

Q: I didn't ask you what you know about it. I am asking you what you heard about it?

A: Well, I can't say as to the time or with regard to it.

Q: Well, I ask you again. Do you now recollect of having heard at any time from any source, that your father did make a will in 1871?

A: I don't know.

The Surrogate: Well, you can answer that yes or no.

A: Well, I don't know anything about it.

Mr. Marshall: Your answer is yes or no; whether you recollect hearing anything about it.

A: I don't recollect; no, sir.

By Mr. Knapp.

Q: Well, do you mean by that, that you may have heard that he had, but don't recollect whether you did?

A: I don't recollect anything about it.

Q: Do you wish to be understood as saying that you didn't hear from any source at any time that he had a will in 1871?

A: I have no recollection of it, sir.

Q: No recollection of hearing of it?

A: No recollection about it.

Q: What do you mean by that?

A: Just what I say.

Q: Well, do you mean that you have no recollection of hearing about it? Is that what you mean?

A: I have answered you all I know about it, sir.

Q: I am not asking you for what you know.

The Surrogate: I think he can answer that question yes or no.

A: Well, as far as my knowledge is,—as far as my remembrance is, I don't know anything about it.

Q: Did you ever hear that your father made a will in 1871?

A: I cannot say that I did [k]now, at that time.

Q: Have you ever heard of it?

A: I can't say.

Q: Have you not since your father's death heard it said that he made a will in 1871?

A: I have heard it stated that he made several wills.

Q: Who stated it in your presence?

(Objected to as entirely immaterial as to who stated anything with reference to the wills, after the death of the testator.)

The Surrogate: I can't see how it is very important, but I will allow him to answer the question.

(Exception taken by Proponent's Counsel.)

A: Well, sir, I can't tell you; it has been talked in conversations since his death, but who told me, I cannot tell you.

By Mr. Knapp.

Q: Was there anything else said than, that he had made several wills?

A: Well, there has been some conversation with different parties, but who told me, I cannot tell you.

Q: Well, what have you been told?

(Objected to as entirely immaterial, incompetent and hearsay.)

A: I think Mr. Wilson has told me that there was several wills drawn, as he understood, and I ain't sure but there was other persons.

By Mr. Marshall.

Q: He stated that he understood it was so claimed?

A: Yes, sir.

By Mr. Knapp.

Q: And you say he is the only person from whom you did receive any such information?

A: That is all I think of now; Mr. Aust[i]n and Knapp [a different Mr. Knapp, Betsy's grandfather, Henry, who fought in the Civil War] claimed to have been witnesses to a will of his; it was the same one we talked about this morning.

Q: Have you had any conversation with Mr. Austin as to the wills which he had witnessed?

A: Yes, sir.

Q: Did he not tell you that he had witnessed more than one will?

A: He may have done so; I don't recollect.

Q: Didn't he tell you that he witnessed a will on one occasion at Mr. Tremain's house?

A: I don't recollected, sir.

Q: He did witness a will in 1874 at The Farmer's Bank?

A: Yes, sir.

Q: When did you have this conversation with Mr. Austin that you refer to?

Mr. Marshall: Now, I submit that it is not material what conversation was had with Mr. Austin and this witness. It is hearsay and incompetent.

The Surrogate: Well, he may answer. I can't see how it is very material.

(Exception taken by Proponent's Counsel.)

A: Some time during this past winter; I couldn't tell you what time.

By Mr. Knapp.

Q: Were you ever informed what were the provisions of any of those others wills?

A: No, sir.

Q: And you have no recollection of hearing that he made a will in 1867 or '68?

A: No, sir.

Q: Did he ever tell you,—did you father ever tell you that he had executed any will except the one made some 40 years ago?

A: I don't recollect anything about it.

Q: If your father had told you about making a will you would have been likely to have remember[ed] it, wouldn't you?

A: I don't recollect anything about it.

Q: Well, if he had told you that he had made his will you would be likely to remember that circumstance, wouldn't you?

A: Possibly.

Q: And you say that you don't recollect that he ever told you that he had made a will?

A: Not at any definite times.

Q: Well, at any indefinite times then?

A: I don't recollect.

Q: Did you have access to this safe of your fathers?

A: No, sir; not previous to his death.

Q: Did that safe lock with a key or combination lock?

A: A key.

Q: Was it a safe that your father had for a good many years?

A: Quite a number of years.

Q: And for a long time before he left the Grove?

A: Some little time.

Q: Where was he accustomed to carry the key of it?

A: In his pocketbook.

Q: So that while he lived at the Grove, you had no access to his safe?

A: No, sir.

Q: None of your papers were kept there?

A: No, sir.

Q: When did your father go to live at your house?

A: I think it was in the fall of 1881; I think so; I don't recollect the date now.

Q: About three years before his death?

A: I should judge so; three or four years; I don't recollect now.

Q: Who comprised your family at the time your father came to live with you?

A: Well, I think there was two of my sons at home and one of my daughters, wife and hired girl; some times some of the boys were home for a time.

Q: Your wife was living at the time your father came to reside with you?

A: Yes, sir.

Q: And your daughter was also there?

A: Yes, sir, and I think perhaps both of them part of the time I know they were part of the time.

Q: They were both unmarried?

A: Well, my oldest daughter was married while he lived there.

Q: And did she continue to live at your house after she was married?

A: She was there part of the time.

Q: Well, were any of your sons living with you at your house at the time your father came there?

A: Yes, sir.

Q: Which ones?

A: The two youngest sons.

Q: What are their names?

A: William and Frank.

Q: Your son Edward and son Charles were not living there then?

A: No, sir.

Q: Were the youngest sons, either of them married?

A: No, sir.

Q: What room in the house did your father occupy when he first went there to live?

A: What we call our parlor.

Q: And did he continue to occupy that room so long as he lived there?

A: Yes, sir.

Q: And was this safe taken from the Grove to your house and put into this room occupied by your father about the time he went there to live?

A: Yes, sir.

Q: Now, who occupied the Grove house after your father came to live with you?

A: Mr. Coon.

Q: What became of the furniture and fixtures that were in the house before that time?

A: Before he came up there?

Q: Yes.

A: I don't know; what he had in his room he brought up when he came.

Q: What became of the rest of it?

A: I don't know.

Q: You don't know what he did with his household furniture?

A: It was left there; I don't know whether it is there now or not; some of it may be there; there was not much value to it.

Q: And from that time on so long as your father lived you say you had no access to this safe?

A: No, sir.

Q: As a matter of fact you never did open it or have anything to do with it?

A: I never opened it for him; I once oiled it so that he could unlock it easier; he was right there; the key turned hard and I oiled it so that he could unlock it easily.

Q: That safe was divided into compartments—pigeon holes?

A: A place for putting boxes and 2 or 3 small drawers.

Q: And in the safe was this tin box?

A: It was the last year of his life.

Q: He didn't have that tin box when he came to live with you?

A: No, sir, not there; he kept his valuable papers in the bank; in the tin box in the bank.

Q: This tin box, as you understand, of valuables, had been for a number of years at the bank?

A: Yes, sir; been there since the organization of the bank.

Q: Now, what was the occasion of bringing it to your house?

A: He wanted to look over the papers that he had there; he wanted I should bring it up for him.

Q: So you went to the bank and brought it up?
A: Yes, sir.
Q: Was the box locked?
A: Yes, sir.
Q: Did you have a key to it?
A: No, sir.
Q: And was there space for that in the safe?
A: Yes, sir.
Q: And after it was brought up from the bank the box was put in the safe?
A: Yes, sir.
Q: And kept in the safe from that time on?
A: Yes, sir.
Q: After your father's death you found this safe locked?
A: I did.
Q: And you took the key and opened it?
A: I did.
Q: And in the safe you found this tin box?
A: Yes, sir.
Q: And that was also locked?
A: Yes, sir.
Q: Where did you get the key to that?
A: That was in the drawer of the box,—in the safe.
Q: And you opened the box?
A: Yes, sir.
Q: And what did you find in it?
A: Well, I found this will in it.
Q: You say that when you found it that it was in an envelope and not sealed?
A: I don't think it was sealed; just as it is now.
Q: Well, is it sealed now?
A: It was cut open at the end.
Q: Well, how was it when you found it?

A: As it is now.

Q: With the end cut off. Just as it is now. Is that what you mean?

A: That is what I said.

Q: I understood you to say this morning that it was unsealed?

A: Well, it is; it was open that way.

Q: That is the first time you had seen this paper since the day it was executed at your father's house in 1876?

A: That I recollected of, sir.

Q: Had you had any occasion to see it?

A: No, sir.

Q: Well, why did you say that you don't recollect,—if you had seen it you would have recollected, wouldn't you?

A: I might now.

Q: Had you had any conversation with your father about it from 1876 down to the time of his death?

A: I don't recollect about it.

Q: You have no recollection of ever having had any conversation with your father upon the subject of his making this will?

A: He made it and got through with it; that is the end of it.

Q: You have no recollection of his saying anything to you about it?

A: He might have talked about it; I cannot now recall up any time.

Q: You say that you have no recollection that he did mention it to you after it was executed?

A: Oh, I have told you what I know about it, sir.

Q: I simply asked you if you have any recollection?

A: Not that I recollect of, but still he may have done so; I didn't recollect at first about Mr. Wilson telling me in regard to these wills.

Q: What did you do with this paper when you found it after your father's death?

A: I brought it here to the Surrogate.

Q: Did you show it to anybody?

A: My son was with me when I took it out.

Q: I asked you if you showed it to anybody?
A: No, sir, not until I showed it to the Surrogate here.
Q: And how long was that after you found it?
A: I don't recollect; a very short time after.
Q: And how long after your father's death did you find it?
A: Well, it was several weeks before I went to the safe at all; until it seemed necessary to have the will to present for probate.
Q: What made it seem necessary to have the will proved?

Mr. Marshall: That is not what he said.
A: Well, I knew he had a will; he said he had made one, and I supposed it was there, but I didn't know until I had looked for it and found it.

By Mr. Knapp.
Q: Why did you wait several weeks before looking for it?
A: I didn't suppose it was necessary to go for it at once; a person's mind is not exactly in condition to go for a will the first thing after losing a fri[e]nd, especially a parent.
Q: What made it seem necessary to you to look for the will?
(Objected to. Objection sustained.)
Q: Do you say that you had any conversation with your father with reference to the execution of his will before this paper was signed by him?
A: I do.
Q: You and he had talked over about his making a will?
A: Yes, sir; he wanted to make his will and have it correct.
Q: And you knew about how he intended to make it?
A: I didn't, sir.
Q: He never talked with you about how he intended to make it at all, I suppose?
A: No, sir.
Q: On what paper,—what kind of paper was this document written upon that you took up to Mr. Cowles? About a month before this?
A: Foolscap paper.

Q: Was that sealed up in an envelope?

A: I don't recollect.

Q: Did you read it yourself?

A: Not until I heard Mr. Cowles read it, sir.

Q: Then did you take it and read it too?

A: I don't recollect; I read it and that was enough.

Q: Did you not talk with your father before this paper was signed with reference to the advances which he had made to your sisters?

A: I can't say, sir.

Q: Why, hadn't the matter of the gifts he had made to your sisters been the subject of conversation between you and your father?

A: More or less, but not with reference to any paper of this character.

Q: I didn't ask you that at all. I simply asked you if the subject of your father's advances to your sisters had been talked over between you and him?

A: Yes, sir.

Q: Before this paper was made?

A: Yes, sir, for years.

Q: And had the subject of the monies paid out by your father for or on account of your brothers-in-law been the subject of conversation between yourself and your father?

A: Occasionally.

Q: Do you know what has become of that paper that you took to Mr. Cowles?

A: I don't.

Q: When you last saw it, it was in Mr. Cowles' possession?

A: It was there.

Q: Was that where you last saw it?

A: Yes, sir.

Q: So far as you know it was never returned to your father?

A: I don't know what became of it.

Q: Well, I say, so far as you know it was never returned to your father?

A: Not as I know of, sir.

Q: You never heard your father say that he had got it back or understood that he had got it back?

A: I don't recollect anything about it, sir.

Q: That paper disposed of your father's property substantially if not exactly as this will does, does it not?

A: I should say there was not much difference, still I cannot say.

Q: In that paper did your father purport to give the reason which induced him to give the property to you and none of your sisters?

A: It did some reasons.

Q: Substantially the same reasons that appear in this will?

A: I should judge so, sir.

Q: It is the best of your recollection then, that in this paper he assigned the same reasons for disposing of his property that he assigned in this paper?

A: Some of that sort, yes, sir.

Q: You are familiar with the reasons he states in this paper for disposing of the property as he does, are you not?

A: I have read it, sir.

Q: And you are aware that he says in that paper that he has paid out for or on account of his sons-in-law and his grand children, about the sum of $30,000? [$616,000]

A: Substantially that.

Q: And you say that the amount that he had paid out for them had been the subject of conversation between your father and yourself prior to this time?

A: Occasionally, sir.

Q: Was it true that your father had paid out about $30,000 for his sons-in-law and grand children?

A: As far as I know, sir, and more.

Q: In addition and not including the gifts or loans to your sisters?

A: Yes, sir.

Q: Which are referred to in this paper?

A: Yes, sir.

Q: You were pretty familiar with your father's affairs for a great many years were you not?

A: No, sir.

Q: Didn't you know what property he had?

A: Yes, sir.

Q: What his investments were?

A: Not all of them.

Q: Well, the most of them?

A: Some of them.

Q: The important ones. The principal ones?

A: Some of them.

Q: You knew what his obligations and liabilities were to a great extent did you not?

A: Yes, sir.

Q: And that monies had been paid out on account of your brothers-in-law,—you had been aware of it, hadn't you?

A: Part of it I had; part of it I didn't until it was paid out.

Q: For the most part of it you knew about, either at the time or afterwards?

A: Yes, sir.

Q: The amounts and the circumstances under which those sums were paid out?

A: Not all of them.

Q: Well, mostly?

A: Yes, sir.

Q: Are you able to state the [it]ems which make up any such aggregate as $30,000? Your father had paid out on account of his sons-in-law and grand children?

A: I can in the aggregate from his statement; that is all I can give you to-day.

Q: Well, do you know yourself from your knowledge of his affairs of payments of the description named in this will to the amount here stated?

A: And larger amounts according to his account which he gave me.

Q: Had you any knowledge of the matter except what he told you?

A: Not the whole of it; I have part of it.

Q: Do you know when those payments commenced?

A: Payments he made?

Q: Payments which he refers to here as having been made for or on account of his sons-in-law and grand children?

A: Well, sir, I couldn't tell you; a long series of years.

Q: You speak of an account. Do you mean in writing?

A: He had a long account with loans and accounts with Mr. Armstrong, a son-in-law of his, that has run for a number of years, and he got Mr. Tremain to settle it; he acted as a sort of an arbitrator between the two; he got their accounts adjusted, which were mixed and left a balance due Father of $14,000 [$287,350] which he was unable to meet.

Q: Now, when was that?

A: I should say that was along about 1870; somewheres about that.

Q: When did Mr. Armstrong die?

A: I should say some 6 or 8 years ago; I don't recollect the time.

Q: And you say there was a settlement brought about through Mr. Tremain between your father and your brother-in-law, Mr. Armstrong about 1870?

A: Well, whenever it was; I could give you the date if I had my papers here.

Q: What papers have you got?

A: I have the receipt which Mr. and Mrs. Armstrong gave my father in regard to it.

Q: A receipt which she gave your father?

A: Yes, sir; Mrs. Armstrong and Mr. Armstrong.

Q: Well, if Mr. Armstrong was owing your father such a large amount why should she give a receipt to him?

A: The receipt explains itself; I can product it if you want it.

Q: Yes, I would like you to produce that Mr. Collin. Was that indebtedness of $14,000.00 from Mr. Armstrong to your father a part of the $30,000.00 referred to in this paper?

A: I don't know, but I presume so.

Q: You so understand it?

A: I so understand it.

Q: There wouldn't be any $30,000.00 without that, would there?

A: Yes, sir.

Q: Oh, there would?

A: Yes, sir.

Q: According to your knowledge of your father's business transactions with him and others?

A: Yes, sir, directly and indirectly.

Q: Well, now, at the time of this settlement were you informed of what was going on? Did you know about the settlement?

A: Yes, sir.

Q: Was there not at the same time an indebtedness from your father to Mrs. Armstrong?

A: It was all brought in.

Q: Was there not an indebtedness?

A: There was an account; I don't know how it was.

Q: And was your father the administrator or rather the executor of the will of Mrs. Armstrong's grand father?

A: Yes, sir.

Q: And as such did he not receive a considerable sum of money which belonged to her under the will of her grand father?

A: I don't know, sir; he paid her in land her interest in the estate, the same as he did some of the rest of us; settled with her.

Q: What was the claim of Mrs. Armstrong against your father at the time of this settlement?

A: I don't know.

Q: There was a claim of indebtedness of Mrs. Armstrong against your father?

A: I don't know; I didn't transact the business.

Q: Did you understand at the time, that that was the fact?

A: I don't know anything about it, sir; I had supposed it was the other way, but I don't know.

Q: Don't you know, that while your father had been making payments to or for Mr. Armstrong, that Mrs. Armstrong had been making payments on account of your father?

A: No, sir.

Q: And wasn't it true that her claim against your father equaled the amount of your father's claim against her husband?

A: No such claim alleged in the settlement.

Q: Do you say, that there was a settlement in which it was conceded by Mrs. Armstrong, that there was an indebtedness of $14,000 or thereabouts to your father over and above the claim of Mrs. Armstrong against him?

A: As I understood it, that settled everything between the parties.

Q: What settled everything?

A: That $14,000; they passed receipts on it. Mr. Armstrong had nothing to [buy] and they passed receipts; I didn't have anything to do with the settlement; Mr. Tremain done the business.

Q: I asked you if you understood that there was a settlement in which it was conceded by Mrs. Armstrong, that there was an indebtedness of $14,000 or thereabouts to your father over and above all claims of Mrs. Armstrong against him?

A: I don't know; her name is to the receipt; they settled all accounts so Mr. Tremain told me and there was that amount due father.

Q: Well, I ask you again if that account was claimed to be due your father over and above what your father owed Mrs. Armstrong?

A: I don't understand he owed her anything.

Q: But you understood that she claimed it?

A: I understood that she claimed it and he claimed the other way.

Q: Well, wasn't it found on that settlement that your father owed Mrs. Armstrong about as much as Mr. Armstrong owed your father?

A: I never heard of it.

Q: And that they passed receipts upon that basis.

A: I never heard of it, sir.

Q: After that settlement and prior,—done to the day of the execution of this will did your father pay out any money for or on account of Mr. Armstrong?

A: Not that I know of.

Q: Or Mrs. Armstrong?

A: Not that I know of; he had to give his notes in part payment of this indebtedness; he wasn't able to pay it until after that, but nothing between those parties.

Q: How was that?

A: He had to give his note in part payment for some of this indebtedness, which he wasn't able to pay in some years.

Q: Who gave the note?

A: My father.

Q: Gave his note to who?

A: Why, to pay this indebtedness that Armstrong had involved him in; where ever he could hire it.

Q: And then, do you mean at the time of the settlement with Armstrong, there were certain contingent liabilities of your father's which were taken into account?

A: My father assumed that.

Q: Was he liable on that at the time?

A: Yes, sir.

Q: What was it,—endorsements?

A: They were notes with Mr. Armstrong's endorsement upon them as I understand it.

Q: Your father's notes with Armstrong's endorsements?

A: Yes, sir; he got him to sign notes so that he could raise money.

Q: And at the time of the settlement your father hadn't taken up and paid all these notes?

A: No, sir.

Q: But did so subsequently?

A: Yes, sir.

Q: And in that settlement he had assumed the payment of these obligations?

A: So I understood it.

Q: Do you know how much of that $14,000 was in obligations than [then] held by your father, and how much of it in those which were outstanding and on which he was liable?

A: I don't.

Q: Have you an idea about that?

A: I have not.

Q: Well, do you know any reason why your father should assume the payment of obligations, which he had incurred for Mr. Armstrong by way of endorsement or otherwise, when that settlem[ent] showed that Armstrong was indebted to him?

A: Those notes were given before this settlement.

Q: Yes, and they were outstanding held by other parties?

A: Yes, sir.

Q: And they had your father's name on them?

A: Yes, sir.

Q: Now, if Armstrong owed your father a large amount why should your father assume the payment of that indebtedness and give Armstrong a release?

A: Why, he was helpless; he couldn't pay them; statements were brought in at the time that he failed of his indebtedness of 80 or 90 thousand dollars [$1,850,000].

Q: What is that you mean? Mr. Armstrong's indebtedness?

A: So reported; I don't know how true it was.

Q: Your father wasn't involved beyond the amount of $14,000. was he?

A: No, sir.

Q: Well, I think you stated there were no payments after that time for or on account of Mr. Armstrong, except as your father subsequently took the obligations which were outstanding at the time of the settlement?

A: That is all I know about it, sir.

Q: No fresh obligations were incurred at that time?

A: I think not; I think he had no business relations with him after that of any account.

Q: Well, what further payments to his sons-in-law were in this $30,000?

A: Well, all I know is what my father told me; that at the time of Charles Tremain's failure [the paper mill], Father became responsible for paper and money, that he had loaned him to the amount of $17,500 [$359,000].

Q: Well, whatever obligations your father incurred for Mr. Tremain by way of endorsements or otherwise had been fixed and determined some time before this paper was executed, had they not?

A: I should say so; I cannot say positively.

What follows is a bickering exchange as to the extent of Charles (Charlie) Tremain's indebtedness to his grandfather over the collapse of the paper mill business and property. It appears that David Jr., in an effort to keep the mill afloat, took on further debts to his father (David Sr.) by taking up another $11,000 [$226,000] of Charlie's debts. While the larger portion of the indebtedness was in cash, approximately one-third was in notes and other papers. Despite Mr. Knapp's persistence, he was unable to get David to amplify in any way the arrangements nor make out that David Sr. had been anything but a generous but tough businessman. In responding to the proponent's counsel, Mr. Marshall, Mr. Knapp responds to the surrogate.

Mr. Knapp: Of course, the Surrogate will perceive that our contention is, that if the old gentlemen believed that his payments to his sons-in-law and to his grand children were of any such amount as $30,000 he was entirely mistaken, and if he was induced to make this will believing that state of facts to exist, why, he was laboring under a very serious misapprehension.

Mr. Marshall: Suppose he was.

Mr. Knapp: Well, then, it may have a very important relation to this controversy.

The debate goes on for a period over minutiae with David continuing to be recalcitrant. Of all the children and grandchildren in debt to David Collin Sr., Charlie Tremain was second only to Miriam and her husband in degree. Mr. Knapp tries unsuccessfully to show that perhaps it wasn't as bad as people had made out. There were at least three mortgages on the paper mill, two owned by the village banks and one which had been assigned to David Jr. by his father. David was the one who eventually had to foreclose on the mortgage. His portion was around $2,000 [$41,000]. In the later sale of the property David realized some profit, but he refused to "recollect" exact numbers for Mr. Knapp. At any rate, David took on the indebtedness of Charlie Tremain for the $11,000, which was broken into $8,000 [$164,000] in one cash portion and the remaining $3,000 in various notes. In the questions that followed from this analysis it becomes clear that Charlie Tremain was never able to repay his debts to David or to his grandfather. And, although he obviously knew, David did not say that Charlie had been involved with his aunt Miriam in the plans of May 1877. The questioning proceeds.

> Q: Now, after that failure and the losses which your father or yourself sustained by reason of it, did Mr. Tremain become indebted to your father for any fresh or subsequent indebtedness?
> A: Not that I ever heard of.
> Q: Nor his mother, Mrs. Tremain?
> A: Not that I ever heard of.
> Q: So that as far as this recited in the will refers to any monies paid out on account of the grand children, meaning thereby Mr. Charles Tremain[,] related wholly to what had been paid for Charles Tremain's failure?
> A: I should judge so, sir.
> Q: And no part of it given after that failure or before the making of the will?
> A: I think it was all enumerated in there; it must have been; because he had no business except his farming there.
> Q: No, don't misunderstand me. There was no other loans or advances to Mr. Tremain after this failure?
> A: Not that I ever heard of.

By Mr. Marshall.
> Q: By your father?
> A: No.

By Mr. Knapp.

Q: At this time two of your sisters were dead leaving children?

A: Yes, sir.

Q: Mrs. Seward and Mrs. Gardener [Gardner]?

A: Yes, sir.

Q: Did your father lose any money or pay out any money for or on account of Mr. Seward?

A: I think not, sir; I never heard of any.

Q: Or Mr. Gardener?

A: I never heard of any.

Q: Had he paid out anything for or on account of the children of Mrs. Seward?

A: I never heard of any.

Q: Or the children of Mrs. Gardener?

A: Only as he gave them property at the time he gave property around to the rest.

Q: I mean that he had met with no losses on account of monies loaned to them or obligations incurred for them?

A: I never heard of it.

Q: Had he for his son-in-law, Mr. Wells?

A: I never heard of it.

Q: So that whatever he had in his mind in reference to this will about $30,000 paid out for and on account of his sons-in-law and grand children related wholly with this [sic] transactions with Mr. Armstrong and Mr. Charles Tremain?

A: The Tremain family.

Q: Had he paid out money for or on account of any other member of the Tremain family except Mr. Charles Tremain?

A: Indirectly he lost by Mr. Porter Tremain.

Q: He was Charles' father?

A: Charles' brother.

Q: What was the nature and extent of the loss?

A: The extent of it was about $11,000; it was not to him directly, but he assumed it.

Q: When did all that happen?

A: Well, sir, shall I explain it?

Q: Yes.

A: My father gave to Mrs. Tremain, Mrs. Wells and myself what is called The Mill Property in Fayetteville and deeded it to us.

Q: The deed running to all three of you?

A: All three of us; and Mr. Porter Tremain became one of the firm with Mr. Wells and myself and in running the business,—saw-mill and shingle-mill, etc., he was the main man; he done the business; he was in business there, I don't know how long; one, two or three years, and it went so fast at that time that we found that the firm had become obligated to the amount of $14,000 and stopped the business; $11,000 of the money was money that we hired of my father,—the indebtedness which Mr. Porter Tremain had made.

Q: That is, the firm represented by Mr. Porter Tremain, who was a member of it, had borrowed $11,000 of your father?

A: Yes, sir, including the interest, and so we were there obligated,—the firm was in to my father for $11,000, and Father saw the way we were in that indebtedness and our inability to meet it and he said he would take the property back and cancel the debt; we done so; we deeded the property back to him.

Q: So that the persons in whom the title stood conveyed the property back to your father and he discharged the indebtedness[?]

A: Yes, sir.

Q: How much was that property worth?

A: I think $8000 was the most I was ever offered for it; I tried to sell it for years.

Q: Well, if your father had got the property back which he had previously given he couldn't be said to have lost $11,000 through Mr. Porter Tremain?

A: If he had carried the business successfully,—

Q: Well, at the end of it all, your father was not out anything more than the difference between the $11,000.00 and the value of the mill?

A: I have given you the fact.

Q: That indebtedness was as much against you and Mr. Wells as it was against anybody else; that is, you were equally liable with the rest.

A: Yes, sir.

Q: Well, that was not any reason why you should get the bulk of your father's property.

(Objected to. Objection sustained.)

Q: Well, then, whatever there is to which this $30,000 refers relates to the matters you have not stated?

A: Yes, sir.

Q: The transactions with Mr. Armstrong and Mr. Charles Tremain and this last one of the mill property and Mr. Porter Tremain?

A: Yes, sir.

Q: Now, did you at any time assume or pay any other obligations of your father except this $11,000 which you have stated?

A: Yes, sir.

For the next ten pages of the court report Mr. Knapp examines several pieces of land scattered across the region owned by David Sr. and transferred to some of his daughters as well as several nieces and nephews in 1874. Some lots were a few acres (fifteen or so) and some several hundred acres (three hundred and more). The interrogator attempts to show, to no real point, that the Armstrongs had in fact sold land back to David Collin Sr. Mr. Knapp also probes for details regarding stock owned by David Sr. in the two banks, particularly the Farmer's Bank. At one point Mr. Marshall, counsel for the proponent, objects to Mr. Knapp's picking over the values of particular acreage ($50 for this, $60 for that).

Mr. Marshall: I don't hardly see the materiality of this testimony; what those were worth in 1874.

The Surrogate: I don't suppose it is very material, but I will allow him to go on. The point is, was this man competent to make a will? Did he make it according to law, and was there any undue influence exercised over him. I will allow him to go on.

(Exception taken by Proponent's Counsel.)

David continues answering with a minimum of words—each fact, dollar, acre having to be pulled out of him. Finally, seeing that this line of questioning is doing little but stacking up an ill-defined pile of numbers, Mr. Knapp moves on. In what follows, the true extent of the Collin estate begins to emerge, as well as the reason for David's reluctance to say more than is necessary.

By Mr. Knapp.
> Q: Well, what else was transferred to you at that time?
> A: That is all at that time that I recollect of.
> Q: Well, at or about that time?
> A: He transferred this mill property to me after that.
> Q: And that mill property was transferred without consideration?
> A: Yes, sir; I paid nothing for it.
> Q: Well, what further?
> A: That is all that I think of, sir; I think that covers the whole.
> Q: Was there any personal property transferred to you at that time?
> A: Yes, sir.
> Q: Well, before I go into that. Was there any personal property transferred to any of your sisters at that time, or to any of their children?
> A: Not that I know of.
> Q: Now state, if you please, what personal property was transferred to you?
> A: He transferred his bank stock.
> Q: To what amount?
> A: $10,000, [$205,000] I think it was.

By Mr. Marshall.
> Q: What bank?
> A: The Farmer's Bank.

By the Surrogate.
> Q: Did that include this $3000 you speak of?
> A: No, sir, it was outside.

By Mr. Knapp.

Q: What else?

A: There was mortgages; $3700 I think it is; and there was railroad bonds,—Western Railroads that I have realized about $300 from, and some Lincoln Coal Company's stock in Missouri, I realized $100 out of it.

Q: On *bona fida* sales?

A: On *bona fida* sales, yes, sir; he paid $1200 for it and I received $100.00.

Q: What else?

A: That is all that I can think of, sir.

Q: That is all the property that was transferred to you?

A: That is all I can think of, sir.

Q: All that property which you say amounts to something over $58,000 [$1,200,00], according to your valuation was transferred to you without consideration beyond the payment of those obligations which you state you assumed and afterwards discharged?

A: I assumed those obligations.

Q: Not exceeding $11,000?

Mr. Marshall: He says $3000 in The Farmer's Bank.

Mr. Knapp: That stock is worth more than the $3000.

Mr. Marshall: No it is not; it is not worth over 50 cents on the dollar.

By Mr. Knapp.

Q: This bank stock of which you speak of as being transferred to you and for which you assumed to be responsible. Is the stock equal in value to the debt?

A: I don't know what it is worth to-day, sir.

Q: Well, what is your best judgment about it?

A: Well, I should not want to give any more than that.

Q: Well, you would not want to take any less would you?

A: Not if I could get it.

Q: That was some stock that the bank had bought up really with its own money, wasn't it?

A: What?

Q: This $3000 of stock was some stock that the bank had bought with its own money?

A: No, sir.

Q: Didn't you so understand it at the time?

A: No, sir.

Q: Where did your father get it?

A: He took it of outside parties.

Q: Do you know from whom he took it?

A: It came from Eli Bangs.

Q: Wasn't he also an officer of the same bank?

A: No, sir, I think not; I don't think he was, but still he may have been when it was organized.

Q: Wasn't this about it. That the bank had bought up some of its own stock with its own hands, and fearing some trouble with the bank department it was divided up among the other stock holders, and it has been carried along in that way for years?

A: I never understood so; Mr. Bangs subscribed for some stock and never took it.—

Q: Have you now mentioned all the property that was transferred to you by your father in 1874?

A: All I think of, sir.

Q: What became of the property mentioned here as The Grove?

A: I have mentioned that.

Q: Is that the 40 acres adjoining the home far?

A: No.

Q: Then you have not mentioned it.

A: There was 40 acres there.

Q: That is The Grove besides?

A: Yes, sir.

Q: The 40 acres?

A: Yes, sir.

Q: Of what value?

A: Well, sir, it is worth $100 an acre.

Q: Isn't there a farm at Manlius Center?
A: Yes, sir.
Q: Have you mentioned that?
A: I think so.
Q: Is that what you mean by the cedar lot 100 acres?
A: Yes, sir; part of it is cleared and part not.
Q: Now, at this time or about this time was any property transferred to your children or any of them from your father without consideration?
A: Not that I know of.
Q: Is the farm which now belongs to your son Edward in Madison County included in this 1000 acres which you have mentioned as having been given to you by your father?
A: He doesn't own any.
Q: Charles?
A: Yes, sir, that is included in it; it was not given to him by my father.
Q: It was included in the 1000 acres which was given to you?
A: Yes, sir.
Q: So that there was no property transferred to your children or any of them by your father?
A: Not that I know of.
Q: About the time of this transfer to you?
A: No, sir.
Q: And then giving you upwards of $60,000 [$1,230,000] worth of property, a little to Mrs. Wells and the Gardener children, is what you mean in your testimony just given, by your father dividing up his property among his children?
A: Yes, sir, when I speak of his dividing up his property in 1874.
Q: Among his children that is what you mean?
A: Yes, sir, certainly.
Q: Do you remember an occasion in 1875,—in May, I think,—where there was a family gathering at the house of your sister, Mrs. Gardener?

A: I don't recollect now that year.

Q: Well, do you recollect any time when the family were convened at Mrs. Gardener's house about that time?

A: Part of them were there, but not that year, that I know of; when they had family gatherings part of the family were around at different times; I don't know what you allude to.

Q: Well, was there a gathering of the family or part of the family at Mrs. Gardener's in 1875, which was attended by your father?

A: There might have been; I don't know.

Q: Well, did you go there and take him away?

A: Not in that year, sir.

Q: What year was it?

A: I think in 1877.

Q: What time in 1877?

A: I don't know it was warm weather; about this time of year I should judge.

Q: What time of the day did it take place,—was it a[n] afternoon or evening gathering?

A: I guess it was a day gathering.

Q: And who were there?

A: I merely drove into the yard in my carriage, but didn't get out; the people were in the house.

Q: Well, your father was there, wasn't he?

A: Yes, sir.

Q: Were your sisters or some of them and other members of the family?

A: I supposed they were there.

Mr. Marshall: Now, what materiality has it? Anything that occurred in 1877, more than a year after the date of this will?

The Surrogate: You may show it.
  (Objected to as incompetent and immaterial.)

The Surrogate: The objection is overruled.
  (Exception taken by Proponent's Counsel.)

By Mr. Knapp.

Q: You did go there and take your father away on this occasion?

A: I called him and asked him to ride out to my house with me; he got in and rode up with me; I didn't take him away. He came volunt[a]rily.

Q: What did you go down there after him for?

A: Because I wanted him to come to my house.

Q: Why did you want him to go to your house at that particular time?

A: I didn't want him down there.

Q: Why didn't you want him down there?

A: Because I had heard reports that it wasn't well to have him there.

Q: I want to know what you had heard?

A: Well, sir, that was on Monday, I think; I was away from home Monday forenoon and when I got home Mr. Burke was just driving away from my house, and Mr. Frank Glover, who had been a partner of the firm of Noxon & Cowles was there at work trying to regain his health and Mr. Burke told him what he came for, and when I got home he told me what he come out for; it was too late for me to go out to Syracuse that day; the next day I came out and had a talk with Mr. Cowles; he said Mr. Wilber M. Brown came to his office Monday morning and told him that he and Charles Tremain, the Sabbath before, during the services in church, where they were singing, had a conversation, in which Charles Tremain told him the plans of the firm was to have a family gathering and have two physicians there and have father pronounced insane and taken to Utica, and have trustees appointed to take care of his property.

Q: And you went down there and took him right away?

A: And took him right away.

Q: And you filled him full of the information that your sisters were going to put him in the lunatic asylum if he didn't leave them?

A: I told him the fact.

Q: Do you mean to say positively that that was after this will was executed?

A: I think it was in 1877.

Q: What makes you think it was in 1877?

A: In referring to my books; the account which I had with Glover at the time he worked for me. I find that that was the time.

Conclusion

> Who loses and who wins; who's in, who's out;
> And take upon's the mystery of things,
> As if we were God's spies: and we will wear out,
> In a walled prison, packs and sects of great ones,
> That ebb and flow by the moon.
> —*King Lear*, 5.3.17–24

That spring afternoon of 1877, when David rescued his father, the two men tore along the road in silence to the homestead, where David Sr. stayed with David Jr. and his family, eventually moving in permanently, until his death seven years later. No longer would whispers have cause to drift about the village like smoke from little fires set by unhappy children. The big house was large enough to accommodate him. After all, he'd built it himself on a large scale. By then many of the grandchildren had moved away, through education or marriage.

David Collin Sr. was ninety when he died in November 1884—a ripe old age even now, but almost unimaginably ancient at the time. And there was prevalent the notion that great age and considerable wealth conferred a certain virtue on the individual, one favored by Fortune, or more nearly, by God. The Collins were not evangelicals and sought no radical alternatives. They had no need to. If it was so, it was ordained to be so. It would not have occurred to David Collin Sr. to doubt that his long labor was proof of his integrity and the truth of his circumstances. Calvin and Luther had long ago laid the groundwork for the ethical efficacy of work and acquisition among the elect.

Throughout this period, some eight years after the "rescue," Miriam maintained a troubled silence over the matter, engaging, as she had since her husband's death in 1878 at the age of sixty-eight (a man leaving behind further financial ruin), in an effort to rebuild the ruins that seemed to appear spontaneously around her. She sought solace in devotion and in writing columns on temperance for the local paper. Miriam nevertheless waited less than six months after her father's death to bring her brother to court to contest the 1874 will. She died of a fever a year later in 1885, aged fifty-eight, her hopes unfulfilled. The will of 1874 remained standing and is on file at the courthouse in Syracuse. The Collins and Armstrongs went their separate ways for a century, the schism hopeless.

When we try to understand the transformation that took place in the mature Roswell Collin, both in the context of his extended family and in the context of the unremitting demands of his work, we arrive at a place where metaphysics, morals, and the down-to-earth bare-handed experience of life come together. Of the two themes that weave the fuguelike nature of this story, Roswell's gives color to both, revealing the finite limits of the moral tragedy of the one, while surrounding the whole with possibility, a possibility found through the cleansing fire of love lost and selfless attention to the details of daily life itself.

Even as a boy, Roswell, as his diaries show, observed the world closely, inclusively, and with respect. It is said it is not perfection that life requires, but completeness, and that everything—each one of us—is the condition by which all else exists. Thus Roswell's legacy.

There is a metaphor that directly addresses this seeming paradox of the timeless within time, of finite individuation of the personal simultaneously resting with the infinite. The sea represents in our imagination our inner sense of the infinite universe. Imagine being on the shore. We can stand in the shallow water and watch each wave as it moves toward us. We see that each of these waves is unique, has its own "personality." But then they crash and disappear. Where do they go? The ocean does not diminish when the wave vanishes, nor is the wave apart from the ocean while it rolls toward us. Any particular wave has a "life" and time of its own on its path toward the shore, but the ocean itself remains constant and unchanged by either the coming or going of the wave or by the time it takes the wave to reach us.

As we glance back over our shoulders into those living waves that make up this selective narrative of the Collin family, we find it is possible to realize a kind of interbeing with Roswell's *nothing,* a conscious state in which everything reflects everything else, while also seeing, as Roswell always did, that everything remains itself and that every journey has neither beginning nor end.

Because we can remember the true stories as they come to us we cannot, in some deep way, finally die. If we can learn that everything is still around we can also learn to live those stories that will help life to continue to emerge between stasis and chaos. Roswell left his stories behind, becoming free by letting go of his history, his ties, and living wholly in the ever-emerging now. The tragedy of Miriam is that she could not let go and so became trapped by the very conditions she had created for herself. Thus the true story of life is without a story. In the end one gives up everything, even one's God, and has it all. This is the great paradox to which we are all heir.

Afterword

I first met Betsy Knapp in a library classroom while I was in graduate school at Syracuse University. It had been fifteen years since I received my undergraduate degree, placing me among the older students by some margin, and I was studying librarianship with a specialization in rare books and manuscripts. My professor and mentor was Antje Lemke, one of the great book people from the precomputer old school. I was taking every class she offered before her upcoming retirement. The atmosphere in the room was always lively as Antje told stories, pulled odd things out of her vast pockets, and imbued in us a passion for the guardianship of the human endeavor, which was how she defined librarians.

This particular class was for archival studies. To complete it we were required to do some field work with an actual archive. Staff from other libraries, the Onondaga Historical Association, the Erie Canal Museum, and so forth had all come looking for recruits. I was often tempted but nothing quite grabbed me. Then one day a very energetic woman appeared. She was oldish, but not elderly, a senior of indeterminate age. She was very direct and forceful and, frankly, she intimidated the class. It appeared she had a huge collection of family papers, which she had taken upon herself to organize into a useful archive and library. She needed help. She explained that when her mother had threatened to discard the disarrayed boxes of stuff, she had cried, "Don't throw anything away!" Now she was trying to make sense of it all. She clearly did not tolerate fools. In our seats around the large seminar table we looked at one another. No one raised a hand. So the woman went on describing the collection, the letters and diaries, the farm records and maps, and the cache of newspapers, deeds, and bonds that had arrived at the Onondaga Historical Association from a distant cousin in the Midwest to add to her work load.

Silence reigned. Antje looked a little embarrassed when no one volunteered. I have no idea what possessed me—perhaps I was feeling particularly foolish—but slowly I raised my hand. Despite my intimidation, perhaps I was also fascinated by the idea of getting inside local history, of being the first to read documents unread for more than a century, to help put some order to the disordered squirreling away of a family's past. Or perhaps it was because I was drawn to the woman herself—her obvious intelligence and self-possession, her confidence that this was good and important stuff. She reminded me of my wife's uncle, a dairy farmer who read Kierkegaard, who was also feisty, remarkably intelligent, curious and practical, earthy, and at the same time a dreamer. I was fond of him. I liked this woman in the same inexplicable way.

She saw my reluctant hand go up. We looked at each other hard for a moment. Then she gave a single, quick nod of her head. Thus began years of friendship, hard work, and affectionate times with Betsy. She became a favorite older (never elderly) aunt to my children. The Christmas holidays couldn't begin before her annual party at which we cut our own tree in the snow from her overgrown tree lot and were then plied with hot cocoa or mulled cider and German holiday cookies put out by her and Antje. I learned from her enormously—not only about archives and historical records, not only about local history from a personal level, but about her struggles as a woman in a world of men—her mother and aunts, for example, had formed the still-extant and locally exclusive group called Coterie to provide an intellectual forum for college-educated women who remained in the home—and her pride in her roots, planted right in the very ground where she stood. In 1986 she had me be guest curator at the Onondaga Historical Association for a major and highly successful exhibition of her collection, not just the documents and books, but clothing, furniture, paintings, and other household artifacts.

Betsy was an unstable diabetic. In the last couple of years, when I would make my weekly Monday night visit to work on the papers with her (a project that continued well after I got my degree), I often found her running low on insulin but far enough gone to be unaware she needed an injection. I'd help her get back to normal, clean up the distracted mess she'd made among the papers, and sit to talk for hours about the family or her own past. My work was no longer archival but rather that of friendship and deep affection.

When she was hospitalized after her last two strokes I'd see her each day after work, as the hospital was a short walk from the university library. She still delighted in giving the staff a hard time and resented when they baby-talked to her, as people sometimes do with the infirm elderly. Everyone was kind to her, though they assumed that since her mind was sharp the rest of her functioned well, too. Her hand shook so badly she could not get the food from her meal tray to her mouth nor the water to moisten her lips, which became cracked and dried. I took to feeding her in the evenings and dabbing her mouth with a damp cloth. We talked as always. She enjoyed remembering the hikes she'd led us on around the Green Lakes. She was thirty-eight years my senior, and I liked to think I was in moderately good shape, but she had had my wife and me panting breathlessly behind her as she lunged with her walking stick through the deep woods her family had owned for 170 years.

I was with her on a stormy day with hugely heavy winds in February 1993, the day she died, at eighty-two, in the arms of the one great love of her life, Antje Lemke. She died in the very room in which her father had died, on the land her forefathers had cleared in 1816, the last of her line. There was a long obituary in the Syracuse newspapers, but her entry in the family genealogy tells a more complete story:

> Daughter of Carroll Duff Knapp and Harriet BeeBee Collin Knapp, born June 6, 1910, Fayetteville, N.Y.; Phi Beta Kappa, Smith, 1932.
>
> Betsy has been actively involved in educating women about the political world [most of her life]. During the early 1930's she was president of the Onondaga County League of Women Voters. She also studied political science and economics at the Syracuse University Maxwell School of Citizenship and was employed by the Works Progress Administration in Washington, D.C., as municipal finance

analyst. In 1937 [she] joined the National League of Women Voters staff in Washington as program secretary and pamphleteer.

During World War II, 1942–48, Betsy was an administrative analyst in the U.S. Bureau of the Budget in Washington [becoming the first woman to help draft the national budget]. In 1949 she was sent to Germany to take part in the reconstruction program as Women's Affairs Consultant under the High Command, and as Cultural Officer in Foreign Service under the State Department. Arriving in Germany without any knowledge of the language, written or spoken, on her first day she was asked to prepare a budget by noon of that day for the bureau she intended to create. With her German counterpart who knew only 14 English nouns and one verb, a budget was prepared and they established a bureau which exists today. [This "counterpart" was Antje B. Lemke, daughter of the theologian Rudolph Bultman, who, with the rest of her family, risked her life to aid Jews escaping the Nazis. She herself just avoided capture while being smuggled into Switzerland, as legend has it, in the trunk of a car. Before the war Antje had been secretary to the novelist Ricarda Huch, often compared with Thomas Mann. This so-called clerical experience qualified her to be brought to Betsy's side. Betsy brought Antje to the States and they remained companions for many years.] This bureau, teaching women's civic and church groups how to influence government officials, was directed by Betsy until 1952 and since then [has been] operated entirely by German women. Betsy was a guest of the German women in 1956, her travel expenses to Germany paid by donations from the women's clubs which had benefitted from contact with the bureau.

Following her return to the Syracuse area [which she felt she must do as an unmarried daughter, who by family tradition was expected to care for her elders], Betsy worked with Cornell University on a program to encourage the participation of labor in [the] Syracuse and Utica areas in their civic affairs. She also planned and directed a study of Onondaga County sponsored by the League of Women Voters, published as a booklet, "Know Your Onondaga

County." Betsy got her masters degree in library science in 1957 from Syracuse University and was circulation manager in the Syracuse University Library until 1967.

During the early 1960's, Betsy organized the Syracuse World Affairs Council, an extremely popular seminar. She also started an adult education program for community leaders called Government in Action, sponsored by the League of Women Voters and Syracuse University. From 1967 until her retirement July 1972, Betsy served as librarian of the Maxwell School of Citizenship.

On Christmas 1986 or 1987 (my memory fails me here a little) Betsy invited her long-estranged cousin Hamilton "Ham" Armstrong to her annual Christmas party and tree cutting. He showed up wearing a strange hat and was delighted to be a part of the festivities. Thus with a simple invitation and its acceptance, one hundred years of silence and mystery ended—in cider, snow, rich baked goods, a renewed sense of shared purpose, and finally, a grudging affection—both for the shared past and for a present in which this old, virtually forgotten family could still have an impact in just the way they always did: food, song, love, and light.

Without Betsy, none of this would have been necessary . . . or possible. I mean that both whimsically and in all seriousness. I did promise her I would write this story some day, and she was not the sort of person to whom one made idle promises. "I came from good stock," she'd often say. She imbued the world around her with the necessity of remembering. We must view the past, she felt, not as it actually was (for that is not possible), but how it made us actually who we are now. Without it we become sentimental, parroting the beliefs of others. Betsy had no time for nor truck with sentiment. She knew exactly who she was and why. She lived in that skin of knowing with vigor and love. And now we know why and how she did.

> So I tell you,
> thus should you think of all this fleeting world:
> A star at dawn, a bubble in a stream;
> A flash of lightning in a summer cloud,
> a flickering lamp, a phantom, and a dream.
> —The Diamond Sutra, v. 32

Source Notes

This informal narrative has been drawn almost entirely from the papers contained in the Collin-Park-Knapp Archive housed at the Onondaga Historical Association in Syracuse, New York. While I worked with many originals and photocopies of original letters, wills, and diaries, I also used typed transcriptions of hundreds of pages from more documents, especially from the diaries of Roswell Park Collin, given to me by Betsy Knapp just before her death. Betsy used many transcribers over the years and their workmanship varied. I cannot vouch that I have found or corrected all the minor errors in the transcriptions—they were almost entirely misspellings or misinterpretations of single words—but I do not think anything of substance has gone missing or been misunderstood.

As a former research librarian, I sometimes have thought of myself as having a mind like a dumpster. An awful lot of junk goes in along with the good stuff on all kinds of subjects, but I couldn't lay claim to where any of it came from nor could I say how successfully I have distinguished between my good and bad finds within. I read a great deal to prepare for this work, considerably more books than I ever used directly. Some sources offered a few scattered notes or facts, items kept in my commonplace book with sketchy references. Others presented certain grounding ideas or details that helped me understand more clearly the material with which I was working. Nevertheless, unless otherwise stated in the text, all quotes from Ellis, Murdoch, Hesse, Lopez, and Fowles, come from the books listed at the end of these notes.

The text in the courtroom chapters is quoted verbatim from the hearing transcript, which was titled as follows: "In Surrogate's Court. In the Matter of Proving the Last Will and Testament of David Collin, Deceased. Hearing before George R. Cook, Esq., Surrogate, at the Surrogate's office in the City of Syracuse, N.Y., Saturday, April 4, 1885."

I would like to make a particular note about the edition of Shakespeare I used for my quotes from *King Lear*. It is an old, now very beat-up 1911 edition by Cumberland Publishers (edited by Clark and Wright) that follows more or less the 1864 Cambridge edition. It does not, of course, include any of the most current scholarship of more recent editions, and the line numbering follows the rather narrow double-column format peculiar to this edition. But I have had this volume for more than forty years and have carried it across the world. It is an old companion and I have felt no shame in using it for this purpose. Also, my villanelle, "What the Wind Said," which makes up the book epigraph, was first published in my chapbook *Where My Feet Meet My Footsteps*, hand set by Allen Hoey, Tamarack Editions, 1986.

In order to convey a very approximate sense of what the amounts of money in the Collin estate would mean to us today I used the online *Inflation Calculator* for rough equivalents. As to the other books and sources, I did not keep a proper list of any of them. Nevertheless, there were some that I returned to often or relied upon completely to provide details about times and events about which I knew very little. What follows is a partial list of such books.

Auden, W. H. Introduction to *The Oxford Book of Light Verse*. Oxford: Oxford Univ. Press, 1938. Reprint, 1973.
Berlin, Isaiah. *Against the Current*. Princeton: Princeton Univ. Press, 1997.
———. *Concepts and Categories*. Princeton: Princeton Univ. Press, 1999.
Berovitch, Sacvan. *The Puritan Origins of the American Self*. New Haven: Yale Univ. Press, 1975.
Brentnall, John M. "Peace and Truth." *The Magazine of the Sovereign* 2001–2 (as excerpted at www.banneroftruth.org. Accessed Jan. 30, 2003).
Ellis, David M., et al. *History of New York State*. Ithaca: Cornell Univ. Press, 1967.
———. *Landlords and Farmers in the Hudson-Mohawk Region, 1790–1850*. Ithaca: Cornell Univ. Press, 1946.
Fischer, David Hackett. *Albion's Seed*. New York: Oxford Univ. Press, 1989.
Fowles, John. *The Tree*. New York: Ecco Press, 1979.
Hedges, Chris. "On War." *New York Review of Books*, Dec. 16, 2004.
Hesse, Hermann. *Magister Ludi*. New York: Frederick Ungar, 1967.
Long, E. B. *The Civil War Day by Day*. Garden City: Doubleday, 1971.
Lopez, Barry. *Resistance*. New York: Knopf, 2004.
Murdoch, Iris. *Metaphysics as a Guide to Morals*. New York: Penguin Books, 1992.
Naipaul, V. S. *A Turn in the South*. New York: Vintage International, 1990.

Nicholson, Adam. *God's Secretaries: The Making of the King James Bible.* New York: Harper-Collins, 2003.
Schopenhauer, Arthur. *The World as Will and Idea.* New York: Charles Scribner's, 1950. Originally published 1819.
Shimano, Eido. "Teisho." *Zen Studies Society Newsletter,* 2004.
Stong, Ruth Collin. *John Collin: Stems and Branches.* Elmira, N.Y., 1980.
Swift, Graham. *Waterland.* New York: Poseidon Press, 1983.
Tatelbaum, Linda. *Yes and No.* Appleton, Maine: About Time Press, 2004.